The Alexander Lectures

HOPKINS, THE SELF, AND GOD

WALTER J. ONG, SJ

Gerard Manley Hopkins was not alone among Victorians ... tention to the human self and to the particularities of things in the world around him, where he savoured the 'selving' or 'inscape' of each individual existent. But the intensity of his interest in the self, as a focus of exuberant joy as well as sometimes of anguish, both in his poetry and in his prose, marks him out as unique even among his contemporaries. In these studies Professor Ong explores some previously unexamined reasons for Hopkins' uniqueness, including unsuspected connections between nineteenth-century sensibility and certain substructures of Christian belief.

Hopkins was less interested in self-discovery or the self-concept than in what might be called the confrontational or obtrusive self – the 'I,' ultimately nameless, that each person wakes up to in the morning to find simply there, directly or indirectly present in every moment of consciousness. Hopkins' concern with the self grew out of a nineteenth-century sensibility which was to give birth to modernity and postmodernity, and which in his case as a Jesuit was especially nourished by the *Spiritual Exercises* of St Ignatius Loyola, concerned at root with the self, free choice, and free self-giving. It was also nourished by the Christian belief in the Three Persons in One God, central to Hopkins' theology courses and personal speculation, and very notable in the *Spiritual Exercises*. Hopkins appropriated and intensified his Christian beliefs with new nineteenth-century awarenesses: he writes of the 'selving' in God of the Father, the Son, and the Holy Spirit. Hopkins' pastoral work, particularly in the confessional, dealing directly with other selves in terms of their free decisions, also gave further force to his preoccupation with the self and freedom. 'What I do,' he writes, 'is me.'

Besides being concerned with the self, the most particular of particulars and the paradigm of all sense of 'presence,' the *Spiritual Exercises* in many ways attend to other particularities with an insistence that has drawn lengthy and rather impassioned commentary from the postmodern literary theorist Roland Barthes.

Hopkins' distinctive and often precocious attention to the self and freedom puts him theologically far ahead of many of his fellow Catholics and other fellow Victorians, and gives him his permanent relevance to the modern and postmodern world.

WALTER J. ONG, SJ, is University Professor of Humanities, William E. Haren Professor of English, and Professor of Humanities in Psychiatry at Saint Louis University, Missouri.

It is the forgèd feature finds me; it is the rehearsal
Of own, of abrúpt sélf so thrusts on, so throngs the ear.
                                        'Henry Purcell'

WALTER J. ONG, SJ

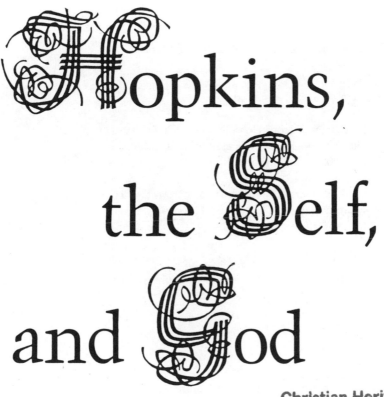

Hopkins, the Self, and God

University of Toronto Press
Toronto Buffalo London

© University of Toronto Press 1986
Toronto Buffalo London
First paperback edition 1993
Printed in Canada
ISBN 0-8020-5688-1 (cloth)
ISBN 0-8020-7413-8 (paper)

Printed on acid-free paper

Canadian Cataloguing in Publication Data

Ong, Walter J.
Hopkins, the self, and God

(The Alexander lectures, ISSN 0065-616X ; 1981)
Includes bibliographical references and index.
ISBN 0-8020-5688-1 (bound) ISBN 0-8020-7413-8 (pbk.)

1. Hopkins, Gerard Manley, 1844–1889 – Criticism
and interpretation. 2. Hopkins, Gerard Manley,
1844–1889 – Religion. 3. Self. I. Title. II. Series.

PR4803.H44Z85 1986   821'.8   C86-093625-2

Quotations from the works of Gerard Manley Hopkins are reprinted by
permission of Oxford University Press on behalf of the Society of Jesus.

Publication of this book is made possible by a grant from University College, University of Toronto.

To the memory of
Charles Kreimer Hofling MD

My selfbeing, my consciousness and feeling of myself, that taste of myself, of *I* and *me* above and in all things, which is more distinctive than the taste of ale or alum, more distinctive than the smell of walnutleaf or camphor, and is incommunicable by any means to another man.

Sermons and Devotional Writings

Self ín self steepèd and páshed.

Let / Me live to my sad self hereafter kind.

Man lives that list, that leaning in the will
No wisdom can forecast by gauge or guess,
The selfless self of self, most strange, most still.

I am gall, I am heartburn. God's most deep decree
Bitter would have me taste: my taste was me.

Life's quick, this kínd, this kéen self-feeling.

Self flashes off frame and face.

The Poems of Gerard Manley Hopkins

Contents

Also by Walter J. Ong

Orality and Literacy: The Technologizing of the Word
John Milton *Logic* (co-editor and co-translator), volume 8 in
    Complete Prose Works of John Milton
Fighting for Life: Contest, Sexuality, and Consciousness
Interfaces of the Word
Why Talk?
Rhetoric, Romance, and Technology
Petrus Ramus *Scholae in Liberales Artes* (editor)
Petrus Ramus *Collectaneae Praefationes, Epistolae, Orationes*
    (editor)
Knowledge and the Future of Man (editor and contributor)
The Presence of the Word
In the Human Grain
The Barbarian Within
Darwin's Vision and Christian Perspectives
American Catholic Crossroads
Ramus, Method, and the Decay of Dialogue
Ramus and Talon Inventory
Frontiers in American Catholicism
Faith and Contexts (2 vols): 1 *Selected Essays and Studies*
    1952–1991; 2 *Supplementary Studies 1946–1989*

HOPKINS, THE SELF, AND GOD

Introduction

ERARD MANLEY HOPKINS' FASCINATION with individuals and individual differences, with particularities, with 'All things counter, original, spare, strange' (*P* 37), is one of the best known and most commented on features of his mind and art. This fascination comes to a head in his intense and often agonizing pre-occupation with the human self, the 'I' that each person knows, 'this kínd, this kéen self-feeling' (*P* 152), and that each person knows as unique and induplicable, accessible directly only to the one who utters this particular 'I' – 'Self ín self, steepèd, and páshed' (*P* 61), the most particular of all particulars. Thanks in part to studies of Hopkins and his milieu, we have become increasingly aware of how widely fascination with particularity and the self marks nineteenth-century thought. It shows not only in the British Isles but also on the Continent, where, even more than Hume, Fichte and Hegel had made the self a major focus of philosophical speculation. Yet the fact that others shared Hopkins' concerns only makes his own case more striking. He is not just a specialist, but a specialist among specialists.

No other Victorian can quite match Hopkins in the intensity of his passion, his insights, and his theories regarding the importance of being different. He is the most relentlessly articulate of Victorians in his attention to differentiation outside, to 'dappled things' (*P* 37), and to differentiation inside, in his acute awareness of the self as ir-reducibly and utterly different from all else, of 'that taste of myself, of *I* and *me* above and in all things, which is more distinctive than the taste of ale or alum, more distinctive than the smell of walnut-leaf or camphor' (*S* 123). However, for Hopkins different beings are not simply constituted out of their differences, as elements would be in Saussurean linguistics. Each being is constituted by its positive selfhood, so positive that there is nothing else like it. Difference, a negative, spectacularly registers but does not bring into being the positive. Ale, alum, walnutleaf, and camphor are what they are not because they are not each other. Each is not the other because it so much *is* what *it* is.

The articulate self-consciousness of the Victorians marked a late stage in the history of human consciousness in the West. The setting off of the individual self or person against the communitarian and ancestral-authoritarian structures that necessarily dominate early cultures lies at the very centre of the history of consciousness, which is to say of the essential history of mankind. Psychogenetically, in each individual the basic sense of self, of 'I' as a positive experience bordered by the opposed 'not-I,' comes into being with the early, but gradual, separation of the mother from the child, who has to learn that he or she has boundaries, exists amongst otherness. From the dawn of humanity each individual's consciousness has of course been introspective: the mere saying of 'I,' which characterizes the human being as far back in time as records go, involves a kind of total interiority and immediacy of self-consciousness that cannot be made more total or more immediate. Yet saying 'I' and talking about the self that this 'I' registers are not the same thing. Over the ages, attention to the self has become more and more discursive. The 'I' learns to expound on itself, particularly after the inward turn of consciousness fostered by the invention of writing and then of print (Ong, *Orality*).

Typically, Hopkins' attention to the 'self' is simply to 'I' or 'me,' not to a 'self-image,' not to a programmed way of thinking about oneself as invested with individual history, certain qualities, or roles – as gentle, firm-minded, reliable, as physician, mother, business person, farmer, priest. The self that Hopkins typically attends to is not something it takes any special constructive effort to know, but something any of us can relate to immediately at any given moment in consciousness. It is the self that obtrudes when one awakens from sleep, the self that does not have to be discovered at all. This self, 'I' or 'me,' is unavoidably there, even when I am attending directly to something else or someone else, asserting its presence to itself and thereby its differentiation from all else. It is the responsible self, accountable, even from early childhood, to itself and to

others, the self that others engage with the term 'you': 'Why did
you do that?' It is the self that must confront itself alone inside
itself – 'self-rung, selfstrung, sheathe- and shelterless' (*P* 61) – even
when it is trying to lose itself in others, the self that is the paradigm
of utter particularity and that Hopkins felt to be the human point of
intimate contact with God.

Hopkins' exquisite and excruciating sense of self and his related
particularism emerge out of the large-scale, centuries-old, movement
toward greater and greater particularization of the exterior world and
deeper and deeper interiorization of consciousness that marks the
evolution of the human psyche in history and that ties in with the
growth of the ego, ontogenetically and phylogenetically, about
which there is such a massive literature today. But certain forces
play on Hopkins' own sensibility that are somewhat special to him.
Those that come from the ancient Greek and Latin classical heritage
he shared with other university-educated Englishmen of his time.
Those that come from Christianity – in the deep self-conscious personalism of its Trinitarian and Christological teachings and of its
liturgical life and private devotional life – he shared with other
Christians and most specifically with Roman Catholics. But Hopkins' acute self-consciousness derives also from his vowed dedication as a priest in the Society of Jesus and especially from his lived
appropriation of the *Spiritual Exercises* of St Ignatius Loyola, with
their focus on free decision making, on the free act of the will
which Hopkins calls 'the selfless self of self, most strange, most
still' (*P* 157). Not only is Hopkins' self-consciousness made more
understandable by examining the forces at work on him, but the
forces themselves are also made more understandable by being seen
as represented by Hopkins. For he himself is a prime exhibit in the
history of consciousness.

The particularization of thought regarding both the exterior world
and the inner psychic world is by no means the only development
that accounts for Victorian self-consciousness or for Hopkins' assertive preoccupation with the self. But this particularization is of major relevance in any thoroughgoing account of Hopkins and in his
case serves as a useful focus for many other issues. Discussion of
the self can proceed in scores of different ways, most, if not all of
them ramified and intertwined, and all of them involuted because of
the very nature of their subject. Some of the well-known ways of
discussing the self have been developed at some length here, but

other ways that today lie open have only been touched on or skirted, notably psychoanalytic thought as such and the complex inter-breeding of Saussurean linguistics and Freudian psychoanalysis found in Jacques Lacan and others. I can only plead that the matters here treated seem to call for attention in the ways they present themselves here and that there is no way to do everything at once. It has been said that all roads lead to the end of the world. Certainly all roads do that lead into and out of the self.

This book is an enlargement of the Alexander Lectures delivered at the University of Toronto in 1981.

ONE

Particularity and Self in Hopkins' Victorian Consciousness

1 HOPKINS VICTORIAN

LIKE ALL HUMAN BEINGS, Gerard Manley Hopkins was the product of his own times. This fact was long obscured, since his fame has all been posthumous, and even belatedly posthumous. His poetry first came to public attention simultaneously with that of the post–World War I creators of 'modern poetry' and was coopted into their achievement, where it fitted convincingly. Recent scholarship has had to correct or supplement early impressions so as to make clear how truly Victorian Hopkins was.

In *Gerard Manley Hopkins and the Victorian Temper*, Alison Sulloway has expertly summed up some major points of correspondence between Hopkins and his coevals, in somewhat different perspectives from those in Wendell Stacy Johnson's earlier *Gerard Manley Hopkins: The Poet as Victorian* (see also Buckley). First, Sulloway notes, Hopkins shared the Victorians' exquisite consciousness of the self as self, a kind of doubly reflective self-consciousness, 'quite new in Christendom' (2). To this newly honed consciousness of self we shall return, for the theme of this work will be that the Victorian reflectiveness about the self marked a development in consciousness which, far from making obligatory for all Victorians the disappearance of God, in fact could and in Hopkins' case did open new depths in Christian belief and understanding.

Hopkins also shared with other Victorians a sense of personal responsibility for remedying social disorders, which would press in on Hopkins particularly in his pastoral work at Bedford Leigh in 1879

and which had brought him earlier to write Bridges (B 27) 'Horrible
to say, in a manner I am a Communist' and thereby unintentionally
to alienate Bridges for some two and a half years. Further, Hopkins
shared the Victorians' passion for comparing their age with other
ages, which marked the intense Victorian sense of history. Contrary
to an impression still common today, his interest in planned change
in poetic expression was not idiosyncratic either, but quite Victorian, though no one else wrought quite the changes that Hopkins
did. Browning, for example, was a stylistic innovator, whose work
even suggests Hopkins': a certain wrenching of expression occurs in
both, though Browning's histrionic rhetoric suggests the public platform, even in the dramatic monologues, while Hopkins' expression,
even at its most bizarre, maintains a close connection with personal
conversation and an intimacy of tone that is rare in Browning.
William Barnes, whom Hopkins liked but Bridges did not (B 221; FL
366, 368–71), was another kind of innovator, an archaizing one who
nevertheless resembled Hopkins in his addiction to spoken and dialectical English and to Anglo-Saxonisms.

   Hopkins was like other Victorians also in his devout patriotism,
which, in his case as in many other cases, combined with what Cotter (61) has called a 'devout nostalgia for the Middle Ages.' This led
Hopkins, as it led other Roman Catholics, to dream of an England
reconstituted in a unity of Catholic faith such as had prevailed in
pre-Reformation times, although, unlike some of his Victorian and
post-Victorian coreligionists, Hopkins was not at all a sentimental
medievalist. He did not want to return to the Middle Ages. He had
no desire to turn back any clocks. At the end of 'The Wreck of the
Deutschland' (P 28), his prayer for a renewedly Catholic England is
as forward-looking as Easter, of which it speaks, as future-oriented
as the conclusion of the Bible in the Book of Revelation (22:20),
'Come, Lord Jesus,' a text on which, as will be seen, this longest
poem of Hopkins centrally focuses. Hopkins does not ambition a
renewed medieval England at all.

2 PANEGYRIC ACCURACY

Beneath all these characteristics lies another that also links
Hopkins' sensibility to that of fellow Victorians and that is for our
present purposes especially significant and perhaps on all scores the
most fundamental: his fascination with what Sulloway calls 'the

panegyric accuracy that Ruskin demanded of all artists' (1972:62). This fascination shows in the subject matter both of his poetry and of his prose. He writes of spring:

> When weeds, in wheels, shoot long and lovely and lush;
> Thrush's eggs look little low heavens. ...   (P 33)
> .

And he describes the rush of a plunging brook (P 56):

> This darksome burn, horseback brown,
> His rollrock highroad roaring down,
> In coop and in comb the fleece of his foam
> Flutes and low to the lake falls home.

A pool in the stream catches his eye:

> A windpuff-bonnet of fáwn fróth
> Turns and twindles over the broth
> Of a pool, so pitchblack, féll-frówning
> It rounds and rounds Despair to drowning.

This is not the epithetic description common in pre-Romantic poetry (Ong, *Rhetoric* 270–82) but the clinical and imaginatively reported description of exactly observed particularities advanced by one schooled under Ruskin and Pater and working often with sketchbook in hand. Hopkins peppered his early diaries and his *Journal* with carefully drawn sketches catching visually this sort of detail (eg, *J* 162, 163, 205, 206 and plates 12, 28), not simply picturesque material.

His meticulous prose descriptions match the sketches in registering exact specificities, in even more scrupulous detail than his poetry does. In his *Journal* for 11 July 1866 (*J* 144), he writes this entry:

Oaks: the organisation of the tree is difficult. Speaking generally no doubt the determining planes are concentric, a system of brief contiguous and continuous tangents, whereas those of the cedar would roughly be called horizontals and those of the beech radiating but modified by droop and by a screw-set towards jutting points. But beyond this since the normal growth of the bough is radiating and the leaves grow some way in there is of course a system of spoke-wise clubs of green – sleeve-pieces.

Try to find something like that in Homer or Hesiod or Columella or Vitruvius or Chaucer or even Vesalius or Newton. Hopkins is working here both perceptively and imaginatively, with a clinical eye trained in geometry ('system of brief contiguous and continuous tangents') and with a sense of practical mechanics hardly articulable in idiomatic vernacular, or indeed in any language, much before the romantic writers. Sir Isaac Newton's seventeenth-century precision was theoretical more than observational. Hopkins achieves here a new and unaffected juncture of dispassionate observation and fresh, often kinaesthetic expression ('radiating,' 'droop,' 'clubs').

In the same *Journal* exactly two years later, 11 July 1868 (*J* 172), we read of the snow on the Swiss Wylerhorn:

The snow is often cross-harrowed and lies too in the straightest paths as though artificial, which again comes from the planing. In the sheet it glistens yellow to the sun. How fond of and warped to the mountains it would be easy to become! For every cliff and limb and edge and jutty has its own nobility. – Two boys came down the mountains yodelling. – We saw the snow in the hollows for the first time. In one the surface was crisped across the direction of the cleft and the other way, that is across the border crisping and down the stream, combed: the stream ran below and smoke came from the hollow: the edge of the snow hewn in curves as if by moulding planes.

This kind of meticulously detailed, particularized description of something under direct observation is quite foreign to verbal expression in oral cultures across the world and it does not come early in the development of writing or even of print. No medieval or Renaissance writer could do this. Such reportorial description was in fact relatively new even in Hopkins' day. It results from a long tradition developed out of the resources of a matured print culture for combining exact verbalization with careful visual observation supported by printed illustrations that provided exactly repeatable visual statement (Ong, *Presence* 50–2, citing Ivins). Close observation alone is not what made modern science or the modern world. Human beings have been observing very closely for tens of thousands of years. If your whole existence depends on caribou or bison, you meticulously familiarize yourself with your quarry's every move and mood. But oral cultures, and for the most part even chirographic cultures until overlaid by print, cannot articulate with precision the close detail they observe and react to with exquisite skill. In early cultures, close observation was not learned from manuals, which verbalize observation, but from field experience, by apprenticeship, with minimal or no verbalization. Before the late eighteenth or early nineteenth century, nowhere in the world could any human mind work the way Hopkins' does to produce his meticulously particularized verbal descriptions. Early description, effective though it quite often is poetically or rhetorically, is quite different from this clinical sort of exactitude, which marked Hopkins' kind of reportorial writing and which was becoming common in Victorian England. Ultimately it would help produce in America the likes of Hemingway and Faulkner. The deliberate and detailed control manifest in such writing both attests and contributes to the growth of ego-consciousness, as will be seen.

3 PARTICULARIST AESTHETICS

The aesthetics of the particular that charmed the Victorians grows out of the Romantic Age. Gardner (90 – citing Walter Jackson Bate), Downes ('Hopkins' 100), and others have pointed this out. Christ (10) cites Blake's precociously romantic gloss in his copy of Reynold's *Discourses*: 'To Generalize is to be an Idiot.' Here the early Romantic writer is putting down the Neo-Classicist. The Romantic poet, in principle at least, does not rework the established, public, communally possessed, commonplaces as oral poets or residually oral poets do, but reconstitutes a particular given out of his or her personal, private, individual experience.

In *The Finer Optic: The Aesthetic of Particularity in Victorian Poetry*, Christ has carefully detailed the many ways in which the Victorians charmed themselves with the particulars of the world around them and the particulars of their particular experiences in the world. She examines the exact fidelity to physical detail that marks the work not only of Hopkins but also of Tennyson, the Pre-Raphaelities, Ruskin, and Dante Gabriel Rossetti. And physical details were not the only highly valued particularities. Political, sociological, demographic (Malthus), and psychological particularities were valued, too, as were historical particularities. John Stuart Mill praises history because it is concerned fundamentally with particulars – the very reason for which Aristotle and other earlier philosophers commonly had downgraded history by comparison with philosophy and even with poetry (Christ, 92), which Aristotle had seen as more 'universal' and therefore, in his scoring, fundamentally better than history. The principle which Aristotle invoked, or set up, is clear: knowledge of universals extends to many things, and so is more completely and sweepingly knowledge. But knowledge of universals also leaves out many things, and thus in another sense is neither complete nor sweeping. Knowledge of universals leaves out the particular details which are always ineluctably part of the really real. Worse, it leaves out individual existence itself, which is all that really is. Without prejudice to Aristotle's insight, we can note that early thinkers esteemed universals largely because, by comparison with our later, infinitesimally detailed scientific and historical knowledge, their knowledge afforded relatively little command of particulars, which modern thinkers can revel in – though of course all thought combines both universal and particular, directly or indirectly. The particularism that Christ treats was not peculiar to the British Isles in Victorian times. It appears in key thinkers in America, as well as elsewhere in the West. Tony Tanner has shown (36) that, while Emerson often pays lip service to universals, his overall effect derives from close vision and attention to 'the best particulars,' while Thoreau sought piercing accuracy in reporting physical facts, however much he mythologized them in the process of reporting them.

The particularist mentality encouraged and was encouraged by the new growth of 'numeracy,' skill in the use of numbers, which became widely diffused in Western Europe and the United States from the seventeenth to the nineteenth century (following on the diffusion of literacy from the sixteenth to the eighteenth century). Numeracy reached epidemic proportions already in the eighteenth century, when, for example, Dr John Lining sent from Charleston, South Carolina, to the Royal Society in London the exact numerical measurements and weights for his total intake of solids and fluids and his total bodily excretions (including perspiration) for one whole year, 1741–2 (Patricia Cline Cohen, 109–10). The Royal Society published Lining's itemized report in their *Philosophical Transactions*. Around the same time the Reverend Ezra Stiles recorded such things as the number of rings on a tree stump he passed, the height of church steeples, and the number of sheep in New Haven, and one autumn in Newport, Rhode Island, succeeded in counting 888 dwelling houses, 439 warehouses, 16 stills, 16 windmills, 177,791 square feet of wharf surface, 3780¼ tons of vessels in the harbour, 77 oxen, 353 cows, and 1601 sheep, capping his activities a few months later by going to Cape Cod and counting all the Indians. Cohen has shown how such seemingly mindless, and very common, aberrations were simply spin-off from the new drive into the statistical thinking that was to shape today's high technology culture. The older mindset, favouring more generic classification, was nonindividualistic: a genus or species normally had an indeterminate number of members (with some exceptions for medieval suppositional logic, precociously quantified – Ong, *Ramus* 65–72). The new numeracy mentality wanted groups with determinate numbers of *individuals*. Hence, paradoxically, today's concern for the loss of individuality in groups, statistical or other. Earlier communal mindsets, for whom numbers were often approximations if not simply symbolic, did not attend to the individuals in groups that closely. Hopkins' father lived in the new world of numeracy: he was, as will be seen, by occupation a statistician, a professional marine-insurance actuary.

The seriousness of the Victorian commitment to the particular shows in the way in which particularism enters as a sine qua non into the fabric of the dominant literary form of the age, the novel. New in the eighteenth century and come into its own in the nineteenth, the novel attends to the details of day-by-day existence with a thoroughness that no earlier verbal art form can approximate (Christ, 77). In *The Rise of the Novel* (15–27) Ian Watt has pointed out the growth of particularizing tendencies in narration and, more generally, in the Western mind from early romanticism on. The particularization not only of the physical environment but also of character traits in the novel made possible literary realism. Watt connects literary realism and philosophical realism, which in turn he ties to the philosophical empiricism of the times, based on attention to particulars of experience. The new intensified sense of historical time, he also notes, was due to particularizing tendencies: more particularized knowledge of changes over time both differentiated periods from one another more sharply and made interconnections of individual events more understandable. Space itself had earlier been only negligibly particularized in narrative. Johnson's remark, quoted by Watt (26), that Shakespeare 'had no regard to distinction of time or space' recalls the Elizabethan dramatist's casual assignment of a seacoast to landlocked Bohemia in *The Winter's Tale* (III.iii). Defoe, by contrast, attends carefully to actual physical environment, though only intermittently, leaving it to Richardson and finally to Balzac to make a particularized environment truly a part of narrative action.

Victorian particularist aesthetics has prospered to the present time, and not only in novels. The isolated, particularized, unique 'good moment' (Christ, 105), the flash of awareness at one particular instant in just the right setting, which Hopkins celebrates in 'The Windhover' (*P* 36) – 'I caught this morning morning's minion' – would program poetics for generations to come, though not always with Hopkins' depth of reflection. It can be recognized in the sudden insight Imagists sought to achieve by the proper juxtaposition of precision-tooled details, in Joyce's idea of 'epiphany,' the flash of illumination made available by a good literary work, in the 'objective correlative' of T.S. Eliot, the precisely conceived creation 'out there' in the poem that elicits a burst of exact response from the reader, in Wallace Stevens' 'supreme fiction,' the unattainable limit point that defines every 'good moment,' in the Bloomsbury aesthetics of G.E. Moore (art produces the 'good moments' unrealizable in mundane life), in Edmund Wilson's *Axel's Castle*, and elsewhere. Today the greater part of lyric poetry written in English and many other languages still undertakes to set up and purvey the 'good moment' through precise physical details all of which are often ultraparticularized by being conspicuously unrelated to one another or to anything else apart from the 'good moment' their conjunction brings into being.

The most generalizable recipe for particularization is ultimately oxymoron, the verbal chimaera, the unrepeatable because unrealizable monster, which present-day culture celebrates ad nauseam not only in avant-garde literature but also even at the more popular level in such creations as its names for race horses (Starbait, Coastal Whisper, Come Up Pence, Seattle Slew, Sonny's Halo) and its names for rock bands (Jefferson Airplane, The Grateful Dead). The total immersion of present culture in particularist aesthetics makes it necessary for us to remind ourselves quite explicitly that particularism was not always the declared goal of poetry or of other art. It represents a state of mind that matured in the Victorian era.

4 EXTERIOR NATURE, INSCAPE, INSTRESS

Ruskin's ideal of particularized 'panegyric accuracy,' in keeping with its romantic sources, applied especially to exterior nature. Like other Romantics and Victorians, Hopkins loved details in nature for their own sake. In the classical tradition nature had been considered at its purest and best when more generalized: as late as in Johnson and Reynolds, when particulars were finally being attended to with great care, this was because they could bring about the sought-after generalized awareness (Christ, 98). But particularized nature and a particularized human being are not always in accord. For some Victorians, such as Tennyson, Arnold, and Carlyle, the distinctively human at times is so particularized that nature becomes a hostile environment, although other Victorians, notably Browning and Hopkins, manage reintegration of the human in a natural setting (see Christ, 104). The modes of reintegration of course differ from one another (Joseph).

Attention to the particular in nature can be variously nuanced. In a youthful essay 'On the Origin of Beauty: A Platonic Dialogue,' from a notebook dated 12 May 1865 (*J* 86–114), Hopkins distinguished two kinds of beauty, the chromatic and the diatonic (*J* 104; cf *J* 120) – a distinction which suggests today the distinction between an analogue and a digital computer respectively, for chromatism (discussed by Miller, *Disappearance* 279), refers to differences that are sliding or unmarked by clear borders, 'analogic,' while diatonism refers to abrupt or digital differences, marked by clearly disparate, distinct cutoff points. In treating nature, early philosophy and science, all the way back to Plato, had favoured the diatonic or digital computer view: Platonic ideas were clear and distinct, the ancient seed-bed of Cartesianism. By contrast, many Victorian philosophies, notably Darwinism, leaned toward the chromatic, denying the reality of clearly marked-off individual classes. In a Darwinian evolutionary world the 'species' of lion and the 'species' of tiger are in fact connected in a kind of genetic continuum: both are descended from common ancestors from which they were gradually differentiated by individual variation generation after generation, so that only arbitrarily can taxonomists say that at this particular point the individuals in one line of descent have become clearly lions or clearly tigers. Of course, there are occasional abrupt genetic changes

brought about by mutation of genes, but the overall effect of the discovery of evolution by natural selection has been to favour a chromatic view of reality.

Slightly later, in an 1867 undergraduate essay on 'The Probable
Future of Metaphysics' Hopkins extended the chromatic-diatonic
distinction from aesthetic objects as such to being itself and proposed his 'new Realism' which would favour the diatonic, arguing
from music and mathematics (J 120):

To the prevalent philosophy and science nature is a string all the differences
in which are really chromatic but certain places in it have become acciden-
tally fixed and the series of fixed points becomes an arbitrary scale. The new
Realism will maintain that in musical strings the roots of chords, to use
technical wording, are mathematically fixed and give a standard by which to
fix all the notes of the appropriate scale: when points between these are
sounded the ear is annoyed by a solecism, or to analyse deeper, the mind
cannot grasp the notes of the scale and the intermediate sound in one conception; so also there are certain forms which have a great hold on the mind
and are always reappearing and seem imperishable, such as the designs of
Greek vases and lyres, the cone upon Indian shawls, the honeysuckle
moulding, the fleur-de-lys. ...

How far Hopkins would have carried this explanation in later life it
is hard to say, but the diatonic view is certainly more congenial to a
mind taken with individual differences. One might argue that there
are in fact differences in the chromatic view, since their number is
potentially infinite. But none of them are salient: in the diatonic
view all of them essentially are. The discovery of quantum physics
in the twentieth century would suggest that at root diatonicity
governs the physical world. It appears significant that in computer
development the diatonic (the digital computer) has in our day far
outrun the chromatic (the analogue computer). Although the
chromatic appears in some fundamental way dominant in the evolving organic world, it seems less so since the discovery of the neat articulations of DNA molecules. Human social structures and the
human unconscious, however, appear chromatic in structure. Perhaps the question of which is more basic will remain permanently
moot. But Hopkins' preference for the most evidently different differences is clear.

This preference shows conspicuously also in what Hopkins says about 'inscape' and 'instress.' Of Hopkins' many neologisms, these are undoubtedly the most commented on. The 'inscape' of a being is the distinctive controlling energy that makes the being itself and connects it distinctively with all else. 'Instress' is the action that takes place when the inscape of a given being fuses itself in a given human consciousness in contact at a given moment with the being (Cotter, 3 and references to Hopkins there). 'Instress,' it will be noted, brings the human self, this particularized human being, into the dynamics of the otherwise 'objective' inscape. As Wendell Stacy Johnson explains (*Gerard Manley Hopkins* 23–4), personal identity, self-consciousness, is 'what Hopkins' poetry of inscape is about.' The given being possessing inscape and generating instress might be virtually anything: a cowslip, a brook, a woodlark, a cloud-flecked sky, a ploughman working a field, a piece of music (*P* 44), or a poem itself. Inscape can refer to an individual existent, to *haecceitas* or, in Hopkins' somewhat Italianate form, *ecceitas* (a Scotist term, the 'thisness' of any being), but it can refer also to species, a common nature, as caught in an individual or even a group of individuals, as of bluebells (Miller, *Disappearance* 293). Inscape, with its corresponding instress, refers to distinctiveness of being not as simply analysed but as intuited in an insight deeper than analysis can go.

The doctrines of instress and inscape, it should be clear from what has already been noted here, are by no means so unprecedented in Hopkins' milieu as they have often been made out to be. They fit the Victorian particularist temperament, though Hopkins introduces his own contours and insistencies, and they have a pre-Victorian history. 'Instress' suggests Coleridge's well-known unifying, detail-fusing 'imagination' as contrasted with mere fancy or fantasy. As Coleridge often did, Hopkins is attending not only to such energy in the human interior but also to the energy concentrated in a given being or beings in the external world as well, that is, to the 'inscape' within the object that catches the poet's attention.

This charged-energy-centred thinking also sits in a large context. Images of concentrated or pent-up foci of energies fascinated Victorians generally (Bruns, 'Idea' 25–42), and Hopkins' vocabulary is studded with terms referring to such energies: besides inscape and instress, one recalls, for example, 'inset' and 'outset' (*S* 127), the 'inlaw' of God's mind compared to the 'inlaw' of the human mind (*S* 127), as well as 'stress,' 'pitch,' 'stigma' (a brand mark), 'gnarls,'

'throng,' 'bole,' 'beechbole,' 'buckle,' 'press,' 'teeming,' 'a ... sloe /
Will, mouthed to fleshburst, / Gush' (of a plum rolled around in the
mouth by the tongue until the peel or rind can hold the pressure no
longer and the plum suddenly bursts, to shock the senses with its
flood of acid sweetness – P 28). Since centres of differentiation or
particularization are power centres, differentiation or particularization itself fits into energy-centred thinking, for it itself can be ex-
plosive: different things often tend to interact powerfully. Frederick
Garber (62–91) has shown how growth in a sense of self-autonomy
from the eighteenth through the nineteenth century had built up the
sense of pent-up, internalized energy.

5 THE INTERIOR WORLD

Victorian particularism extends also to the interior world, directing
attention not only to external objects perceived but also to perception and other psychological processes themselves. Introspectiveness
had of course characterized many Romantic writers, notably Coleridge and Wordsworth, but the Victorians, and Hopkins with them,
went further. In close observation and exact verbal description of interior states of mind they were well on the way to depth psychology
and present-day phenomenology, to clinically meticulous description
of conscious and unconscious activity, and of the self as self, known
from within to itself.

Pater, one of Hopkins' tutors at Oxford and enduringly Hopkins'
friend, specialized in minutely scientific description of interior
states of mind (Christ, 106), typifying a widespread Victorian objective attention to subjectivity. Tennyson's 'Maud' advertises the
primacy of perception (Christ, 25), and others of Tennyson's poems,
such as 'Mariana' and 'Oenone' and 'The Lotos-Eaters,' carry the
reader into an intense emotional state that holds a character im-
prisoned in itself and suggests, as Martin Dodsworth has pointed out
(Christ, 25), that the external world is little more than the material-
ization of subjectivity. Browning explored states of consciousness in
dramatic monologues, where the single speaker lays open, wittingly
or unwittingly, his inner state of soul. The Oxford Movement had
encouraged arduous introspection, and not alone among religious
movements, for revivalism had done the same in another way in
many Protestant ecclesial communities. Newman carefully dissected
states of mind and degrees of freedom in *An Essay in Aid of a Gram-*

mar of Assent and bared his soul in his *Apologia pro Vita Sua*. But religious introspection was only one manifestation of the diffuse drive to introspection and self-consciousness which marked the Victorian temper in more generalized fashion, too. John Stuart Mill could write with conviction 'Of Individuality as One of the Elements of Well-Being' in his work *On Liberty*. Hopkins' own attention to inner states of mind will be discussed at length later.

6   KNOWLEDGE EXPLOSION AND CONSPICUOUS SELFHOOD

Nineteenth-century talk about the self was both new and old. The commandment 'Know thyself,' which was urged by the Stoics and which goes back to Socrates or even, it appears, beyond his age to the ancient Delphic oracles, shows a considerable depth of reflection about the self quite far back in Western antiquity. Yet, as late as Plotinus (AD 205–70) and later, the Greeks had no way of saying 'self' or 'person' as such (O'Daly, 89, quoting P. Henry). Plotinus has 'no *concept*, strictly speaking – for "self," ' though he and other Greek speakers could of course say the Greek equivalents of 'yourself,' 'himself,' 'herself,' and the like, as in the Stoic formulation just cited.

St Augustine's *Confessions*, with which autobiography as a genre in effect begins, draws on biblical tradition to develop an urgent sense of the human interior or heart in confrontation with the living God and simultaneously with itself. 'Inquietum cor nostrum, donec requiescat in te' – Our heart is restless until it rests in you' (*Confessions* I, i). Augustinianism saturates the Middle Ages, when St Anselm of Canterbury (1033–1109) in his *Proslogium* and St Bonaventure (1221–1274), in his devotional writings, among many others, continue Augustine's sense of God's presence to the interior human person. But the formally cultivated rhetoric which was ubiquitous from classical antiquity on always carried a suggestion of public platform performance (rhetoric was essentially the art of public speaking). 'Too late have I loved you, O Beauty so ancient and so new, too late have I loved you! ... You were with me, but I was not with you' (X, 27). The assertive parallelisms, expostulations, and other conspicuous tropes and figures are incompatible with the informal intimacies that would develop in later centuries. Even Augustine's 'What is closer to me than I myself?' (X, 16) is delivered in the carefully tooled classical rhetorical style, grown out of the cultivation of public speaking, histrionic in its balanced tensions, but at the same time often beautifully urgent. For all this is not to say that Augustine's rhetorical manner was any less genuine or effective than less conspicuously rhetorical, less residually oral, writing of the period after Romanticism (Ong, *Rhetoric, Romance, and Technology*; also *Presence* and *Orality*). It is to say that the oratorical tonality and the state of consciousness it incorporated was not yet open to certain kinds of privacy and the sense of the particularity of the self that later expression could deal with.

The great Trinitarian and Christological disputes of the patristic age immediately after Augustine's death in 430 developed the concept of 'person' and directly or indirectly laid the foundation for virtually all subsequent discourse in the West about person or self. The Middle Ages were steeped in Trinitarian theology of the Persons in God and in Augustine's thought, but they still did not yet have our twentieth-century concept of the 'individual' or the 'personality.' They attended to the *anima* or 'interior human being' (*homo interior*) not explicitly as a particular self, unique, unlike other selves, but as an 'image of God,' *imago Dei*, conceived of essentially rather than existentially, as the same for all human beings and as innately tending toward God (Bynum, 'Jesus as Mother' 87, citing John Benton). In the twelfth-century *Ancrene Wisse*, an ascetic 'rule' for women hermits, Linda Georgianna finds a growing attention to interior awareness (that occasioned, among other things, a redirection in the discipline of the sacrament of penance), but no direct discourse at all about the 'self' as self.

The introspection that grew through the Middle Ages and the Renaissance (as Pater's famous essay on Leonardo da Vinci makes clear) and that in the seventeenth century marks Descartes' thought, achieved its fuller explicitness in eighteenth-century discourse about the self which accompanied the 'inward turn' (Kahler) of consciousness as writing lost more and more of its declamatory oral residue. A recent book on this period by John O. Lyons bears a significant title, *The Invention of the Self: The Hinges of Consciousness in the Eighteenth Century* (1978). By the Victorian age, consciousness had achieved an even deeper inwardness, a new stress or intensity – what Hopkins would call a new 'pitch.' The inward turn of consciousness continues through the nineteenth century into still more recent times with the emergence of depth psychology, phenomenological psychology, personalist existentialism – Martin Buber's *I and Thou* – and related developments.

The Victorian fascination with external particulars of all sorts and the related Victorian fascination with the interior self both come to peak intensity in Hopkins. Moreover, in Hopkins they interlock firmly with one another. Because of this interlocking, Hopkins' case suggests to the modern reader, perhaps more strongly than does the case of any other writer, including classic philosophers of the self such as Hume or Fichte or Hegel, a principal reason for the growth of explicitness about the self over the centuries: the demise of the old rhetorical tradition (Horner) that had so dominated the intellectual world from antiquity and the rise of the new world of science. The new science depended on close analysis of the kind of detailed knowledge made possible by writing and, even more, by print.

The art of rhetoric, which governed and styled so much of academic training and intellectual life until the Age of Romanticism (Ong, *Rhetoric*), had focused on public performance. Initially, the art of rhetoric was the art of public speaking, of platform oratory, looking to externally effective leadership, such as should mark the political leader, the mover in human affairs. Lanham has indicated how the rhetorical tradition kept the self as such in wraps. Because it was concerned with public performance, rhetorical argumentation had to be based not on great masses of scientific detail but on more or less generalized considerations – the ubiquitous *topoi, loci communes* or commonplaces – which could be brought to bear on the particular case under consideration. The vast accumulation of knowledge made possible over the centuries by writing, and even more by print, ate away at this public, generalized framework, though of course it would not destroy it completely, since oratory is still with us. But oratory gradually lost its dominance as a focus for education and the sciences rose to greater prominence, filled with the vast amounts of particularized detail that could be accumulated and retrieved by writing and, even more efficiently, by print. Scientific knowledge was not perfected in public, as rhetoric was, but was a matter of private study and research. Books privatized intellectual activity as oratory had once publicized it. In this new climate of privatized study of particulars, it is understandable that the private self should command detailed, analytic attention as never before. Consciousness had taken a new turn.

7 SELF-CONFRONTATION RATHER THAN SELF-DISCOVERY

At one time or another Hopkins uses the term 'self' and its cognates, in many or perhaps most of the various senses which were,
and still are, conveyed by the term and its cognates in English. But
when he treats intensively of the self, as he so often does in both his
poetry and his prose, he typically does so by confrontation: 'that inmost self of mine which has been said to be and to be felt to be, to
taste, more distinctive than the taste of clove or alum, the smell of
walnutleaf or hart'shorn' (S 125; cf S 123), 'of own, of abrúpt self' (P
45), 'self ín self steepèd and páshed' (P 61), 'Come, poor Jackself' (P
69), 'let / Me live to my sad self hereafter kind' (P 69). Often the
self is related to the superindividuation of 'inscape' or 'instress': 'A
nature to "function" and determine, to selve and instress' (S 125).

As these examples show, Hopkins typically treats of the self as
face-to-face with itself, confrontationally. This does not mean that
he is typically concerned with the 'self-identity' that Jacques Derrida and other deconstructionists treat. Hopkins' typical self or 'I' is
not identifying itself with itself nor regarding itself à la Descartes as
a starting point for anything. It is simply what one faces up to, experiences, 'tastes,' and expresses in each saying of 'I' or 'me.'
Although Hopkins expresses genuine, if reserved, admiration for
Walt Whitman's poetry (B 154–7, 262), he does not share a sense of
the expansive, omnibus self that Whitman so much celebrates in his
'Song of Myself' and elsewhere. Hopkins writes Bridges (B 157) that
Whitman 'eats his [cake] offhand, I keep mine. It makes a great dif-
ference.' But Hopkins insists that he does not mean to run down
Whitman. You have to make your choice.

Nor is Hopkins centrally concerned with 'self-discovery' or with
the 'self-concept' so commonly discussed in psychological literature
today. One can do violence to oneself, as Caradoc does in slaying
Winefred (P 152), or one can better oneself, become a 'nobler me' (P
60), or one can come to a more mature recognition of oneself as the
little girl Margaret will (P 55), but in all these cases the self is not
something one is en route to finding but the given one knows and
works with. In 'Spring and Fall' (P 55), Margaret's self is not under
construction: she is told she will become more consciously aware of
the self she already is: 'It is Margaret you mourn for' – right now.

Rosenberg has defined the 'self-concept' as 'the totality of the individual's thoughts and feelings having reference to himself as an

object' (Rosenberg, 17). This is the sort of 'self' that Paul Jay finds under construction in autobiographical, explanatory literary texts from Wordsworth (and earlier) through Roland Barthes. The self-concept that regards the self as object involves social identity (one's age, sex, race, nationality, occupation, etc), attitudes (liberal, conservative, etc), character traits (bravery, generosity, morality), abilities (musical skills, intelligence), values, personality traits (compulsiveness, extroversion), specific habits (working five days a week), likes or preferences, or 'tendencies' (Rosenberg, 15). The formation of the 'self-concept' is closely tied to one's place in the history of culture.

The self-concept treated by Rosenberg is approximately what William James considers the 'empirical self,' a complex construct of which we all have several versions (James, *Principles* 309, cited by Rosenberg, 19) – and with which, of course, our interior 'I' gets involved. Kierkegaard's concern with the self seems to have been largely a matter of shaping a satisfactory self-concept (Collins, 1981).

The factors listed by Rosenberg and the 'construct' described by James, however, are radically exterior to Hopkins' typical interior, subjective self, which is not looked for or 'discovered' or constructed, but is simply present to each human person as taste is present, the confronting self, something given, simply *there* in the 'I' which each of us feels and utters, or equivalently utters (as in the case of congenitally deaf or other human persons using signing or other nonverbal means of expression). This self is not what Harding (13) styles 'the personal "I," ' that is, 'a kind of skin, a mask' whereby an individual adjusts to an environment: rather, it is the abrupt, unprotected, naked 'I.'

Nor is Hopkins' confrontational self the self analysed out of social structures by Paul Ricoeur, after Heidegger, or earlier by Jean-Paul Sartre. Articulate attention to Hopkins' confrontational self becomes possible in the stage of consciousness at which such writers emerge, but such a sense of self does not command their direct attention, as it does Hopkins'.

Like all of us, Hopkins in some way of course formed a 'self-concept' or 'self-image' by bringing elements such as Rosenberg mentions into a unity, centred ultimately for Hopkins clearly in his deep commitment to Catholic belief (Robinson, ix–xi: Miller, *Disappearance* 352), although this self-concept is adventitious to the 'I' which each person speaks and which is Hopkins' radical meaning for self. The self-image develops and can change. The 'I' that I say now is the 'I' that I have said from the start of my 'I'-consciousness as a child. 'When I was a child I used to ask myself: What must it be like to be someone else?' (S 123). The 'I' of his boyhood whom Hopkins here refers to is unmistakably the same 'I' now looking back on his childhood adventures and savouring them and himself afresh. The two 'I's in the sentence totally coincide. In his recent book, *The I* Norman Holland reports (ix) that 'Not long ago I found a journal that I had kept when I was in my twenties.' In this journal he reflected how 'Someday I shall look back, ... and wonder what the now-I was like, just as the now-I wonders, about the then-I. ...' But the same 'I' speaks all the way across the thirty-three years of new experiences, wondering about the same 'I', and now writing a book *The I*.

Hopkins' mature self-concept or self-image, formed over the years, was dominantly and unabashedly that of a Roman Catholic Jesuit priest, as conceivable in the tradition that he knew. The image was worked out more or less gradually in his family context, in his early religious and educational contexts, and in other contexts of his life, and it reached decisive stages at his reception by John Henry Newman into the Roman Catholic Church and, a bit later, in his decision to enter the Society of Jesus in 1868 (this involved settling on a central detail of his self-image, for he had also seriously considered entering the Order of St. Benedict – 'becoming' a Benedictine instead of 'becoming' a Jesuit), and at his ordination in 1877.

In an 1884 letter to Bridges (B 197) Hopkins reports an incident involving a young Irish Jesuit scholastic who had only recently taken his vows ('lately from his noviceship'). In a cricket game, the 'lad ... was at the wicket and another bowling to him. He thought there was no one within hearing, but from behind the wicket he was overheard after a good stroke to cry out, "Arrah, sweet myself?" ' The incident was so utterly genuine and human and attuned to Hopkins' sensibility that, he tells Bridges, 'it amuses me in bed.' One might try to argue that the 'myself' here was the young man's self-image which he felt was fulfilled by his good stroke, but it seems to ring truer as an instance of self-confrontation, of a person's 'tasting' or savouring with exquisite joy the 'me' or 'I' that he has always been, here immediately and freshly realized in an action in which for the moment he had invested his whole being. 'Each mor-

tal thing ... / Deals out that being indoors each one dwells: / Selves
– goes itself; *myself* it speaks and spells, / Crying *What I do is me:
for that I came*' (P 57).

Hopkins' mature self-image included his wish for as full as possible 'identification' with Christ. All Christians are in faith identified
with Christ in the grace of Christian faith, not in the sense that
their personalities are absorbed by his but in the sense that through
responding to divine grace in faith and hope and love they undertake
to unite themselves with him and perfect their own individuality
through this union – as a married couple can perfect one another
without absorbing one another. 'Put on the Lord Jesus Christ,' Paul
urges all Christians (Romans 13:14). The ideal of realizing oneself in
Christ and Christ in oneself, which is common to all Christian
teaching, is particularly highlighted in Jesuit spirituality. One of the
deepest experiences in the life of Ignatius Loyola was the one he
reports as a vision in which God the Father 'placed him with his
Son' (*Autobiography* 89). The name Society (or, better, Companions)
of Jesus, which Ignatius insisted upon for his group, though it could
apply to all Christians, attests the Christocentricity of the Jesuit
ideal. 'What have I done for Christ? What am I doing for Christ?
What ought I to do for Christ?' are questions the retreatant is to ask
himself or herself in the First Exercise of Ignatius Loyola's *Spiritual
Exercises* (53). Yet when Hopkins writes of the self in relationship
with Christ, as he often does, he does not write of the self as constructed out of this relationship but rather as there, a given that
enters into the relationship, though the relationship can always be
deepened and selfhood more accentuated as one becomes continu-
ally, day after day, 'More Christ. ... / New self and nobler me'
(P 59), for the self, once given to Christ, can be renewed every instant in Christ. This renewal is not always easy, and it can be agonizing, as it was for Hopkins during the loneliness of his Dublin
years, when he writes (P 66), 'To seem the stranger lies my lot'
through 'dark heaven's baffling ban.' One's self-concept is an ideal
rather than a full realization.

Hopkins' self-concept built in his faith relationship with Christ is
a part of his conviction in faith that all things have their fullest
meaning and selfhood in relationship to Christ. This is eminently
true of human beings, but true also *mutatis mutandis* of every being
in God's creation. 'The Windhover' (P 36) Hopkins dedicates 'To

Christ Our Lord,' for the little falcon's spending of himself echoes Christ's spending of himself. Elsewhere (*P* 57) 'The just man ... / Acts in God's eye what in God's eye he is – / Chríst.'

But, as always, Hopkins insists that this does not mean that the individual person is absorbed into Christ so that his or her self is lost. For the individual person is not his or her self-image. The individual person is simply 'I' or 'me.' Each individual self is enhanced in its individuality and even Christ's individuality is enhanced in the individuality of all those who represent him. An 'I' related personally to a 'you' is not less an 'I,' but more. 'For Christ plays in ten thousand places / Lovely in limbs, and lovely in eyes not his' (*P* 57). The eyes remain 'not his' but the eyes of the person, the self, whom Christ inhabits and who inhabits Christ. Here again, in the realization of each self in Christ and of Christ in each self, Hopkins attends not to the search for identity as such but to the fact of identity, not to self-discovery but to self-possession and self-confrontation. 'Each mortal thing does one thing and the same: / Deals out that being indoors each one dwells; / Selves – goes itself' (*P* 57). There the self is, not needing to be discovered, but already a given, deep within, so that each being simply 'deals out' what is in it: it 'selves,' or 'goes itself.' And sometimes with agony as, again, mostly in Hopkins' last years in Dublin.

If Hopkins is little concerned with self-discovery or the 'empirical self,' much less is he concerned with a 'bundle or collection of different perceptions which succeed one another with inconceivable rapidity and are in a perpetual flux movement' within the stream of consciousness, in the midst of which David Hume (152) futilely tries to pin down the self (634) as though it were just one or another of the items in the flow rather than something utterly unique to each separate person. Hopkins' self is not the self Nietzsche constructs in undertaking to deconstruct the self. It is the 'I' in which all Nietzsche's deconstruction is enfolded and which the deconstruction never eliminates and, in fact, never even touches. For Nietzsche is deconstructing a fiction, and the 'I' is the 'contrasting' reality that shows up fictions as fictitious (Miller, 'Disarticulation'). The self Hopkins refers to is of course still more remote from later ideas of Claude Lévi-Strauss (3–4) and other semiotic structuralists who would maintain that the self is simply a 'crossroads,' a structure of recurrence. The self for Hopkins is something utterly immediate and unavoidable. He characteristically attends to the self much in the way in which William James wrote of it the year after Hopkins died (289):

The altogether unique kind of interest which the human mind feels in those parts of creation which it calls *me* or *mine* may be a moral riddle, but it is a fundamental psychological fact. No mind can take the same interest in his neighbor's *me* as in his own. The neighbor's *me* falls together with all the rest of things in one foreign mass against which his own *me* stands out in startling relief.

Hopkins provided earlier a strikingly parallel statement (*S* 123):

We say that any two things however unlike are in something like. This is the one exception: when I compare my self, my being-myself, with anything else whatsoever, all things alike, all in the same degree, rebuff me with blank unlikeness.

Neither James' nor Hopkins' statement is an attempted definition of the self. Both are simple instantiations, comparable to that in Martin Buber's *I and Thou* or in other recent phenomenological literature. For the confrontational self, the 'I' or 'me,' cannot be defined, only pointed to. It cannot be broken down into simpler components: it is the ultimate, existential point of reference in our concept of unity.

For Hopkins, the creation of the universe is centred ultimately in God's bringing into being interiorized, utterly differentiated human selves. In his notes on the introductory 'First Principle and Foundation,' concerning creation, in Ignatius Loyola's *Spiritual Exercises* Hopkins turns the focus of attention even more clearly and forcefully inward than Ignatius had done, or could have done. Hopkins writes (*S* 123):

We may learn that all things are created by consideration of the world without or of ourselves the world within. The former is the consideration commonly dwelt on, but the latter takes on the mind more hold. I find myself both as man and as myself something most determined and distinctive, at pitch, more distinctive and higher pitched than anything else I see. ... And when I ask where does all this throng and stack of being, so rich, so distinctive, so important, come from / nothing I see can answer me ... When I consider my selfbeing, my consciousness and feeling of myself, that taste of myself, of *I* and *me* above and in all things, which is more distinctive than the taste of ale or alum, more distinctive than the smell of walnutleaf or camphor ... Nothing else in nature comes near this unspeakable stress of pitch, distinctiveness, and selving, this selfbeing of my own.

Taste is a discriminating or differentiating sense, in its direct and in its metaphorical meanings (Ong, *Presence* 45, 170–1). Taste tells us what to intussuscept into our bodies as food and what to reject. Metaphorical taste, similarly, tells us what is to be welcomed and what is to be rejected in art or literature or lifestyle. Again and again Hopkins uses this most discriminating of senses, taste, as a metaphor to express how utterly different is each self from every other and thus how superlatively isolating is the experience of being with oneself alone (*P* 67):

I wake and feel the fell of dark, not day.
What hours, O what black hoürs we have spent
This night! ...
...
I am gall, I am heartburn. God's most deep decree
Bitter would have me taste, my taste was me.

The 'me' or 'I' which Hopkins tastes here and typically elsewhere is certainly related to but is not exactly the same as the Freudian ego, which is an analytic construct fitted into an elaborate theory, although in Freud's own original German somewhat closer to 'I' than the English rendition 'ego' would suggest. (Freud used the German *ich*, not the Latin borrowing *ego*, as Bettelheim has pointed out.) Neither is Hopkins' 'me' or 'I' the same as the 'self' seen as a whole of which the id, the ego, and the superego are parts, for this self, too, is a scientific construct. The self, the 'me' or 'I,' that Hopkins 'tastes' is not amenable to direct scientific analysis: it is experienced as immediately present, without parts, and as essentially nameless, as we shall later see. Of course, a psychoanalytic study of Hopkins' sense of self could be undertaken, in Freudian or Jungian or other perspectives. But this book is not directly undertaking such a study, although it uses much material which a directly psychoanalytic study would doubtless find relevant.

8 'MY TASTE WAS ME': REFLECTIONS ON HOPKINS' 'SELF' AND 'I'

The self has a positive content limited by a border, the most peremptory border in human consciousness, that separating the 'not-I' from the 'I.' Weakening of this border signals no less than total psychological collapse. The border is established shortly after infancy. Having during infancy acquired a positive consciousness of self-and-mother as unitary, the child later becomes capable of saying 'I,' usually in the third year of life, by establishing a border between himself or herself and mother (Harding; Mahler), or a mother substitute in some cases, marking off an 'other' outside the self. Hopkins' sense of self, as all sense of self, bears the cachet of this initial border-creation or separation, as well as, complementarily, of memory and promise of union. Because self-consciousness comes into its own through separation or division, a marked interest in differentiation, in particularities, in specificities, in 'Pied Beauty' (P 37), in 'dappled things,' in 'things original, spare, strange,' such as we find in Hopkins and in many other Victorians, can readily go hand-in-hand with greater and greater articulation of self-consciousness.

Still, when all this is said about separation and borders, the experience registered in the saying of 'I' that Hopkins typically attends to is positive and more fundamental and immediate than the sense of border. The child comes gradually to experience direct, positive control over some of his or her own bodily movements, and learns to split off mother as different because her movements escape this central self-control. Borders are thus generated out of the positive content of self-consciousness: the self is not generated out of borders, but merely shaped or limited by them. It is a positive reality. What can be said about this interior positive reality, this immediacy, the self or the 'I' to which Hopkins so vigorously responds?

The Proto-Indo-European root of self is *seu-*, a pronoun of the third person that is reflexive, referring something else in a sentence back to the subject of the sentence. The root *seu-* generates many words all through the Indo-European family of languages from Old Norse *sveinn* (English 'swain' – one's own man) and Latin *solus* (solitary, by one's self, alone) to Sanskrit *svamin* (English 'swami' –

one's own master, owner, prince) and Old Irish *fein* (selves – Sinn
Fein, 'we ourselves'). As some of these examples show, the term
'own' tends to attach to 'self.' 'Own' is a reflexive possessive also
referring to something already mentioned, and thus also a repetitive
intensifier of 'self.' Some of the examples also illustrate how possessive pronouns ('my,' 'our') also attach to 'self.' Possession means
appropriation of something by the possessor, that is, identifying
something somehow with the possessor. What 'my' appropriates
here to me is 'self,' which, without the addition of the 'my' is
already a reflexive 'me.' 'Myself' thus in effect says 'I' or 'me' three
times over. Adding 'own,' as in 'my own self,' repeats the reflexiveness again. 'I my own self' is equivalent to saying 'I' or 'me' four
times. Reflexiveness fosters and defines itself by further and further
reflexiveness. There is no alternative procedure. Nothing shows better the essential reflexiveness or inwardness of the individual human
consciousness than does the management of this term 'self' (and its
equivalents or near-equivalents in various languages other than
English).

Yet, despite its value in advertising the essential reflexiveness or
inwardness of 'I' or 'me,' as employed by you or me or anyone else
who says 'I,' the term 'self' is in a certain way deficient. It does not
relate to human experience at all so directly as 'I' does. 'Self loves
other self' is no equivalent for 'I love you.' Even 'I myself love you
yourself' deadens the message.

The concept of self builds on the experience of reflectivity already
expressed by 'I,' in such a way as to generalize the reflectiveness
most immediately, but unreflectively, known in one's own 'first'
person. From the first person, where reflexiveness or inwardness
palpably lives, where we have direct knowledge of reflectiveness or
inwardness, a similar reflexiveness or inwardness can be imputed
proximately to a 'second' person (yourself) and more remotely to a
'third' person (himself, herself, itself). Knowing reflexiveness, the
'self,' from my own self-consciousness, I find that I can identify or
impute a corresponding 'self' elsewhere. As I am a self, you are a
self. The 'self' is in this way generalizable and to that extent less
utterly distinctive than 'I.' I can speak of 'you yourself' but not of
'you your-I,' for I cannot detach 'I' from me to apply it to you so
conveniently as I can 'self.' Much less can I speak of 'the tree its-I,'
although I can and do say 'the tree itself.' 'Self' objectifies somewhat the subject 'I' or 'me.'

By comparison with 'I' or 'me' or even 'you,' the term 'self' is thus a kind of abstraction, impersonal even though used to refer to a person, who is not and cannot be abstract at all. 'The self' is conceived of as in some way an 'it'; speaking of 'I' as 'the self' reduces the first-person 'I' to a 'third' person, and a kind of impersonal third person at that: we refer to the 'self' as 'it' rather than 'he' or 'she.' (The gendered pronouns are radically personal, suggesting that sexuality is at its peak of significance in human beings, as indeed it is.)

As compared to the term 'I,' it is well to note that the term 'person,' too, has disabilities, comparable to but not identical to those attaching to 'self.' Like 'self,' it is an abstraction when compared with 'I,' that is, it is a kind of name. But it is in a way more personal than 'self,' as can be seen from the way it relates to gender (in English, for example): whereas 'the self' is rather likely to be referred to as 'it,' 'the person' is more likely to evoke a 'he' or a 'she.' We regularly say, 'A self is conscious of itself' (not himself or herself), but 'A person is conscious of himself or herself' (but not of itself).

By contrast with 'self' and 'person,' the uniqueness of each 'I' is absolute. Though physically it sounds the same in different mouths, everyone who uses 'I' or its equivalent in any language means something utterly different by it from what anyone else means or can ever mean. Some four billion persons in the world today can say 'I' or its equivalent, and every one of them means something different by the term. The term can be given any of its some four billion current referents only by noting who says it: it simply means whoever says it. Moreover, no one else can use the term 'I' and make it mean what another person means when he or she says 'I.' You do not know what it feels like ('tastes' like) to be me, nor do I know what it feels like ('tastes' like) to be you. I can of course say, 'What *you* mean when you say "I." ' But then the term that bears the burden of meaning, the term in my words pointing immediately to you, is precisely 'you,' not the 'I' which I say *you* say. In 'What you mean when you say "I," ' the meaning of the 'I' derives from the 'you,' whereas in my own saying of 'I' the meaning is directly from the 'I' itself. The 'you' is of course generated out of your relationship to me, to the 'I' that I say, but it is not an 'I.'

Every 'I' or 'me' is socially, genetically, and historically free-floating. Socially free-floating: other human beings have no direct access to it in the sense that they are totally barred from experiencing it directly. Genetically free-floating: whereas your biological constitution is related to that of your mother and father, so that you in some way resemble them physically, the 'I' that you say is no more related to the 'I' of your mother or to the 'I' of your father than it is to the 'I' of an utter stranger. Historically free-floating: there was a time, and not long ago, when this self-conscious 'I' that I say simply did not exist even in germ. There were no historical antecedents out of which it was built. First it was not, and now it is. My body is historically continuous with the universe in clearly verifiable ways. The 'I' that I say is totally discontinuous with all around in its origins (although one can of course project any number of purely fanciful theories such as metempsychosis, which gratuitously assert continuity on no verifiable or even testable grounds). Oddly, once it is in existence, each free-floating 'I' can become in its own unique way continuous with the universe, present and past, for each 'I' can ingest through culture and memory, recorded and unrecorded, the experience of others, even others long deceased. I can know where I am in time and space by reference to times and spaces in which I did not exist.

The free-floating condition of the 'I' seems to be the state of affairs underlying Sartre's well-known contention, and, before him, José Ortega y Gasset's, that the human being has no 'nature.' Each person must 'make' himself or herself. The relationship of each human 'I' to whatever human 'nature' may be is radically different, detached, by comparison with the relationship of any other animal to its 'nature.'

The free-floating condition of the 'I' baffles those who want to reduce the 'I' to something other than itself. Hume's report, 'I can never catch *myself* at any time without a perception, and never can observe anything but the perception' (252) registers disappointment – to my mind distressingly naïve – that the self does not appear to itself as other things do. Why should it? It is utterly unique and knows itself most intimately in its uniqueness. It is common today to maintain, somewhat à la Hume, that there is no such thing as a self – that the self is only a kind of floating crossroads, only an inbetweenness. Because experience of it cannot be shown to be like experience of anything else, the self must not be there at all. The conclusion hardly follows. What is distinctive of the self as self, of the 'I' aware of itself as 'I,' is precisely that it is not like anything else, as we have seen William James and Hopkins both straightforwardly note. The self is the interior to which all else is in some way exterior and 'other,' although it can open to and accommodate the exterior otherness around it.

9 THE NAMELESS 'I' AND THE CONCEPT OF 'PRESENCE'

The 'I' has no name, at the very point at which it is best known, in its own self-consciousness. Names show that beings exist in classes or at least, in proper names, establish relations between one being and another. Proper names relate a person to a culture and to history. 'I' does not of itself relate to any other existent (except to God, Hopkins would say), though historically it may come to relate to many. 'I' is an unavoidable declaration of independence, of separateness, of particularity. My name 'Walter' is purely adventitious. Even though it is my proper name, it could in fact as well be applied to someone else. If I am called Tom or Dick or Harry, I remain the same 'I.' No name of itself refers to me as me. The 'I' that I utter does, with deadly aim.

'I' is a pronoun. 'Noun' comes from the Latin word *nomen*, which means name and also noun. A noun is a name. *Pronomen* in Latin, which gives us our English word 'pronoun,' means something that stands in place of (*pro*) a name. Here we have caught in the conceptualizing process the basic, unalterable reason why the 'I' as 'I' remains forever scientifically unprocessible. There is no real name for it, no class it belongs to. Instead of a noun that would put it in a class, you have only a personal pronoun, defined from inside itself. This fact makes the 'I,' the individual person, permanently resistant to any strictly scientific treatment. There is no way to measure the difference between my 'I' and yours.

The radical namelessness of the 'I' in its presence to itself is of major importance in view of the deconstructionist doctrine that belief in 'presence' is a naïvely entertained by-product of our use of names, of 'logocentricism.' Quite to the contrary, the supreme instance of presence in each person's life, the presence of the 'I' to itself, involves no name at all. A child becomes truly present to himself or herself when, usually during the third year of life, it ceases to refer to itself by a name – 'baby' or 'Nancy' – and begins to say 'I' (Harding, 11).

The novelist and essayist Walker Percy, who is also a physician, catches some of the paradoxes at work here (22):

Science cannot utter a single word about an individual molecule, thing, or creature in so far as it is an individual but only so far as it is like other individuals. The layman thinks that only science can utter the true word about anything, individuals included. But the layman is an individual. So science cannot say a word to him or about him except as he resembles others. It comes to pass then that the denizen of a scientific-technological society finds himself in the strangest of predicaments: he lives in a cocoon of dead silence, in which no one can speak to him nor can he reply.

The 'I' (with its variable corresponding 'you') holds a privileged place in discourse through all ages. 'I' is in a sense diachronic. It comes into being at a point in history, and without antecedents, but, once in being, it penetrates all history. When we have, say, a thousand-year-old written record of someone saying 'I' (or the equivalent in any language), we have immediately a point of purchase: whoever this is/was, he or she is/was a self-conscious being referring to his or her self. 'I' is defined by being self-referential, and our own 'I' snaps to attention and relates immediately, sensing the other as other, dead or alive, and identifying the other as 'you.' This is not to say that we know much at all about this 'I' in the thousand-year-old text. But neither do we know much at all about a living 'I' whom we have never met before and who accosts us in conversation, setting up immediately an I-you relationship, whether we welcome the relationship or not. The self-referential 'I' defines itself in your world by relating 'you' to your own self-referential 'I.' Names provide no such immediacy of reference. Their reference has to be ascertained indirectly. Who is/was Perkin Warbeck? I have to find out from sources other than simply the designation 'Perkin Warbeck.' 'I' carries its own reference within it.

Paradoxically, although persons are radically distinct from one another in the 'I' that each knows and utters, they relate profoundly to one another through the same 'I,' not via science (as the quotation from Percy makes clear) but via the correlative of 'I,' that is, 'you,' which, like 'I,' is not a name. To put it another way, 'I' is not a label, but a voice, a cry, calling for response from a 'you' who can cry out his or her own 'I.' Not through names, which science uses and must use, but through name-substitutes, *pronomina*, pronouns, we know intimacy. 'I love you' is more intimate than 'I, John, love you, Mary,' or a fortiori than 'John loves Mary.' 'John' can apply to another or to any number of other human beings, as *this* John's 'I' cannot. A proper name applied to a given 'you' can serve as a reservoir of emotion, but always subordinately to the 'you.' A name can interfere with intimacy, though it makes the legal document ('I, John Doe, ...'). The legal document must treat persons less personally than objectively.

Nouns, names, even proper nouns, proper names, Mary or John, are in a way intrusions in personal address, although we may love another person's name by association. In conversation we 'set off' names with pauses, indicated in written texts by commas, which might as well be parentheses. Like parenthetical remarks, the nouns or names are inserts, necessary for discourse but at the same time breaking the deeper continuity of the discourse. A person who regularly thinks and speaks of himself or herself by a proper name – 'John does not want to,' 'Mary is not feeling well today' – is alienated from his or her own self, reducing the 'I' to a third person, and is in need of psychotherapy.

Nameless pronouns that most deeply establish inner unity simultaneously make community with others possible, for community is opening to others, and only beings who can say 'I' have an interior to open.

The autocratic obtrusiveness of the 'I,' the way his or her own 'I' 'thrusts' and 'throngs' into each person's attention (cf *P* 45), makes 'I' utterly inescapable. We cannot deny it without asserting it: 'I deny that I exist' is the ultimate exercise in futility (and consequently has always been a fascinating routine to go through). Anselm found the 'I' so incontrovertible that he undertook to use it as a starting point to prove the existence of God. With his 'I think, therefore I am,' Descartes posited the fully personalized 'I' as the zero-point for all the coordinates of philosophical speculation. It is easy to attribute magic powers to the obtrusive, confrontational self.

The 'I,' the self, as sensed by Hopkins, is a pent-up force within us. Gerald Bruns, in an article earlier referred to ('Idea' 25), has shown that the Victorian consciousness was much taken with taut 'patterned energies' – the knot, the vortex (which spun its way into the Imagist and Vorticist movements of the next century), Tennyson's eagle in the poem of that name, clutching the crag, ready to plunge, not to mention Hopkins' ploughman ('Rope-over thigh, knee-nave, and barrelled shank' – *P* 71) or windhover ('Buckle!' – *P* 36) or, as earlier noted, his concept of instress and inscape. In Hopkins' poetry and prose the human self is the ultimate among such patterned energies, its forces moving inwardly as well as outwardly.

> ... self ín self steepèd and páshed (*P* 61)

> ... Self | flashes off frame and face (*P* 62)

> Soul, self; come, poor Jackself, I do advise
> You, jaded, let be; call off thoughts awhile
> Elsewhere ...   (*P* 69)

> To his own selfbent so bound, so tied to his turn   (*P* 58)

> ... this soul
> Life's quick, this kínd, this kéen self-feeling   (*P* 152)

Paul Mariani ('Hopkins'; cf ch 4 below) has noted the great strength of Hopkins' own ego structures, a strength which helps explain Hopkins' ability to deal so vigorously with the self-confronting, other-confronting 'I,' the energy source which no one can avoid but which some persons may wish, in vain, to ward off or shield themselves from. For the self can be a threat to itself. Above all, as will be seen, it threatens itself with freedom.

Hopkins can entangle discussion of self in scholastic theories about individuation and the person, as he does when he writes, 'Now a bare self, to which no nature has yet been added, which is not yet clothed or overlaid with a nature, is indeed nothing, a zero, in the score or account of existence' (*S* 146; cf Miller, *Disappearance* 331). Such discussion is an attempt to throw light on philosophical questions about the self ('about,' that is, 'around' the self, questions treating not the urgent 'I' one feels, but the circumference of the 'I'). Such speculations fascinate Hopkins because the self is such a live issue for him that anything 'about' it is also a live issue. But such speculations do not at all define his sense of self, which is quite direct and untheoretical: 'this kéen self-feeling.'

Hopkins was well aware that 'self' applies properly or paradigmatically to human beings. In his 1881–2 notes on the *Spiritual Exercises* he writes that 'Self is the intrinsic oneness of a thing' and that 'selves are from the first intrinsically different,' and then goes on to add that 'this intrinsic difference, though it always exists, can-not appear except in a rational, to speak more to the point / in a free / nature' (S 146, 147). Hopkins here also elaborates a theory of individuation out of Beothius' definition of person and scholastic commentaries, but his theorizing, though always interesting if not always watertight, in any event is secondary and need not detain us here: we are concerned here with what he points to in the living ex-perience of each individual. Human beings alone can turn back on themselves consciously, and thereby say 'I.' The potential for such reflexiveness is what distinguishes a human person from other infra-human existences. 'Manshape ... / Sheer off, disseveral, a star' (P 72).

Every human person who is physiologically and pyschologically mature and unimpaired can say 'I,' and does. Other living beings quite evidently cannot do this. It is naïve to say that maybe they can, only we cannot tell, as some have said of the pongid apes. For one of the quite evident paradoxes of the self-conscious self, which 'I' expresses, is that, although it is directly accessible only from its interior to itself – only I know what it feels like to be me – it is irre-sistibly driven to make itself known exteriorly, to other self-con-sciousnesses. If a chimpanzee could say 'I,' you can be sure that he or she would let other 'I's' hear of his or her 'I' without delay. A self-conscious self is desperately concerned to make sure that other selves can tell that it knows itself. Otherwise, other selves treat it as a thing, an exterior, not as the reflexive interior that it is, and this is a self, a person, cannot bear, for such treatment equivalently denies the self its very existence. Hegel's discussion of the need of a self to be recognized by other selves has made this truth a common-place, though the reciprocity of such recognition in Hopkins is not the same thing as Hegel's power-modelled and back-firing master-slave dialectic.

10 INTERACTION WITH OTHER PERSONS

For Hopkins, the 'inscape' of a being, however individualized, moves outward by its 'instress' to register in human consciousness. All beings have a kind of outreach, and especially to human beings. Hopkins' reflections on the term 'sake,' which figures pivotally in 'The Wreck of the Deutschland' (P 28, stanza 22), make his sense of this outreach clear. He writes to Bridges 26 May 1879 (B 83):

Sake is a word I find it convenient to use: I did not know when I did so first that it is common in German in the form *sach*. It is the *sake* of 'for the sake of,' forsake, namesake, keepsake. I mean by it the being a thing has outside itself, as a voice by its echo, a face by its reflection, a body by its shadow, a man by his name, fame, or memory *and also* that in the thing by virtue of which it has this being abroad, and that is something distinctive, marked, specifically or individually speaking, as for a voice and echo clearness; for a reflected image light, brightness; for a shadow-casting body, bulk; for a man genius, great achievements, amiability, and so on.

Doing something 'for my sake' is doing something for me in so far as I have an outreach to you. What is distinctive about 'my sake' is not that I am totally self-contained in a solipsistic, self-sufficient world but that the outreach to you is in this case the outreach that comes from me and only from me, that is distinctive of me, not found in any other.

The appeal of one being to another being is not an imperious, stand-offish, dispassionate, uninvolved appeal, based on 'power,' but rather the appeal of something that is involved with me and with which I am involved. Interaction of persons in Hopkins is often presented in explicit terms of self, of the relation of one self to another self. Only through such interaction does the self come into its own. Thus in Hopkins' unfinished 'St. Winefred's Well' (P 152) Caradoc, who has just slain Winefred, moans:

> I all my being have hacked | in half with hér neck: one part,
> Reason, selfdisposal, | choice of better or worse way,
> Is corpse now, cannot change; | my other self, this soul,
> Life's quick, this kínd, this kéen self-feeling,
> With dreadful distillation | of thoughts sour as blood,
> Must all day long taste murder.

Here Caradoc's self, once identified empathetically with Winefred, interacting with her self, has regressed from interaction with other selves into isolation and guilt.

The self that, unlike Caradoc here, shares itself with others lives more fully in itself as well as in them. Each Christian open to Christ in his or her daily life, as Mary was at the time she conceived him in Nazareth, finds (P 60) that Christ takes on

> Not flesh but spirit now
> And makes, O marvellous!
> New Nazareths in us.
> ...
> ... born so, comes to be
> New self and nobler me.

Christian redemption is not absorption of self into God, but union with God that intensifies the uniqueness of each self. The 'me,' there before it accepted Christ, is there even more after giving itself to union with him. Mariani ('Hopkins') has discussed the way in which Hopkins, with great effort, sets himself to self-fulfilment through emptying himself so as to open himself to God and others (following the example of Christ's emptying of himself in Philippians 2:7 – treated at length in chapter 3 here below). Mariani has pointed out that such self-giving calls for strong ego-structures. And Sutton has shown how in Hopkins' poems self achieves its maximum perfection of actuality by such self-giving, and has related the process to Jungian archetypes of self-giving typified in the Virgin Mary and various saintly women such as St Winefred or Margaret Clitheroe (the subject of one of Hopkins' poems, *P* 145 – since Hopkins' time become St Margaret Clitheroe).

11 INTERPENETRATION WITH MATTER

The self, moreover, for all its personal, unique interiority, not only interrelates with other selves but also carries on traffic with the material world. It does so through the human body. Hopkins does not set the self nakedly against the object, as Morse Peckham (136, 277, 291, 302) notes Carlyle, Flaubert, Ruskin and other nineteenth-century authors do. The human body is both part of the self and part of the material object world. In his retreat notes on the 'First Principle and Foundation' of Ignatius Loyola's *Spiritual Exercises* (*S* 127) Hopkins writes:

For, to speak generally, whatever can with truth be called a self – not merely in logic or grammar, as if one said Nothingness itself – , such as individuals and persons must be, it is not a mere centre or point of reference for consciousness or action attributed to it, everything else, all that it is conscious of or acts on being its object only and outside it. Part of this world of objects, this object-world, is also part of the very self in question, as in man's case his own body, which each man not only feels in and acts with but also feels and acts on. If the centre of reference spoken of has concentric circles round it, one of these, the inmost, say, is its own, is óf it, the rest are tó it only. Within a certain bounding line all will be self, outside of it nothing: with it self begins from one side and ends from the other. I look through my eye and the window and the air; the eye is my eye and of me and me, the windowpane is my windowpane but not of me nor me. A self then will consist of a centre *and* a surrounding area or circumference, of a point of reference *and* a belonging field, the latter set out, as surveyors etc say, from the former; of two elements, which we may call the inset and the outsetting or the display.

This description is based not on theories of soul-body relation-ships but on data available from individuals' ordinary experience. It faces honestly our paradoxical relationship to our bodies, which each person 'feels in and acts with but also feels and acts on.' Hopkins treats this relationship in a reportorial, phenomenological manner more common in the mid-twentieth century than it was in Hopkins' lifetime. By contrast, another Jesuit, George Tyrrell (97 – italics in original), fourteen years after Hopkins' death, seems still fixed in a more dogmatic Cartesian tradition:

Not only must we perforce think of the spirit or *real* self, in terms of the body or *apparent* self, but we must also think of its timeless and indivisible action in terms of those appearances to which its action relates.

Tyrrell's neat disjunction between the spiritual 'real self' and the body does not allow for the unhandy, structurally recalcitrant state of human existence. When someone kicks my body, I do not say, 'Quit kicking my apparent self,' but, 'Quit kicking *me*.' Though I feel myself as somehow inside my body, so that my body is in some real way vaguely external, my body is still in another real way unmistakably an integral part of me, actually included in my con-sciousness of self. 'Part of this world of objects ... is also part of the very self,' as Hopkins puts it in the passage just quoted. My body is the frontier in which I am embedded and which is embedded in me: my body mediates between what is myself and everything else: it is both 'me' and otherness. The self for Hopkins is not solipsistic or even disengaged from the world. Despite its inwardness, its privacy, its isolation, it appropriates and exists in the material world.

12 CHRISTIANITY AND SELFHOOD

From his training as a Jesuit as well as from a certain amount of earlier reading, Hopkins knew a great deal of the vast literature relating to the self in the Christian, and particularly the Roman Catholic, ascetical tradition, which besides its fundamentally biblical sources had many other relevant sources in antiquity, most notably perhaps the Stoic tradition, with its *gnothi seauton*, 'know thyself.' The great difference between Christian thought and that of other widespread religions has often turned on the basic stance toward the self. Is the self to be minimized or maximized? In certain forms of Buddhist and other Indian philosophy, the self is to be minimized to the point of elimination: nirvana is achieved with the disappearance of the self (Organ, 108–15, 132); Dumoulin, 102, 119, 166–83). Worship of a personal God is only for the beginning of spiritual life; those who know more meditate on the Impersonal Absolute (Organ, 114). In the Bible, on the contrary, the human self as a distinct self or person is valued as such permanently by a personal God: 'I have called you by your name, though you know me not,' Yahweh announces to the Deutero-Isaiah (Isaiah 45:4). And again, in the Second Servant Song, 'The Lord called me from my birth, from my mother's womb he gave me my name' (Isaiah 49:1). 'I ... you ... ,' 'The Lord ... me': in the Old Testament the human person and God are constantly in dialogue with one another. Job and Jeremiah actually interrogate and debate with God, though reverently, as Hopkins does, too (*P* 74).

The reciprocal love between God and the human person testifies to their permanent distinctness in their union with one another. One can give Hopkins a Jungian reading which is deeply informative, yet at points such a reading will not fit, since for Hopkins God is not, as God seems to be for Jung, simply identified with psychic content, but quite separate from the psyche (Sutton), even though within it. God is one who loves us and whom we love – in biblical conceptualization, as husband and wife love one another, different but united persons. The numinous God is the ultimate 'not-I' as M. Esther Harding has explained (173, 179–80). A human person's identification of his or her 'I' with the numinous (one or another divine figure) can be a clear mark of insanity. Religions ambitioning absorption into the absolute commonly conceive of this as occurring by elimination of the 'I.'

Christianity also maximizes the self in a special way through its teaching on the Trinity of three Persons in God and its related teaching on the Incarnation, to both of which teachings Hopkins was exquisitely responsive (eg, *S* 95–100). As the result of the Incarnation of the Second Person, the Son or Word, individual human beings are adopted into Jesus' unique, filial, personal relationship with the Father. Jesus gives human beings the Lord's Prayer, telling them to call his Father 'our Father.' The self of each individual Christian is thus caught up with the self or Person of Jesus Christ, structured into what Hopkins calls the 'selving in God' (*S* 197): the Father-Son-Holy Spirit personal relations.

Christianity further maximizes the self by its belief in personal immortality capped by the resurrection of the body of each individual person into the transformed state where each person endures forever precisely as a person. In the 'communion of saints' noted in the Apostles' Creed as integral to Christian belief, persons, living and deceased, all belong to the same community. After death all persons still remain as individually distinct as in mortal life, relating to the Person of God the Father through the Person of the Son in the Person of the Holy Spirit and to one another as persons or selves both now and after the resurrection through all eternity.

Despite the permanent, and indeed eternal, value Christianity places on the human self, however, Christian asceticism also in well-known ways minimizes the self. It advocates self-abnegation, self-denial, refusal to accede to all the self's desires. Purely selfish desires and habits are to be 'mortified,' that is, put to death. But the self as such is never to be annihilated, however imperfect and in need of correction it may be. The anonymous author of the fourteenth-century treatise written in English, *The Cloud of Unknowing* (modern English version, ed Johnston, 103–4 – ch 44), after urging with precocious Hopkinsian anguish the loathsomeness of the 'naked knowing and feeling of your own being,' goes on to extol the existence of the self, though he still does not yet have available the explicit concept or term 'the self' but must rely on circumlocutions:

And yet in all this, never does [the devout Christian] desire to not-be, for this is the devil's madness and blasphemy against God. In fact, he rejoices that he is and from the fullness of a grateful heart he gives thanks to God for the gift and the goodness of his existence. At the same time, however, he desires unceasingly to be freed from the knowing and feeling of his being.

'Naked knowing and feeling of your own being' (ie, one's own self) without even a touch of God or of any other human person was not a pleasant experience in the fourteenth century any more than it was in the nineteenth.

I know of no evidence that Hopkins had read *The Cloud of Un-knowing* – the first edition, the only edition published during his lifetime was the modernized version of Henry Collins published in 1871 under the title *The Divine Cloud*. But Hopkins lived and did his thinking in the same deeply personal ascetical tradition as its author. In Christian teaching, through all the austerities one is encouraged to practice, the self looks forward not to annihilation but to fulfilment. Fulfilment of the self is to be achieved finally through the resurrection, which confirms one's selfhood, not as any longer naked but as united in distinctness to God. The recent editor of *The Cloud of Unknowing*, William Johnston, who is also a Buddhist scholar, makes the point that 'Christian mysticism can be understood only in the light of the resurrection, just as Buddhist mysticism can be understood only in the light of nirvana' (11). Sensitive to the deep resemblances between Buddhist mystical writings and the *Cloud*, Johnston is equally sensitive to their deep differences, and points out that in Christian teaching, 'until the resurrection, man's personality, his true self is incomplete' and that 'this holds even for Christ, of whom Paul says that "he was constituted Son of God by a glorious act in that he rose from the dead"' (Rom. 1:4).' Devlin summarizes Hopkins' own view (in Hopkins S 350): 'Personality is thus a journey into ever-increasing, never-ending self-realization.'

The resurrection of Jesus, paradigm of the coming resurrection of all men and women, was not a mere resuscitation, such as was effected by Jesus in the Gospel account of Lazarus (John 11:1–54). In this account, Lazarus' body, and with it Lazarus himself, was simply restored by Jesus to its previous, natural, antemorten state. Jesus' body was not simply restored to its antemortem state by his resurrection. His body was mysteriously transformed by his resurrection, though in Catholic teaching it was – and still is – his real body: 'Look at my hands and my feet; it is really I,' Luke (24:39) reports Jesus as saying when he appeared to his disciples. In John (20:27), the risen Jesus directs doubting Thomas, 'Take your finger and examine my hands. Put your hand into my side.' Though mysteriously transformed in his body, he does have the same body and is also the same person: 'It is really I.' So in Catholic teaching, the selves, the persons, of his followers, other human beings, are at the final resurrection to be somehow transformed as he was on the first Easter, not dissolved but confirmed in their selfhood as individual persons.

Hopkins is more explicit than the author of *The Cloud of Unknowing* about the transforming self-realization of the resurrection. He writes characteristically of each utterly distinct person before death as a 'Manshape, that shone / Sheer off, disseveral, a star,' which nevertheless 'death blots black out.' The dead do not come back to the life they left. Yet the self is not annihilated. On the contrary, with the resurrection, the self, curtailed in its very selfhood by death, which deprives the body of its soul, and the soul of its body, is reintegrated in a real but transformed body rejoined to the soul (P 72):

> In a flash, at a trumpet crash,
> I am all at once what Christ is, | since he was what I am, and
> This Jack, joke, poor potsherd, | patch, matchwood, immortal diamond
>   Is immortal diamond.

If, however, the self is to be fulfilled in the transformation of the resurrection, it is to be fulfilled not by centring on itself, but by opening and giving itself to others. 'He who loses his life for my sake will find it' (Matthew 10:39). Jesus' followers are to do as he did: 'Greater love than this no man has that he lay down his life for his friends' (John 15:13). This was the kind of self-fulfilment that Hopkins knew from the *Spiritual Exercises* of St Ignatius Loyola, where the 'Contemplation for Attaining Love' (102), the prayer climaxing the entire *Exercises*, attends entirely to a free act of complete self-giving:

Take, Lord, and receive all liberty, my memory, my understanding, and my entire will, all that I have and possess. You have given all to me. To you, O Lord, I return it. All is yours, dispose of it wholly according to your will. Give me only your love and your grace, for this is sufficient for me.

Free self-giving is the goal, but, paradoxically, the self remains after the giving: 'this is sufficient for me.' In Christian teaching such self-giving is the opposite of annihilation: it is a sharing and thereby is self-realization. Hillis Miller has put it well ('Creation' 318): 'Even when transubstantiated into Christ, a man still remains himself, since it is that mere positive infinitesimal which the man is aware of in his first self-consciousness which is so filled with Christ.' Another Jesuit whose life overlapped Hopkins' by some eight years, Pierre Teilhard de Chardin, has pointedly stated the principle at work here: in the realm of personality, 'union differentiates' (63, 64, 67, 144, 152) – or even 'super-differentiates' (42). One is never more one's own distinctive self than when one is in love with another or others, to whom one's self is given.

13   FREEDOM: 'WHAT I DO IS ME'

Where is 'individuality' or the differentiation of self from others most distinctively realized? Hopkins gives his response to this question a characteristic focus. The distinctiveness or particularity of the self he links (S 147) to the power of free choice (which he calls freedom of play) in a field offering options (which he calls freedom of pitch).

Selves are from the first intrinsically different. But this intrinsic difference, though it always exists, cannot appear except in a rational, to speak more to the point / in a free / nature. Two eggs precisely alike, two birds precisely alike: will behave precisely alike; if they had been exchanged no difference would have been made. It is the self then that supplies the exercise, and in these two things freedom consists. This is what I have before somewhere worked out in a paper [of which nothing is now known – Devlin, in S 293, n 147] on freedom and personality and I think I used the terms *freedom of pitch* and *freedom of play*: they are good at all events and the two together express moral freedom.

Since all things are differentiated, particular, have inscape, since each thing has its own ineradicable uniqueness, all things in some sense have a kind of self. But as seen in Hopkins' text earlier quoted (S 146–7), in infrahuman beings the self is not self-manifesting and thus less fully a self than the human self because it is not free, cannot exercise free choice. Human beings are fully selves because they are free. It is in choosing freely that being is most isolated, most particularized, and thereby most itself. The will, with the act of free choice the will produces, is for Hopkins 'the selfless self of self, most strange, most still' (P 157) – 'selfless' because it is not the self, since I do not say that I am my will or that my act of choice is me, but still the 'self of self' because it is in the exercise of free choice that the 'I' realizes its own distinctive, separate being most of all. Henry Johnstone's definition of the self as the 'locus of contradiction' (23) seems allied to Hopkins' view of the self as condemned to choose between alternatives.

Hopkins' conviction that freedom manifests the particularity of the self suggests precociously certain existentialist awareness of the twentieth century, such as Heidegger's and Sartre's persuasion that we create ourselves by the choices we make, that we are our own projects, built out of freedom, that we are what we do. Hopkins puts it thus in so many words, and thus anticipates twentieth-century thinkers (P57):

> Each mortal thing does one thing and the same:
> Deals out that being indoors each one dwells:
> Selves – goes itself; *myself* it speaks and spells
> Crying *What I do is me: for that I came.*

14 THE SELF AND SHIPWRECKS

Hopkins' urge and ability to confront the self directly in the ways he does registers a new stage in the history of consciousness. Like other stages in this history, that in which Hopkins finds himself has roots which are not simply psychic but also interactively social and technological. Some significant social and technological connections can be seen in 'The Wreck of the Deutschland.' To bring them out, it is useful to compare this, Hopkins' most ambitious and longest poem, with Milton's 'Lycidas,' the only other shipwreck poem in English that has occasioned a comparable number of comments. Indeed, as Glavin has convincingly maintained, the mass of particular resemblances, parallelisms, conspicuous reversals, and other contrasts that reveal themselves when the poems are closely compared show that Hopkins had 'Lycidas' consciously or unconsciously in mind when he wrote this poem. Hopkins was later to write to Dixon (D 13) that 'Milton's art is incomparable, not only in English literature, but, I shd. think, almost in any; equal, if not more than equal, to the finest Greek or Roman.' Hopkins knew that there was no way to deal with his heroic death-by-drowning theme without confronting Milton's poem, and he ended by 'usurping "Lycidas" and imposing upon it the features of his own choice,' exhibiting 'in "The Wreck" a stance and strength as willful as it is brilliantly successful' (Glavin 542). The cardinal points of comparison which I develop here are not quite those developed by Glavin, but they would seem to make his points only more cogent.

Both poems are about ships that in actual fact foundered off the coast of England and brought death to those aboard. Milton's poem focuses on the death of one passenger only, Edward King, a young clergyman and ertswhile friend of Milton's at Cambridge. Hopkins', too, focuses on one passenger who likewise is especially dedicated to the Church, the tall Franciscan sister whom Hopkins never met, but it does not focus only on her. The rest of the passengers also command attention in considerable detail. Both poems move out from their immediate historical subject matter to attend to larger questions: Milton's, to denunciation of the corruption which Puritans found pretty well everywhere in the Church where they were not in charge; Hopkins', to reflections on God's providence and mercy regarding all those on the *Deutschland* who died, both those of the Roman Catholic faith and all others besides, 'the comfortless unconfessed of them,' whom Hopkins was sure 'lovely-felicitous Providence' took care of, too, despite the horror that attended their deaths. Milton concludes by reflecting on the place of his hero in a somewhat classicized Kingdom of God and, rather debonairly, upon himself, the poet, and what awaits him: 'Tomorrow to fresh Woods, and Pastures new.' Hopkins concludes by celebrating his heroine's union with Christ, who had come in the awful tempest to claim her as his own, and by begging her, the German sister, to pray for his country, England, and especially for the reunion of the English people with the Roman Catholic Church.

Milton classicizes his hero; Hopkins psychologizes his heroine. The amount of circumstantial detail concerning the shipwreck and King's death in Milton's poem is virtually nil. Details were probably not available to him. He makes up for lack of detail by enriching his text out of the store of topoi which the rhetorical tradition had accumulated from classical times. King's death is presented in melodiously tuned commonplaces: he is 'dead ere his prime,' he is said to 'float upon his watery bier,' where he must not be 'unwept.' The 'remorseless deep' clos'd o'er the head' of this beloved of the sea Nymphs. In thus resorting to commonplace treatment, Milton was following accepted poetic practice which could produce out of the accumulated wisdom of the past work not only profound but also original (Ong, *Interfaces* 148–88). A hundred years later, Alexander Pope would still advocate such practice in his *Essay on Criticism*: poets were reprocessors who improved what they fell heir to, writing of 'What oft was thought, but ne'er so well expressed.' But Milton was also making the best of a difficult situation. He was compensating for lack of detail by supplying attractive and effective commonplace generalities. This not only poets but also rhetoricians and even trial lawyers had typically been forced to do in the pre-modern world. Cicero had followed this procedure. In a low-technology culture access to facts even in cases of national and international importance is extremely limited, almost infinitesimal by Watergate standards, and Cicero had to flesh out his argument with all-purpose purple patches: 'O tempora! O mores!' And he did it well, as few can do anymore and as Hopkins was disinclined to do. Commonplace treatment diminishes as access to particularities grows.

Hopkins had abundant and almost immediate access to particulars about his wreck. Newspapers were collecting eyewitness reports and distributing them as fast as they could across the British Isles. The entire nation was consciously involved in the disaster while it was still going on. St Beuno's College in Wales, on the western edge of Great Britain, where Hopkins was studying theology, was in contact with the eastern coast, where the doomed ship was breaking up. A technological revolution which had brought into being the steam locomotive and the telegraph had altered human beings' feeling for the world around them and for the presence of themselves in the world. It had changed the face of poetry as well and made possible Hopkins' poem.

Hopkins' family had felt intimately the effects of this technological revolution. From boyhood Gerard had been conditioned, more than all but a very few other Victorians, to a synchronic awareness of events from across the globe. His father, Manley Hopkins, as earlier noted here, was a marine insurance 'average adjuster' (Mariani, *Commentary* xi), a person apportioning among multiple insurers charges regarding loss of jettisoned goods on a given ship, one professionally alert to shipwreck or other marine crises. The Hopkins family, more than most families, lived in constant alertness to events, especially large-scale catastrophic events, occurring across the globe. In a letter to Bridges 21 May 1878, Hopkins refers to insensitive oral reading of 'The Loss of the Eurydice' (P 41) as 'mere Lloyd's Shipping Intelligence' (B 52). The imperial British net was cast wide, and a pull on the meshes in the South Pacific or the Indian Ocean would immediately register on the London exchange and send tremors through the Hopkins household.

Hopkins' two longest mature and complete poems are about distant shipwrecks, 'The Wreck of the Deutschland' and 'The Loss of the Eurydice,' and his feeling for the human suffering in both, and most notably in the former, is not for something long over with but for something going on, as Milton's 'Lycidas' could not be. Hopkins had been getting day-by-day on-the-spot reports of the Deutschland's disaster from the Times, thanks to the telegraph (mentioned repeatedly in the Times reports) and to the British railways connecting London with Wales. He felt the human suffering on the grounded and disintegrating ship in the North Seas as simultaneous with the activities, trivial by contrast, that he was engaged in at the same time when many of the passengers and crew were dying (P 28):

> Away in the loveable west,
> On a pastoral forehead of Wales,
> I was under a roof here, I was at rest,
> And they the prey of the gales.

The poem is packed with precise, near-synchronic details from the Times accounts of the wreck, as can be seen by examining these accounts reprinted in Weyand (353–74). In the wealth of its physical and human specificities, the 'Deutschland' easily matches the Times stories. Moreover, Hopkins writes himself into the poem as reportorially as he does the physical particularities of the wreck: his unique self is there in all the personal awareness of particularities it involves. 'I may add for your greater interest and edification,' he writes in his letter to Bridges on 21 August 1877 (B 47), 'that what refers to myself in the poem is all strictly and literally true and did all occur; nothing is added for poetical padding.' Carol Christ has pointed out (105–49) that the Victorian vaunting of particularism affected the reporting not only of exterior reality but also of personal experience, including interior states of consciousness. Hopkins' other, and later, shipwreck poem, 'The Loss of the Eurydice,' was written also at the time of the shipwreck and is equally laden with details from the *Times* accounts of that disaster, again all reprinted in Weyand (375–92), though Hopkins' personal involvement here is less conspicuously autobiographical, showing chiefly in his prayer, which certainly involves his own personal feeling.

The immediacy provided by rapid telegraphic communication was a new experience in human life. It would deeply influence literary style, producing, in the post–World War I generation who resonated immediately to Hopkins, the widely imitated participatory narrative of Hemingway – you, the reader, and I, the writer, are here in it together (Ong, *Interfaces* 62–9). Hemingway had been schooled in synchronic writing as a Toronto *Star* war reporter, producing texts for telegraphic transmission that gave readers all-but-instantaneous access to distant events. 'The Wreck of the Deutschland' is Ur-Hemingway in the sense that it is the first great telegraphically conditioned poem in English, and perhaps in any language. Electricity even surfaces explicitly in the text: against the protracted sufferings of life, 'time's tasking,' Hopkins sets in contrast what he calls 'electrical horror,' the sudden urgency of the storm at sea. In 'The Loss of the Eurydice,' likewise, Boreas, the north wind, 'came equipped, deadly-electric.' Hopkins found electricity in the form of lightning and thunder a spectacular instance of the concentrated, suddenly releasable energies that appealed so much to the Victorian sensibility. Although he does not advert explicitly to the use of electricity for the telegraph, certainly this and its other growing uses were making electricity an element in the sensibility of Hopkins' age.

John Robinson (124) points out that in some of Hopkins' poems, even in the early 'Nondum' (1866), 'It was not his own fate which caused such a shudder of loneliness but a feeling of the ultimate inaccessibility of others' lives and deaths.' Other selves: the isolated 'I.' Rapid communication, by making the experience of others in disaster so immediately present, had advertised more than ever this inaccessibility. The German sister, faced with the 'electrical horror,' cried out, 'O Christ, Christ, come quickly' (P.28) – in the *Times* account, 'O Christ, come quickly.' And Hopkins anguishes: 'The majesty! What did she mean?' How is this isolated 'I' in the storm really reacting in the secret interior of herself? 'What did she mean?' Her 'selfless self of self,' her will, her power of free choice, how was it leaning in this instant of time? By bringing her and the other ship-wrecked persons so close to him, rapid communication had given new reality to the selves of others.

Hopkins found the answer to his question, 'What did she mean?' by deciding that the Franciscan sister's cry, as reported in the *Times*, was her recognition that Christ was coming in the storm to take her to himself in her death that, like his, would open a new life. She freely accepts her death. Hopkins was drawn to this magnificent, though anguished, free acceptance. Precocious again: for free acceptance of one's own death was to become the ultimate freedom in some later existentialist thinking. Although, oddly enough, no commentator has heretofore adverted to this fact, so far as I am aware, this embattled woman's last or near-last words are equivalently the last words of the Bible itself, where, just before its one-verse formal blessing ('The grace of the Lord Jesus be with you. Amen.'), the Book of Revelation concludes with the cry 'Come, Lord Jesus.'

This is the perennial cry of Christian faith. With this utterance in Revelation, eschatological time is ushered into full consciousness: the time in which the resurrected Christ now lives according to Christian faith, a time which is curiously both future to us and present to us, for the resurrected Christ lives both in eternity (which we feel as future, though it is not) and in the now that human beings know. Christ is coming to bring life to this anguished and courageous woman in her death – in the Roman Martyrology the day of death is called the saint's 'birthday,' when she or he is born into eternal life. With these words, Hopkins finally concludes, the woman showed that she was aware that this horrible scene was in fact the coming of Jesus at this moment to bring her with himself to his Father and her Father, just as he had entered into the Resurrection through suffering on the cross. 'The cross to her, she calls Christ to her.' 'There was a heart right! / There was single eye! / Read the unshapable shock night and knew the who and the way.' God comes into our lives in all sorts of ways, Hopkins brings himself to acknowledge in part I of the poem: he comes with 'a lingering-out sweet skill' as to Augustine, or 'at once, as once at a crash' to Paul or as 'lightning and love' or 'With an anvil-ding / And with fire.' Adding the 'quickly' to the biblical text, the sister was asking Christ to speed his arrival. In the midst of terror she was destined for the 'heaven-haven of the reward.' Hopkins allusively likens the nun's story to Mary's response at the Annunciation, which he later comments on (*S* 172 – see ch 2, no 11 below). With her 'Be it done to me according to your will' (Luke 1:38), Mary had first conceived Jesus by faith in her mind and thereby opened the way to conceiving him in her body (the Incarnation came about, the Son became man, consequently to this 'Yes' of Mary's). In her cry recognizing Christ's advent at her life's end this German sister also first conceived Christ in faith in her mind and thereupon received him for eternity as she met her bodily death. 'Here was heart-throe, birth of a brain, / Word, that heard and kept thee and uttered thee outright.'

Unlike his fellow Jesuit-to-be, Pierre Teilhard de Chardin (born six years after the *Deutschland* disaster, eight years old when Hopkins died), Hopkins showed little if any conscious awareness of the effects of technological advance on consciousness. On the contrary, he often feels technological progress as a possible threat to nature, whose treatment by human beings he laments: 'even where we mean / To mend her we end her' (*P* 43). Bedford Leigh, the manufacturing city where Hopkins spent some of his happiest days among his working-class parishioners, did not alter Hopkins' ecological concern, expressed in an earlier poem (*P* 31):

> Generations have trod, have trod, have trod;
>> And all is shared with trade; bleared, smeared with toil;
>> And wears man's smudge and shares man's smell.

There was indeed unquenchable hope, but it lodged in nature as overseen by God:

> ... for all this, nature is never spent;
>> There lives the dearest freshness deep down things;
> And though the last lights off the black West went
>> Oh, morning, at the brown brink eastward, springs –
> Because the Holy Ghost over the bent
>> World broods with warm breast and with ah! bright wings.

However, although Hopkins fails to note the fact, the new technology, telegraphic communication, had actually brought human beings together in significant ways more than before. By making associations between human beings across the globe closer and closer, it had curiously intensified the Victorian sense of the self, joined in its isolation with other isolated and yet intersubjectively related selves, and had given to Christian concern for others a new immediacy. Access to more and more external particulars had paradoxically internalized Hopkins' focus in ways impossible for Milton. Aware of the detailed circumstances of the disaster and of the exact words of the distressed woman, Hopkins thought immediately and intently of her interior life, her self, of her effort to communicate amidst her agonies: 'The majesty! What did she mean?' By contrast, Milton reflects on his associations with King at Cambridge in beautifully turned, but distanced, classical commonplaces: 'For we were nurst upon the self-same hill / Fed the same flock.'

In contrast to Milton, who had wondered what the mythological sea Nymphs were doing when King was drowning without their attentions, Hopkins reflects ruefully on what he himself was doing: 'On a pastoral forehead in Wales / ... under a roof ... at rest' at the very time when the *Deutschland* passengers and crew were 'the prey of the gales.' His felt identity with the victims of the disaster in the detailed circumstances he could picture from the *Times* reports made Hopkins acutely uncomfortable about his own quite comfortable situation contemporary with theirs. Hopkins expresses a far stronger personal relationship with all the victims of the disaster, whom he did not know, than Milton does with King, whom Milton had known. This is not to say that Milton's conventionalism interfered with his expression of the self, but that it gave this expression certain contours different from those of Hopkins.

Processed through Hopkins' sensibility, the new experience of time and self had not done Christian teachings or the Christian sensibility any harm. Quite the contrary, for Hopkins it had been a means of realizing and expressing more urgently than before both the isolation of each person and the unity of isolated persons with one another in Christ. By its new realization of near-simultaneity, technology had afforded a new kind of synchronizing model to aid in thinking of eschatological time, which combines the present and eternity.

TWO   Self and Decision
                    in Ascetic Tradition

1   VICTORIAN PARTICULARISM AND
    JESUIT ASCETICISM

HOPKINS' CONSCIOUSNESS OF SELF was fed not only
out of the Victorian milieu generally, but also by certain elements
in the ascetical tradition in which he lived from the time he entered
the Society of Jesus as a novice at the age of twenty-four. The
ascetical tradition of the Society of Jesus is at the root no more than
the Christian ascetical tradition, as are the ascetical traditions of
other Catholic religious orders, Benedictine, Franciscan, Dominican,
and others. Religious orders seek approval of the Church, in effect,
to receive assurance that their aims and way of life accord with the
Gospel. But the various religious orders emphasize various features
of Christian ascetical tradition. In the Jesuit tradition most of the
characteristic emphases are set by the *Spiritual Exercises* of the
founder of the Society, Ignatius Loyola.

The *Spiritual Exercises* of Ignatius Loyola (1491–1556) were
worked out in a sixteenth-century context and the contours they
give the human self are not those of the nineteenth century. Yet in
their own way the *Spiritual Exercises* focus with precocious intensity on the self and on human freedom as centring the self, and do
so with a particularism that has recently fascinated Roland Barthes.
Their particularist procedures and their focus on self and freedom reinforced in depth the particularism and self-consciousness which
Hopkins first picked up from the Victorian milieu in which he lived.
Downes (*Gerard Manley Hopkins*), Mariani (*Commentary*), Cotter,

Robinson, and many other literary exegetes have assessed various effects of the *Spiritual Exercises* on Hopkins, but no one appears to have examined them as contributing to Hopkins' intense and articulate self-consciousness. The vast ascetical and other theological literature on the *Exercises* is of little help, for until recently, this literature has treated ascetical and other theological history only within a narrow theological context, generally disregarding the larger psychodynamics in the history of consciousness and culture which help determine what theological issues and what ascetical practices come to the fore at any given time. Unless related both to theological formulations and to the larger history of consciousness and culture, studies of Hopkins and the *Spiritual Exercises* can prove pretty jejune.

The influence of the *Spiritual Exercises* on Hopkins was immeasurably more intense and extensive than the influence of a literary work or of a literary tradition. The Spiritual Exercises of St Ignatius Loyola, as a series of ascetical activities described in Ignatius' book of the same name, penetrated Hopkins' entire life, including of course his writings, as a literary work or literary tradition hardly could. (Here, references to the book, the *Spiritual Exercises*, are italicized, references to the Spiritual Exercises as the ascetical activities described in the book are not.) Hopkins 'made' the Exercises, as the expression goes – that is, thought and prayed his way through them – every year of his Jesuit life, in their full thirty-day form twice, in 1868 and 1881, and in an abridged eight-day form (B 59, 194) in each of the other nineteen years. He 'gave' or helped many others through retreats based on the *Spiritual Exercises* (D 69; B 147). All the other Jesuits he lived with were similarly saturated by the Exercises. The Exercises entered into Hopkins' preaching, his daily meditation and other prayers, his correspondence, and his poetry, as well into much of his prose. His commentaries on the *Excercises* constitute his major theological writings.

The present undertaking does not propose to account for the full effects of the *Spiritual Exercises* on Hopkins but rather to examine ways in which they fostered the intensive particularism and self-consciousness in which he outdid even other Victorians. This particularism and self-consciousness, however, is not an isolated effect of the *Exercises*. It is a central effect, with which many other effects are associated.

2 THE 'SPIRITUAL EXERCISES,' TIME, AND HERMENEUTICS

Those who know the Spiritual Exercises more from hearsay than
from direct experience may think of them as a kind of behavioural
template, calculated to produce always the same patterns in
Hopkins and in everyone else who goes through them or 'makes'
them. In actuality, however, the Exercises are not designed to work
as a template. Individual Jesuits have always had quite different personality structures, both before and after they have gone through the
Spiritual Exercises. No other Jesuit ever wrote poetry like Hopkins',
as no other Jesuit ever produced a world view like that of the
sixteenth-century Brother Alphonsus Rodríguez, to whom Hopkins
devoted one of his poems (P 73). Ignatius believed in 'union of
minds and hearts' but not identity of personality structures or
behaviour.

As they have grown diversely into the lives of different persons,
so have the Spiritual Exercises grown diversely into different ages
and cultures. A Victorian came to the Spiritual Exercises, whether
as a book or as a tradition, out of a Victorian setting, with foci of attention partly the same and partly different from those of the sixteenth century, when the Exercises originated. Later ages often surface meanings in a text which the text could express at its point of
origin only by implication, inarticulately or subconsciously. Examining Ignatius' little volume in the light of later awareness, here
in particular that of Hopkins' own world, we can see it and the
tradition it builds not only as a major landmark in the Christian
ascetical tradition but also as a major landmark in the development
of Western consciousness – though not necessarily a major determi-
nant, for its influence was of limited range. The *Exercises* show
Western consciousness maximizing more and more explicitly the
human person and that particularizing centre of the person which is
free human decision, the act of will, which Hopkins identified as
'the selfless self of self' (P 157).

3 THE NATURE OF THE 'SPIRITUAL EXERCISES'

As has just been suggested, the term 'Spiritual Exercises' can refer to
a certain set of activities or to a book entitled *Spiritual Exercises*
that treats of these activities. In the first of these senses, as a set of
activities, the Spiritual Exercises of St Ignatius Loyola consist

basically in sequences of meditative prayer and related activities calculated to assist the one who works through them, the exercitant or
retreatant, to make and confirm a decision, especially a decision
regarding basic orientations in life – marriage or the single state, a
life with personal material possessions or a life of evangelical poverty, and so on – knowing not only what one is doing but also, so
far as possible, one's motivations, without being influenced by 'any
inordinate attachment' (21), which is to say in complete freedom
before God (De Guibert, 122–32). The Exercises are commonly gone
through with the help of a director, but those already experienced in
them can go through them alone. When repeated annually, they are
adapted most often to realizing better or improving or extending
decisions earlier made.

Starting from the stated premise that God is creator, that he
created human beings to praise, reverence, and serve him and thus
to achieve union with him, and that all things on earth are there to
help human beings attain this union, the Exercises take the retreatant in prayerful meditation successively through sin and its consequences, the incarnation and the life of Jesus, his passion and death,
his resurrection and ascension, and through fundamental implications of these events for the individual, to end with the holistic
'Contemplation for Attaining Love' through seeing God working in
all things. Toward the middle of the Exercises, the exercitant must
face the *electio* or decision that he or she finds central in life at the
period when the Exercises are being undertaken. In their complete
form the Exercises take the exercitant's full time for more or less
thirty successive days – divided into four 'weeks' of adjustable
lengths, for the exact duration of the various parts Ignatius deliberately and explicitly leaves flexible. But the Exercises are also
variously abridged, often into an eight-day period. Besides meditative prayer, the Exercises include such other matters as examination
of conscious, repentence for sins and confession of sins, and reception of Communion, as well as consideration of various ascetical
guidelines (to be noted here later).

The Spiritual Exercises are isolating. They are devotional, but,
unlike the liturgy, which is communal, they are basically gone
through all alone, with the exception of their liturgical components,
Mass, Communion, and confession. If they are gone through in accord with Ignatius' plan and not in some adapted form, all during
the days devoted to the Exercises the exercitant speaks with no one

but the director, and then only briefly and infrequently, perhaps once a day. The encounters with the director all bear on the exercitant's particular, and variable, reactions to the Exercises. The rest of the time the exercitant spends in isolation and in silence, in prayer and reflection. The Exercises pivot on the *electio* or the making of a decision, inevitably an isolating and lonely act. The director, Ignatius insists, must not attempt to influence the decision, which is the business of the exercitant alone before God (15).

The book entitled *Spiritual Exercises* is a manual-like, rather brief work for the use of a person helping the exercitant go through the Exercises, that is, for the person commonly called the director. It provides the sequences of subjects for meditation and prayer, sketches how the director is to present to the exercitant the matters proposed for meditative prayer, and provides other instructions and suggestions at some length.

The Spiritual Exercises as such and the book bearing that title both grew out of Ignatius' own conversion from the life of a soldier-courtier to a life of total dedication to God – ultimately, as it worked out, to total dedication to God in the priesthood in a religious order which he and his associates founded, *Societas Jesu*, the Society of Jesus, or, to convey the feel of the Latin name somewhat better in today's English idiom, the Companions of Jesus.

The sources of the Spiritual Exercises are manifold, of course (Marjorie O'Rourke Boyle, 'Angels' 242–7; Joseph de Guibert, 152–81. We do not know all of them and never will, for real influences are often obscure and often work idiosyncratically. But we know some of the literary sources. Ignatius had read in Spanish the fourteenth-century *Life of Christ* by the Carthusian Ludolph of Saxony and the Spanish translation of the *Golden Legend* of Jacobus de Voragine (d 1298) known also as the *Flos Sanctorum*, a collection of saints' lives and legends. From the time of his conversion on, he read frequently in the *Imitation of Christ*, attributed in Ignatius' day to John Charlier, also called John de Gerson (1363–1429) but now known to be almost certainly by Thomas à Kempis (1379 or 1380–1471), though massive appropriation of material from the commonplace tradition often makes 'authorship' of this work in places a moot question. Specific sources proposed for various features of the *Exercises* include also the *Arte de servir a Dios* of Alfonso de Madrid, Erasmus' *Enchiridion Militis Christiani*, and several other works. Besides such literary works, a popular 'crusade spirituality' also distinctively marked Ignatius' mindset (Wolter), as will be seen.

Ignatius' spirituality is in the mainstream of Christian spirituality but is also strongly influenced by pious humanist currents of his day (Evennett, and references therein). Its literary sources can perhaps best be situated historically with reference to the Devotio Moderna, the fifteenth- and sixteenth-century ascetical movement in the Low Countries which produced both the *Imitation of Christ*, which Ignatius always recommended highly, and the work of Erasmus, which Ignatius came to dislike.

The well-known devotional compilation *Imitatio Christi* or *The Imitation of Christ* arose in the context of the Devotio Moderna and shows many of the movement's special features. Ricardo Garcia Villoslada (1956) lists ten of these features, all relevant here. The Devotio Moderna was (1) Christocentric, focusing more on Christ's humanity than on the divine nature and attributes – hence the 'imitation' to which human beings are called. It stressed (2) an affectivity allied with rationality rather than with what would much later be styled 'enthusiasm.' It sought to introduce some kind of (3) method into meditation and life generally, and thus was to some degree monastic. It stressed (4) self-knowledge and obligation, in a way suggesting the strong Stoic influence that marked much late medieval and, even more, Renaissance thought, religious and other. Its concern with mysticism had a strong (5) moralistic cast, stressing self-abnegation and effort – more Stoic influence, though combined with biblical. It was (6) anti-speculative: knowledge was inconsequential and indeed useless without fear of God. 'I would rather feel compunction than know how to define it,' *The Imitation of Christ* states (bk 1, ch 1, sec 3). It was (7) deeply interiorized and subjective in focus: external works and ritual were far less important than intention, reflection, and inner fervour. It favoured (8) solitude and silence. The Devotio Moderna encouraged (9) Bible reading for devotional purposes, not for scientific research. It was (10) anti-humanistic to the extent that it despised not only merely human values but also secular knowledge generally. To these features noted by García Villoslada one might add: it regarded reception of (11) Holy Communion as crucial to devotional life.

These characteristics of the Devotio Moderna do not define the Spiritual Exercises but they identify a setting in which Ignatius thought and prayed and worked. Ignatius would modify several of the emphases that García Villoslada identifies. External works he would upgrade in importance, but only if they proceeded from the deep interior where the person stood before God (7). Solitude and silence (8) were to be valued, but not at the expense of work for one's neighbour. The ideal was *contemplatio in actione*, being contemplative, keeping attentive to God, while working for others. Humanism (10), the study of human beings in their works, cultural and artistic, was not rejected but authenticated. Secular knowledge was recognized as having positive value, though a decidedly lesser value than knowledge of God and his revelation in his Son, Jesus Christ, to whom secular knowledge, like everything else, is related. 'Through him all things come into being' (John 1:3). On this score Ignatius had misgivings about Erasmus, who had been trained in the Devotio Moderna but whose *Enchiridion Militis Christiani* Ignatius found caused him to lose his devotion, leaving him spiritually cold (De Guibert, 165–6, n 36). The relationship of Ignatius and Erasmus has been much discussed (Villoslada, 'San Ignacio ... y Erasmo'; Bataillon), and it does appear that Erasmus actually influenced Ignatius, but it seems clear that Erasmus did not make secular knowledge subservient to knowledge of God in a fashion that would satisfy Ignatius. Ignatius, on the other hand, had no experience of advancing learning such as Erasmus had, and seems to have sensed no urgent need to advance secular knowledge or even to have considered the possibility that it might be advanced. Although he held the degree of Master of Arts from the University of Paris, and had subsequently studied some little theology there (he had no degree in theology), Ignatius in fact was hardly an intellectual academic, as Erasmus definitely was. Ignatius' antipathy to Protestantism was not based on confrontation of doctrinal issues – Ignatius says virtually nothing anywhere about Protestant doctrine – but on a desire to minimize disturbances in the Church, which he felt impeded evangelization and devotional life. He 'conceived doctrine almost entirely with a view to pastoral effectiveness' (O'Malley, 'The Fourth Vow' 11), in this way profoundly resembling his polar opposite Martin Luther.

Despite these and a few other variances, Ignatius preserved the essential Devotio Moderna tradition. His spirituality, and the Spiritual Exercises, would be Christocentric, deeply affective but not wildly so, not restricted to reason but consonant with reason, attentive to self-knowledge, self-abnegation, and effort, more concerned with inner fervour than with speculative web-spinning, focused resolutely and methodically but also adaptively on the inner life even when attentive to the exterior, valuing solitude and silence and prayer even when committed also to work with others, stressing frequent and even daily reception of the Eucharist, attending to the word of God in the Bible for its devotional effects rather than its intellectual piquancy, rating human knowledge positively but placing it at infinite cut below knowledge had through faith and God's gracious giving.

But other kinds of influences also affected Ignatius. The Devotio Moderna grew around an academic and literary core. Ignatius was not a bookish person, and certainly not theologically bookish. His Master of Arts degree at the University of Paris did not involve the study of theology at all, but the logic, 'physics' (or 'natural philosophy,' the then equivalent, more or less, of our modern natural sciences and 'faculty' psychology), and, on a much lesser scale, some ethics and metaphysics (Ong, *Ramus* 141). Ignatius attended some lectures in theology only for around a year and a half after his MA (Clancy, 38). The roots of his devotional life were largely in popular piety, and Karl Rahner has called it a 'real miracle' that a person with so little theology other than that found in 'popular works of piety never broke the rules of theology' ('Ignatian Process' 282). One Paris doctor of theology, Martiall Mazurier, to whom Ignatius gave the Exercises, stated, 'I never heard a single man speak on theological matters with such a mastery and reverence' (quoted by Clancy, 38).

The strain of popular piety which left perhaps the most distinctive marks on Ignatius has lately been called 'crusade spirituality.' This late medieval development exhibits many features that overlap with or interact with the Devotio Moderna, so that the two traditions, the Devotio Moderna largely literary and the 'crusade spirituality' popular, can account together for much of the characteristic outlook of the Spiritual Exercises and of the Jesuit spirituality the Exercises shaped. 'Crusade spirituality' grew naturally out of the crusades and their complex religious, social, and psychological effects. The crusade mentality of course was very much alive still in the life of Ignatius' Spain, following the reconquest of Granada from the Moors and the unification of Granada and Castille under Ferdinand and Isabella in the late 1400s.

The 'crusade spirituality' inherited by Ignatius has been described as 'rich in intensity and weaknesses, in depths of feeling and super-

ficiality, in a variety of religious gestures, in the power to organize
forms of devotion – from the stay-at-home pilgrimage, in which a
proxy was sent, to the Franciscan Way of the Cross, from the crusade indulgence to the blessing of those who fought the Turks'
(Wolter, 103). After the victory over the Turks at the siege of
Vienna, 'crusade spirituality' declines, to be submerged finally at
the Enlightenment. But it was very much alive during the youth of
St Ignatius, and especially in the Iberian peninsula, where it fed,
among other things, the Spanish and Portuguese expansion into
lands of the 'heathen.' Ignatius inherited from 'crusade spirituality'
such things as (1) a sense of the call of Christ to do hard things for
him because of the hard things he had chosen to do for human
beings, (2) hence a strong Christocentrism (as also in the Devotio
Moderna), (3) concern with the penitential pilgrimage and readiness
for poverty and the marked early Ignatian commitment to work in
hospitals (these had proliferated along crusading routes), (4) strong
allegiance to the papacy, for the pope was felt to be central to the
Christian unity the crusades demanded, (5) a sense of the interrela-
tionship between the defence and the spread of the faith, (6) concern
for 'the glory of God,' affronted by the heathen, (7) the need to bring
interior motivation to bear on exterior action – committing oneself
to a crusade, with all the hardship this involved, had to be interiorly
motivated or it spiritually was useless (Wolter, 134 and passim).

Despite its connection with the popular 'crusader' mentality, it
should be noted that Ignatian spirituality is not 'military' in the
sense in which it is often supposed to be: committed to rigid external conformity, draconian rules of conduct, lock-step order, relent-
less authoritarianism, undeviating pursuit of goals conceived of in
terms of power. More than one author (De Guibert, 172–4; Clancy,
267–79) has shown that Ignatian spirituality is not of this sort at all,
despite recurrent cloak-and-dagger accounts such as René Fülop-
Müller's *The Power and Secret of the Jesuits* (1930) or an occasional
aside such as one in John Robinson's *In Extremity* (2). This point is
important with regard to Hopkins because commentators, mostly
earlier ones, have supposed that the anguish in some of his later
poems, the 'terrible sonnets,' was connected with some sort of
repressions brought on by the 'military' character of Jesuit life.

The biblical tradition affords Ignatius, as it affords many other
ascetical writers, an occasional military image or expression, which
Ignatius often enhances with chivalric trappings, frequently con-

nected with the 'crusade spirituality' just mentioned, as in the meditations on the Two Standards and on the Kingdom, but Ignatius' famous letter on obedience does not contain a single military analogy. Ignatius had been a soldier, but deducing from this that the Society of Jesus is 'military,' as Thomas Clancy has amusingly noted, makes about as much sense as to attribute to the Kennedy and Nixon administrations 'naval' ideologies because Kennedy and Nixon had been naval officers. Moreover, sharply defined ranks, close-order drill, rigidly stylized values, and clicking heels – which 'military' commonly suggests today – were unknown in the soldiering of Ignatius' age. His soldiering had been rather more in the *Three Musketeers* style, noted for daring venturesomeness rather than for lock-step discipline. In my own entire experience of Jesuits' spiritual exhortations to other Jesuits, I do not recall ever having heard the Society of Jesus presented to its own members as distinctively military. Quite to the contrary, the basis of its obedience, as that of all Roman Catholic religious institutes, is caught in a saying often heard among Jesuits, when Latin and formulaic expressions were more common than either now is: *Societas Jesu, societas amoris,* 'the Society of Jesus, a society of love.'

'Military' suggests, of course, among other things, total accountability of lower to higher personnel. Such accountability marks, more or less, all Catholic religious institutes. However, accountability, though real, is far more personalized in religious life than in the military. Religious accountability is set in a dialogic relationship between superior and subject. Each Jesuit provincial superior must meet each year privately, in complete confidentiality, with each of his subjects (who may number as many as three or four hundred in a province) for as long as the individual subject may wish. Such 'visitations' constitute a major part of the religious superior's work. Each local superior also must arrange similar heart-to-heart conferences with each Jesuit priest, scholastic (a Jesuit, with vows, studying for the priesthood but not yet ordained), and lay brother in his community. Of course, if by military is meant dedicated, responsible service in a socially organized structure even in the face of hardship, then the Society of Jesus is military, but so are health service organizations, companies of actors ('the show must go on'), groups of explorers, and countless other groups. Ignatius made a great deal of obedience not out of any desire to militarize the Society of Jesus but because Jesus was obedient and redeemed human beings by his obedience offered in love to his Father (Philippians 2:8) and also because in the absence of any fixed style of dress (Jesuits wear no special 'habit') and of a routinized external way of life such as was common in other religious orders, obedience, tying all persons together under one head, was the principal implement and sign of fraternal union of minds and hearts.

Ignatian obedience relates intimately to the self because it is personally grounded and implemented. The superior and his subjects are to be united in love and in objectives so that a command is something to be obeyed not mechanically, but with one's whole being. Hopkins' relations with his novice master, Father Peter Gallwey (*FL* 112–13) reflect the Ignatian ideal (see also Thomas, *Hopkins* 59, 90, 126, 129, 149, 152, 172–3). In *The Constitutions of the Society of Jesus* Ignatius took pains to suggest ways of resolving conflicts which in good faith would inevitably arise to block union of minds and hearts (167, 242, 271–3). If a superior tells you to do something morally wrong, he of course is not to be obeyed. This is taken for granted in Catholic moral teaching, and the Jesuit *Constitutions* also state it explicitly (164, 248). But otherwise, if a directive goes against your grain, you should make every honest effort to construe it positively and to see the superior's point of view. Obedience is to be not merely mechanical, but internalized. Any problems one has with a directive from a superior can be discussed with him in an open, filial way. This internalized obedience is more demanding than merely perfunctory, external compliance. It is central to Jesuit asceticism and the key to Hopkins' own vocation (Thomas, *Hopkins* 211).

Ignatius' concern with internalization or subjectivity here also links him to the Devotio Moderna. While in humanist fashion accepting the external world with less trepidation than some earlier Christian ascetics, Ignatius assumes, and the Constitutions of the Society of Jesus explicitly state (813), that the interior psychic world, where self-consciousness lodges, is more important, more crucial in each human person than are the human body and its physical world, on which exterior consciousness is nevertheless dependent. Ignatius' and Hopkins' basic intuitions of existence here meet somehow in depth, although Ignatius' age, as has already been suggested, was by no means so adept as Hopkins' in clinical descriptions of interior states of consciousness.

4 MANUALS AND DETAILS

Ignatius' little book, *Spiritual Exercises*, is noteworthy for its
manual-like arrangement, its precise attention to detail, and its constant partition of its subject matter. But his particularized detail in
organization is not so entirely novel as a recent commentator, the
late Roland Barthes (58–70), has tried to make it out to be. De
Guibert (167–8) has pointed out that the *Rhetorica Divina* of
William of Paris (d 1202) taught the organization of mental prayer
according to the principles of Quintilian's *Institutiones Oratoriae*.
More recently, Whelan has shown how much in Renaissance religious meditation manuals connects with ancient, medieval, and Renaissance rhetoric, which inculcated careful division of subject
matter and other detailed organizational practices. Ignatius' method
of meditation by use of the three faculties of memory, intellect, and
will had been worked out by St Bonaventure (d 1274) and Ramon
Lull (d 1315). Programmed imaginative contemplation of events in
Jesus' life had been taught four and a half centuries before Ignatius
by Aelred of Rievaulx (d 1166) and further developed in the *Meditations on the Life of Christ* attributed to the fourteenth century to St
Bonaventure and transmitted to Ignatius during his convalescence
through Ludolph of Saxony's *Life of Christ*, mentioned earlier.

Attention to detail had long marked religious life in countless
ways. Rules of religious orders are filled with specifics about physical settings, behaviour, and much else. The tradition even runs back
to the minute prescriptions set down by the Priestly Writer in Exodus for the construction of the tabernacle and for liturgical procedures, as well as to other minute prescriptions for all sorts of
behaviour in Numbers and Deuteronomy. Clerks, biblical and other,
are writers and writing facilitates and encourages the multiplying of
detailed rules: a text itself is a paradigm of fixity and the very
possibility of setting down fixed written prescriptions encourages
the desire to reduce life itself to textual regularity.

De Guibert (168) states that Ignatius' achievement consisted in
simplifying, varying, and making flexible the methods in spiritual
life to which he fell heir. Certainly the *Spiritual Exercises* strike today's reader immediately as more clearly and conspicuously organized than earlier ascetical or other religious treatises – which largely
means, in effect, arranged for easy visual retrieval in clear-cut sort-

ings and divisions under appropriate headings, with elaborate and trustworthy cross-references. This kind of manual-style clarity we today take quite for granted, though it resulted from the tight control of textual space made possible by print. Before print, handwritten texts entitled manuals or handbooks, such as Epictetus' *Enchiridion* of Stoicism, lack this crisp, visually governed, compartment-like format.

Ignatius was born most probably in 1491, when printing from movable alphabetic type was less than fifty years old, but spreading fast. Everywhere authors and editors, sometimes deliberately though often unreflectively, through subconscious adjustment, were organizing or reorganizing materials for an imagination subtly restructuring itself for visual rather than oral-aural processing and retrieval of knowledge (Ong, *Ramus* and *Orality*). It must be noted, however, that Ignatius lived early enough to be not fully into typographic organization of materials: the *Spiritual Exercises* have no title page, an invention of print, and indeed not even a title until after the reader has covered some two thousand words of *Annotations* or Introductory Observations. They simply start with the text itself, as do most pre-typographic manuscripts, which, lacking not only title pages but also lacking even clear-cut titles, normally have to be indexed each under its opening words, which bibliographers call its 'incipit' (the Latin third person singular verb meaning 'it begins').

What is most distinctive of Ignatius, however, is not simply his exploitation of typographic organization but his exploitation of it and of elements in Christian asceticism for the very specific and clearly stated purpose earlier noted, namely, the coming to a fully free decision before God, primarily about the choice of one's state of life but also on occasion about other important matters. The focus on free choice means inevitably sharp focus on the self, for the human person is the only decision-maker there is on earth. Ignatius' preoccupation with organized detail bears, surprisingly perhaps but really, on the self as self.

5 FLEXIBLE PARTICULARISM

Because it focuses on decision making, the particularism in the *Spiritual Exercises* is not rigid. The illusion that it is has often been kept alive by the complementary illusion, already noted, that the Society of Jesus has a 'military' spirituality. All the hundreds of directors of the Spiritual Exercises whom I know personally or have ever heard of, following Ignatius himself (6–10, 15, 18–19, etc), insist on the flexibility of the directives in Ignatius' little book. The *Spiritual Exercises* are not like yoga in aim or spirit, in that their directives are not keyed ultimately to foreseen results but are only helps to open the soul to God's grace. Who knows what the results of grace will be? 'The wind blows where it will' (John 3:8). Ignatius was not a Pelagian, and he knew there is no way to set up an inflexible method that will guarantee the action of grace or even the best response to grace. Grace is a free offering of God, made for the human being's free acceptance, and one has always to attend to the way God works with this particular person, for he works with no two the same way. Hence Ignatius' sections in the *Exercises* on 'The Two Standards' and 'The Discernment of Spirits' to help the exercitant be sensitive to the often puzzling movements of the Spirit in the exercitant's life. The *Spiritual Exercises* are at the service of grace, not a mechanism for grace. There is no mechanism for grace.

Nevertheless, the Exercises are full of particularities, and their particularism is relevant to Hopkins' particularist mindset. The most salient particularities in the *Spiritual Exercises* are methodological or procedural particularities. These are minute. Ignatius goes into painstaking detail about the way to do the general examination of conscience, in which the exercitant twice a day reviews his or her thoughts, words, and actions. He provides a five-point method for the examination: thanksgiving to God for his goodness, petition for grace to know one's sins and rid oneself of them, the actual account-taking of one's actions since the last examination of conscience, asking God for forgiveness, and the resolution, with God's grace, to amend one's life. In addition, Ignatius explains a carefully elaborated 'particular examination' of conscience that aims at extirpating the exercitant's various failings one after the other by working on each successively, day by day. The exercitant chooses one fault – yielding to impatience, speaking unkindly, and so on – recalls it on rising in the morning and twice a day tallies up how many times he or she has fallen into it. Ignatius' text presents a simple graph – graphs were rare in manuscripts but becoming common in print – for visibly recording the tally day-by-day and week-by-week. When a person has eliminated one fault, he or she begins on the next. During the course of the Exercises, the exercitant is to direct the particular examination of conscience to an especially particularized end, using it 'to remove faults and negligences' in the following of the Exercises themselves (90). The particular examination of conscience is bluntly practical, focusing sharply on the here and now.

Each period of meditative prayer is highly structured, beginning always with a preparatory prayer asking God that 'all my intentions, actions, and operations' may be directed purely to his 'praise and service.' Next come the 'preludes,' generally three, the first a review of the scriptural event being meditated on (this prelude is omitted in the few cases where meditation is on some more generalized subject such as sin), next a mise-en-scène, the well-known 'composition of place,' about which more will be said later, where a scene, usually in the life of Christ, is imagined in as specific physical detail as can be commanded, and then a third prelude in which the exercitant prays to God for the grace desired. Ignatius is at pains to indicate what the exercitant should ask in particular of God at various places in the Exercises: at one time knowledge of one's own sinfulness, at other times sorrow for one's own sins, deep interior knowledge of Jesus, highly personalized (as we would put it today) identification with Jesus in his sadness and passion, participation in the joy of his Resurrection, a knowledge of God's goodness to me and others and of God's presence everywhere, the grace to love and serve him in everything, and so on. After the preludes comes matter for the body of the prayer, that is, the various 'points' or divisions of the subject to be meditated on or contemplated. (This division into 'points' is one of the many divisions that Ignatius got in one way or another, or in many ways, from the Western rhetorical tradition – Whelan).

Last comes the 'colloquy,' to which all else builds up. The colloquy, paradoxically, downgrades all the antecedent particularized divisions and procedures, for it is essentially a holistic activity, a spontaneous, intimate encounter 'made by speaking exactly as one friend speaks to another, or a servant speaks to a master.' The colloquy consists of person-to-person encounter. It is addressed to a particular person or particular persons: to Jesus Christ, to God the Father, to the Three Divine Persons (Father, Son, and Holy Spirit), a few times optionally to Mary, the Mother of Jesus, and in the 'triple colloquy,' at crucially intimate points in the Exercises, first to Mary, then to her Son, and then ultimately to the Father.

Other details spin out on all sides in the book of the *Spiritual Ex-*

ercises. Ignatius advises how to adjust the physical environment to the mood suitable for one or another subject of prayer, darkening the room for meditations on sin and hell, letting in light for contemplations on Christ's resurrection, and so on. He goes into great detail regarding the character of Christ's kingdom and of Lucifer's methods, specifications for choosing a way of life, favourable times for personal decision-making (the *electio*), three typical responses to obstacles to freedom ('Three Classes of Persons'), three degrees of 'humility' (after endless commentary, still a maverick term; by it Ignatius means, in effect, degrees of generous response or self-giving), rules for the discernment of spirits (that is, for deciding whether a given attraction to a particular action or sort of behaviour is truly from God or not), rules for doing penance for one's sins, rules for the giving of alms, rules for dealing with scrupulosity, rules for thinking with the Church, and many more specificities.

Ignatius' particularities bred more particularities in his followers. Early directors generated various baroque and highly idiosyncratic elaborations of what Ignatius specified (Iparraguirre, *Historia*, vols 2, 3). There is no time to go into all these idiosyncrasies here. They do suggest, however, how the *Exercises* adapted or even fostered highly individualistic tendencies well before Hopkins.

6 HOPKINS' APPROPRIATION OF IGNATIAN DETAIL

Ignatius' particularist prescriptivism in the *Spiritual Exercises* represents not simply a religious phenomenon but an advanced analytic consciousness in some general way en route to Victorian particularism. But the Victorian particularist state of mind, as has been seen, characteristically concerned itself not so much with methodological or procedural detail as with exactly articulated attention to physical particularities and to interior states of mind, both of which intrigued Hopkins. Is there anything in the *Spiritual Exercises* that would encourage precisely these concerns? There is, and certain effects are spectacularly evident in Hopkins.

In the well-known 'composition of place,' already mentioned briefly, the exercitant, in accord with Ignatius' instruction, is to represent to himself or herself the place in which the event occurs that is to be meditated on or contemplated. Ignatius insists on detailed representation though he leaves it to the individual retreatant to generate the details. Thus, to take one example among many, in meditating on the Nativity (111), the exercitant is to construct, by way of a Second Prelude to the prayer proper,

a mental representation of the place. It will consist here in seeing in imagination the way from Nazareth to Bethlehem. Consider its length, its breadth; whether level, or through valleys, and over hills. Observe also the place or cave where Christ is born; whether big or little; whether high or low; and how it is arranged.

The purpose, of course, is to help the ensuing concentration on the matter of prayer.

Not all matter for prayer in the Exercises is equally amenable to the composition of place, which most readily suits prayer about visible phenomena, such as events in the life of Christ. Prayer about such events Ignatius calls contemplation (*contemplatio*). Prayer about matters not visible – which Ignatius calls meditation (*meditatio*) – creates certain representational problems. In such cases, however, Ignatius is equally insistent on some sort of sensible representation, often of a kind thoroughly familiar to those who know the Renaissance emblem book milieu. Thus, in meditating on sin (47), the retreatant, by way of prelude, is

to see in imagination my soul as a prisoner in this corruptible body, and to consider my whole composite being as an exile here on earth, cast out to live among brute beasts. I said my whole composite being, body and soul.

The last sentence here appears to be added as a disclaimer of Platonism or extreme dualism, which the previous sentence rather helplessly slips into, for it was still hard not to be Manichaean (Ong, 'St Ignatius' Prison-Cage'). That is, the sentence 'I said my whole composite being, body and soul' seems calculated to show that Ignatius is aware that, contrary to dualist teachings, the soul and body belong together, despite the tensions between them, that the whole human being is not just a soul but soul and body conjointly.

Two other procedures in the *Exercises* match the composition of place in their attention to physical detail. Thus in the contemplation of the Nativity the three 'points' to consider are, first, to see the persons – Mary, Joseph, the extrascriptural maid who, Ignatius says, it 'may be piously believed' accompanied them from Nazareth to Bethlehem, and the child Jesus after his birth; second, to hear and reflect on what they are saying; and, third, to see and reflect on what they are doing. Or again, in a repetition of the same contemplation, he calls for the intensive 'application of the five senses': imagining the persons and their circumstances visually, then hearing in the imagination what they might say, then (here the senses become more indirectly or metaphorically operative) 'to smell the infinite fragrance, and taste the infinite sweetness of the divinity,' and finally 'to apply the sense of touch, for example, by embracing and kissing the place where the persons stand or are seated.' Imaginative attention to physical detail is here involved with emotional and other psychological consequences, but it is unmistakably prescribed.

Commentators on the *Exercises* have devoted much time to the composition of place, the contemplation of persons, words, and actions, and the application of the senses, but seldom do they discuss the cultural matrix or the stages of consciousness out of which such procedures arise. The two later procedures, contemplation of persons, words, and actions, and the application of the five senses belonged to the entire culture: they are obviously of a piece with the formulary rhetoric which, as Wilbur Samuel Howell explains (138–45, 335–40), suffused the academic tradition from classical antiquity long before and beyond Ignatius' lifetime.

The composition of place likewise has a general cultural matrix, but one not at all so old. It is not biblical or classical: early cultures do not attend with this conscious clinical objectivity to specific visual detail, and they certainly do not verbalize careful visual descriptions. Roland Barthes (60) associates the composition of place with the 'view' paintings becoming current in Ignatius' day, such as *A View of Naples* – although Ignatius is not particularly interested in landscape as such, but rather in physical surroundings as bearing on persons, who are his basic interest. Ignatius' detailed verbalized attention to picturable detail does, however, strongly suggest the printed emblem books circulated during his lifetime in thousands upon thousands of printed copies and emanating in large numbers particularly from the Spanish Netherlands (where the Spanish ascetical tradition and the *Devotio Moderna* mingled). Emblem books, which greatly influenced many literary genres (Daly), presented individual illustrations in woodcuts or metal engravings accompanied by detailed commentary pointing out the particular persons or animals or objects or actions in a given print from which moralizing or other useful conclusions were to be drawn. They do bring physical surroundings (often allegorical) to bear on the human lifeworld. Emblem books were a new genre because they are a print product: they require that the graphic presentation be the same in every copy so that the text, which is the same in every copy, has exactly the same target for its commentary. Manuscript culture can produce identical texts (with a few errors), but hand-produced drawings vacillate in their handling of detail, so that soon the text is referring to details that are not present or are present in impossibly altered form. So far as I know, the patent correspondences between features of Ignatian prayer and emblem books has never been studied or even previously adverted to. Interestingly, Ignatius was Spanish and the Spanish Netherlands were a major centre of emblem book publishing.

Whatever its earlier sources or allegiances, Ignatius' attention to physical detail certainly encouraged Hopkins' cultivated Victorian particularizations. Here, for example, are some excerpts from Hopkins' retreat notes in 1888, the year before his death, regarding meditation on Jesus' baptism by John as suggested in the *Spiritual Exercises* (S 267–8; see also the fuller notes of 1881–2, S 122–209, esp 171–3). Hopkins follows in his own way Ignatius' instructions to particularize, but in typical Hopkinsonian Victorian fashion he also articulates physical detail with a circumstantiality beyond the capability, and even the concern, of the sixteenth century.

The penitents then went down into the water, but this was their own act and for the symbol this was far from enough. John was the Baptist and must baptise them. For this probably he used *affusion*, throwing water on them, and for this some shell or scoop, as he is represented. And he seems to allude to this in contrasting himself with Christ; *ego quidem aqua baptizo ... cuius ventilabrum in manu eius* Luke iii. 16, 17. – *he* baptises with breath and fire, as wheat is winnowed in the wind and sun, and uses no shell like this which only washes once but a fan that thoroughly and forever parts the wheat from the chaff. For the fan is a sort of scoop, a shallow basket with a low back, sides sloping down from the back forwards, and no rim in front, like our dustpans, it is said. The grain is either scooped into this or thrown in by another, then tossed out against the wind, and this vehement action St. John compares to his own repeated 'dousing' or affusion. The separation it makes is very visible too: the grain lies heaped on the side, the chaff blows away the other, between them the winnower stands; after that nothing is more combustible than the chaff, and yet the fire he calls unquenchable. It will do its work at once and yet last, as this river runs forever, but has to do its work over again. Everything about himself is weak and ineffective, he and his instruments; everything about Christ strong. He dwelt with enthusiasm on this thought, representing Christ as a heroic figure, of gigantic size, strength, and equipment; to whom he was a pygmy child. ... But now he uses terms of force and, though he was well understood, he speaks of moral greatness and dignity, yet, in terms of physical force. I take your garments and your footgear from you when you go down into the water; all sorts of men come to me and I know the difference between a light sandal and the soldier's heavy *caliga*: I tell you my fingers have not the force to wring open this man's laces, though I stoop and bend my body to the task; if he washed himself, my arms have not the strength to lift his boots. He uses this imagery because he was the forerunner and smoothed the way; not, he would have said, for his sake, for it is nothing to him where he treads, but for yours, hard hearts, which like sandstone, his tread may grind to powder; brood of adders whose heads they may crush in blood. He would be well shod as a traveller, soldier on the march, or farm-labourer in the forest (*securis ad radicem arboris posita est*).

There may be added the contrast between baptising one by one and tossing the whole basketful of grain, each grain a man, at one throw empty

Another passage in Hopkins' commentary on the *Spiritual Exercises*, here concerned with the composition of place for the contemplation on the Last Supper, shows even more clearly how Ignatius' attention to physical particulars not only grows into the more advanced Victorian sense of particularity but also advances to explicated personhood or selfhood. Ignatius directs the exercitant (194) to 'see the persons at the Supper,' to 'listen to their conversation,' and 'to see what they are doing.' Hopkins elaborates (S 186):

As all places are at some point of the compass and we may face towards them: so every real person living or dead or to come has his quarter in the round of being, is lodged onewhere and not anywhere, and the mind has a real direction towards him. We are to realise this here of 'the persons of the Supper': as we have got the orientation of the room, its true measurements and specifications, properly furnished it and so on, so now we are properly 'to people it and give it its true personallings. It is in this way that Scotus says God revealed the mystery of the Trinity that His servants might direct their thoughts in worship toward, determine them, pit them, upon the real terms, which are the Persons, of His being the object of that worship.

Ignatius' directives have been incisively noted: the exercitant is to orient the room, measure it and otherwise specify it, furnish it – altogether particularize it. But, as earlier explained, the most particular of particulars is the self, the human person, each one of whom is forever unique, induplicable. Hopkins takes note, as Ignatius had not explictly done, that peopling the room, seeing in the imagination the persons in it, giving it 'its true personallings' is the greatest particularizing of all.

Moreover, as on this same page of commentary (S186; see p 118 here below), Hopkins moves from the Three Persons in God to 'the play of personality in man below them,' so he moves from the particularizing effected by human personality to the particularizing of the Persons in the mystery of the Trinity. 'That His servants might direct their thoughts in worship toward, determine them, pit them, upon the real terms, which are the Persons.'

Ignatius' attention to physical and psychological detail, which Hopkins intensifies here and in countless other places, has deep theological roots. It is encouraged by Christian teaching regarding the incarnation of the Word of God as an historically real human being. Since Jesus' life consisted of real events in real places and time, to grasp its full meaning it helps to make his life as realistically concrete in detail as possible. At least, it helps once the psyche has interiorized print-processed information: before print, the more oral world of the Bible – and of ancient literature generally, with its writing that carried always a massive oral residue – had almost no such concerns with reportorially itemized physical detail. No one bothered to report at all what Jesus looked like or exact physical details of his surroundings: indeed, until modern times minute verbal description of any physical details such as we take for granted today in today's descriptive and expository writing was beyond any writer's competence or inclination.

Nevertheless, both prayer and theological speculation fostered a certain intense specificity in Catholic spiritual literature and thought because each and every one of the specific actions in Jesus' life was, individually, infinitely salvific as leading to the cross and resurrection. Jesus was in his Person the Word of God, and every one of his actions both spoke truth and was truth, being a concrete manifestation of the Father's Word. We know Ignatius' own determination to verify as much as he could exact specifics in the life of Jesus. Avid for facts, he inevitably at times grasped even for evidence since discredited. In his *Autobiography* (50-1) he reports how he returned to the purported locale of Jesus' ascension in Jerusalem because he had forgotten to make a mental note of the direction in which the supposed last footprints of Jesus pointed when he left this earth. He gave the guards a desk knife he had with him to persuade them to let him back in for a final check.

This last-mentioned incident suggests the basic reason for Ignatius' concern with physical particulars. It was not unlike the Victorian concern with 'the panegyric accuracy' that Ruskin was to demand of Victorian artists, for it was rooted in concern with the sensibly, historically real. Like Ruskin, Ignatius wanted to get at things the way they really are, or were. But with Ignatius any desire for 'panegyric' accuracy was centred on the person of Jesus, who had told his disciples, 'Do this in memory of me.' Details for Ignatius were important not for themselves but for memory's sake, and specifically for the sake of personal memory of Jesus. In this incident just mentioned from Ignatius' real life, as in the composition of place, Ignatius zeroes in on detail as a means of implementing or recalling or extending a personal relationship. Memory connects with real events. Ignatius, like the Victorians, valued an accurate report of reality, but whereas their concerns were most often essentially aesthetic, his were devotional and existential, profoundly personal, concerning the self of Jesus in relation to one's own self.

7 INTERIOR STATES

Ignatius can also be compared with the Victorians not only in his attention to physical detail but also in his attention to states of mind. Here he follows a long ascetical and mystical tradition. Most notably, his 'Rules for the Discernment of Spirits' call for close observation of the 'whole course of our thoughts' in their relationship to states of disquiet and disturbance, or of quiet, peace, and tranquillity. For the *Exercises*, despite the aseptic rationalist interpretations of them not uncommon even in Jesuit circles during the nineteenth and early twentieth centuries, are very much concerned with feelings or moods, though their purpose and effects are not at all to set up psychedelically altered states of consciousness, which would interfere with or completely block free choice.

The *Exercises* do not, however, describe states of mind with an eye to a psychological realism such as Christ (40–6) finds in Dante Gabriel Rossetti and other Victorians. Rather, Ignatius is interested in feelings or moods as they may indicate what is going on in the depth of the relationship between the exercitant and God. His interest was obviously a Catholic parallel to the contemporary Protestant particularist concern with identifying the conversion experience, but it was not so centred on one hypothetical event in the individual's life. Rather, it examines a variety of experiences, undertaking to identify throughout the course of the Exercises, and indeed throughout the individual's lifetime, which particular inclinations or attractions, some of them quite obscure or elusive, are indeed graces from God, so that they can be trusted, and which are from Satan, the 'adversary.'

Ultimately, the particularities of mood which engage Ignatius have to do with his sense of the human self in personal relationship with Jesus Christ and through Jesus Christ to the Father in the Holy Spirit. His concern with procedural detail and with physical detail likewise comes to a head in this same personalist concern. The specific procedures in the meditations and contemplations as well as the use of physical detail to root the imagination and affections in something which can be felt as real are ultimately to free the soul so that the individual can respond to the grace that offers 'intimate knowlege of our Lord,' love of Jesus Christ, a desire to follow him, and hence a personal intimacy with God the Father derivative from Jesus' own intimacy with the Father. Responsiveness to God's grace involves the gift of tears, not randomly sought or hoped for (De Guibert, 24) but growing, if God wishes it to grow at all, out of real repentance, based on deeply personal love, and a desire to give oneself to God in some way echoing Jesus' giving of himself. The Exercises throughout are presented by Ignatius as exercises in love, in personal exchange, in person-to-person, self-to-self, mutual giving. They build up to the famous *Suscipe* prayer, earlier cited, in which the exercitant, in a free offering, places himself or herself entirely in God's hands. The *Exercises* are to help remove the obstacles to a perfect surrender of one's entire self to a personal God, a surrender not at all passive, as though one were an inert inanimate object, despite Ignatius' often cited borrowing of the well-worn ascetical topos, 'a stick in an old man's hand,' but an active surrender as a complete person, responding out of love to God's love. This is the way Hopkins understood the *Exercises*.

8 SEPARATION AND FREE CHOICE

Particularization shows in the *Spiritual Exercises* in one notable way which has occasioned a great deal of comment, most recently and most intensively by the late Roland Barthes in his *Sade, Fourier, Loyola* (58–70). Barthes comments at length on Ignatius' passion for separation or division of his material, that is, its greater and greater particularization. Ignatius' separation or division, writes Barthes, is 'unceasing, meticulous, and seemingly obsessive' ('séparation incessante, méticuleuse, et comme obsessionelle' [55]). Everything in the *Exercises* is divided, subdivided, classified, numbered, and sorted out: introductory notes, four weeks, meditations with three or four 'points' to be covered in each, three classes of men, eight rules regarding eating, fourteen for the discernment of spirits, seven for the distribution of alms, eighteen for thinking with the Church, and so on endlessly. Ignatius also works in old standard numbered lists: the Ten Commandments, the seven capital sins, the five senses.

Acknowledging the rhetorical and scholastic forces at work on Ignatius (though inattentive to any effect of print), Barthes makes the *Exercises* out to be nothing but separation: 'The *Exercises* are this separation itself, antecedent to which there is nothing' (58). Barthes's concerns are linguistic and thoroughly reductionist: linguistics, he has it in Saussurean fashion, builds on separation or sectioning: 'Tout ce qui est linguistique est articulé' (58). It does not follow, however, that everything that is articulated is linguistic, as Barthes seems to assume. God, as referred to in the *Exercises*, is himself coopted by Barthes as part of the articulating linguistic machinery: 'structurally, he is the Marker, the one who impresses a difference' on alternatives presenting themselves to choice, which Barthes reduces to a binary choice (77).

This seems in effect to reduce to a textual adjunct whatever significance 'God' has for Ignatius – and, by implication, for Hopkins, who in his writings on the *Exercises* follows Ignatius' divisions religiously (*S* 122–209). But choice, which Barthes openly introduces into his description, is not at all a textual matter. Texts cannot choose. Persons can. For Ignatius, 'God' has meaning in volitional acts of choosing and loving rather than in textual or linguistic dysfunctions. Since Barthes is really interested only in the text as text, he completely passes over the volitional holism into which the 'separations' or diaeretic structures of the text feed. However much their organization is divided and subdivided, Ignatius' meditations and contemplations and all else in the *Exercises* come to a head not in separations and divisions but in the nondiaeretic, holistic colloquies in which each contemplation and meditation ends. As has been seen, here (71) the retreatant is to 'enter into conversation' with God the Father or Christ or occasionally with Mary, 'speaking exactly as a friend speaks to another, or as a servant speaks to a master, now asking him for a favor, now blaming himself for some misdeed, now making known his affairs to him, and seeking advise in them' (54). The *Exercises* culminate not in locating God as a 'Marker' – a kind of particularizer – but in a free extratextual act offering the self to God: 'Take, Lord, and receive all my liberty, my memory, my understanding, and my entire will. ... Give me only your love and your grace, for this is sufficient for me' (234). This is the consummation of the *Exercises*, and there is no separation at all here. Ignatius situates the climactic contact of the exercitant with God in a free offering wherein one finds God in oneself and in others and in the whole world. Thus Ignatius' focus on freedom generates in Hopkins' notes on the *Exercises* his section 'On Personality, Grace and Free Will' (*S* 146–59).

To put it in currently critical terms, here at the end the author of the *Exercises* deliberately and consciously deconstructs all his attention to division or separation in favour of holistic person-to-person transactions. Ultimately, Ignatius' particularism attends not to particularizations achieved by division but to the particularism of the individual self – the ultimate particularization. It is surprising that a brilliant and skilled modern literary critic would not have attended to what was going on here.

9   'TO THE GREATER GLORY OF GOD'

It is especially surprising that, having noted so perceptively that Ignatius' separations or divisions tend to reduce to the binary, Barthes fails even to mention the best-known example of binary division in Ignatius' thought, which appears over and over again in the *Spiritual Exercises* (185, 189, 339, etc) and even more often in the *Constitutions of the Society of Jesus* – namely, the famous expression *ad majorem Dei gloriam*, often abbreviated 'A.M.D.G.,' 'to the greater glory of God.' Both Jesuits and others commonly take this expression as virtually defining the Society of Jesus and 'Jesuitness.' The expression hinges on a comparative – *majorem*, 'greater' – and thus clearly involves binary separation or division and, most radically, free choice between separate alternatives. Perhaps Barthes did not advert to this expression because in Ignatius it is so close to the volitional, which Barthes' linguistic concerns do not touch but which is absolutely essential to the *Exercises* and to Hopkins' use of them. 'A.M.D.G.' is a recipe for choosing, but an open-ended recipe, for Ignatius uses it when he leaves it to the exercitant to come to the decision as to which of any two given alternatives is to the greater glory of God. 'A.M.D.G.' tells exactly what the *Exercises* and what Ignatius' binarism are about and shows how insistently the *Exercises* feed Hopkins' nineteenth-century explicit preoccupation with freedom.

Often today the expression 'to the greater glory of God,' or 'A.M.D.G.,' is felt, as indeed it has commonly been felt for some generations, even by Jesuits, to be a kind of epigraph or dedication to be applied to one's actions. Hopkins himself occasionally follows a late tradition in using the expression that way (*S* 225, 241). One affixes the expression to the object or activity as a kind of celestial address label to launch it heavenward: 'to the greater glory of God,' or 'A.M.D.G.' Or one writes 'A.M.D.G.' at the head of a letter to consecrate its contents to God.

The trouble with this use of 'A.M.D.G.' is that it is insensitive to the comparative 'greater.' Why not 'to the glory of God'? This would make the point without overtones of vanity. Using 'to the greater glory of God' as an epigraph seems to suggest that what I have done for God's 'greater glory' is of more importance than what others have done simply 'to the glory of God.'

Such usage of the expression as a dedication is a post-Ignatian development. Ignatius did not use 'A.M.D.G.' this way, as an epigraph or dedication. At the head of letters he commonly wrote the same epigraph that St Teresa of Avila used and indeed that Martin Luther used, either the name 'Jesus' or its first three letters, JES or, one form of the Greek alphabet, IHS. *Ad majorem Dei gloriam* occurs and recurs in the *Spiritual Exercises* and the *Constitutions of the Society of Jesus* and in other writings of Ignatius, so far as I can discover, never as a dedicatory epigraph but rather in a context of decision-making (Ong, ' "A.M.D.G." '). Faced with alternatives, one is to choose the one which is for the greater glory of God.

The recipe focuses decision-making not on oneself or on one's own actions, but on the God of faith to whom one gives oneself in love. The procedure here may be marker-like but it is also dialectical: to decide whether to perform action A or B, I must negotiate the actions themselves in terms of something else, or, rather, of someone else, as Fessard has shown. Should I give all my possessions to the poor or not? Do not look to the possessions but to something else, or, rather, to someone else, to God in his glory, who effectively enters one's life precisely at the point of decision-making.

One might argue that it is possible to prefix 'A.M.D.G.' to a letter or affix it to a building without obviating its decision-making function. At the head of a letter it might be interpreted as saying, 'May the choices I am going to have to make in drafting this letter be such as will promote the greater glory of God rather than derogate from or minimize this glory. I intend to make them on this basis.' Or, 'This building was constructed as the result of a decision that it would be more to the greater glory of God to construct it than not to construct it, or to construct it this way rather than another way.' These interpretations would honour the fact that 'A.M.D.G.' is anticipatory rather than postfactum. I hope that when 'A.M.D.G.' is used in an epigraph it is so interpreted and that Hopkins so interpreted it when, following the by then current Jesuit practice, he used the initials as an epigraph at the head of a 'dominical' sermon draft (S 225). But I have never to the best of my recollection met anyone who thus explicitly interpreted the epigraphic use of the expression. Affixed to an object, rather than operating within one's heart when the heart is torn now one way and now another, as Hopkins' heart was over and over again, *Ad majorem Dei gloriam* seems to be saying, 'Here it is, and we now give it to God.' This mentality is product-oriented, not decision-oriented, as Ignatius' use of the expression uniformly was.

The biblical background of Ignatius' expression is informative. The expression 'glory of God' occurs well over twenty times in the Bible, and related expressions such as 'his glory' and 'your (thy) glory' many times oftener, but the expression 'the greater glory of God' or, 'his greater glory' or 'your (thy) – that is, God's – greater glory' never at all. The contexts for most of these noncomparative biblical references to glory are not decision-oriented or action-oriented – in many 'glory' translates *shekinah*, the luminous cloud that indicates God's presence (Exodus 19:9, 24:15–16) so that 'the glory of God' (*shekinah*) in the Temple is equivalent simply to 'God.' The one biblical passage which is clearly action-oriented (1 Cor 10:31) is not decision-oriented: 'The fact is that whether you eat or drink – whatever you do – you should do for the glory of God.' Paul's words here contain no comparative: they thus might accommodate to epigraphic use more readily than would the expression 'to the greater glory of God,' although they seem to mean not 'dedicate your work, whatever it is, to the glory of God' so much as 'do your work in such a way that it will be to God's glory.' Something of decision-making is implied here, though much less openly than in Ignatius' expression. Biblical usage thus provides only a remote foundation for Ignatius' *ad majorem Dei gloriam*. Ignatius' expression is parabiblical rather than biblical: it uses biblical language and a biblical frame of thought to address decision-making represented more self-consciously than biblical times had allowed for.

10 DECISION-MAKING, RATIONAL AND PARARATIONAL

Although in one way or another decision-making employs diaeretic processes – splitting the field of attention into this issue versus that issue, setting up reasons pro and reasons con, ultimately suspending the subject himself or herself between yes and no – the decision with which the process terminates, like every decision, is holistic, doing away with the diaresis and throwing weight on the whole human person of the decision-maker. A decision resolves dichotomies by incorporating one or another option into the total density of lived existence, letting the others fall away. Decisions are often stressful, involving unknown consequences. 'The die is cast.' 'Here I take my stand.' 'The buck stops here.' 'Lay your body on the line.' Such utterances indicate the point at which the divided attention, hesitating between or among alternatives, is transcended and the decider 'takes' a position, makes one position a part of his or her own existence.

The holistic force of Ignatius' 'deconstruction' of the diaeretic or separative organization in the *Exercises* shows in his own reflections on decision-making procedures. Although he sees usefulness in articulating the pros and cons for coming to one or another decision, so far as such articulation may be possible (178–83), such a procedure seems to be for him a last resort, the third of the 'three times when a correct and good choice of a way of life may be made.' The first time is 'when God our Lord so moves and attracts the will that a devout soul without hesitation, or the possibility of hesitation, follows what has been manifested to it. St Paul and St Matthew acted this way in following Christ our Lord.' The second time is 'when much light and understanding are derived through experience of desolations and consolations and the discernment of diverse spirits' – that is, the identification, through experiential as well as rational means, of the sources of one's inclinations and moods, whether from God or from elsewhere, Satan, as Ignatius puts it. The third time is when the pros and cons of alternatives are consciously adverted to, is the least emotional time, 'a time of tranquility,' when 'one considers first for what purpose man is born, that is, for the praise of God our Lord and the salvation of his soul.' Ignatius goes on (178–88) to suggest various ways of organizing the pros and cons, but in doing so he includes in his suggestions this rule: 'The love that moves and causes one to choose must descend from above, that is, from the love of God, so that before one chooses he should perceive that the greater or less attachment for the object of his choice is solely because of his Creator and Lord.' This is another wording of 'to the greater glory of God.' It makes clear that Ignatius grounded decision making in the *Exercises* ultimately not in rational considerations themselves, however these may enter into decision, but in something that reason can relate to only indirectly: the loving encounter in faith of self with self, of the human being with God. In a sense, God is a 'marker' here, but we are far from the articulations of textuality in a world of nonverbalizable numinous presence. Karl Rahner ('Ignatian Process') and Harvey Egan have treated in detail Ignatius' position here.

It should be noted that, although the self is private and intimate and the relationship of the self to God is presented by Ignatius as private and intimate, Ignatius' concept of God is not workable simply as a private projection, an imaginary figure generated by the individual psyche out of its own private needs with no reference to other human beings. The *Spiritual Exercises* include 'Rules for Thinking with the Church' (352–70), which are, among other things, reality-testing rules that relate personal decisions to a community – and indeed to a widespread and diachronic community, self-consciously Catholic, that is, 'through-the-whole' (*katholikos*). Maintaining union with this community, 'thinking with the Church,' prevents the psyche from isolating itself within its own projections. For Ignatius, in thinking of God, of Christ, and of the truths of the Christian faith, and most notably in its faith-decisions, the psyche has to accommodate itself massively to others, maintaining at least implicit dialogue with the community of living persons, the Church, whose dialogue over the ages reaches back to Jesus' companions and to Jesus himself. In its drastically communal as well as utterly personal grounding, the decision-making in the *Exercises* is holistic in a radically social as well as personal way: the individual self, the individual human person, drawing on all resources available, offers himself or herself to God but does so within a community of other human persons, as a unique self who is related uniquely to a larger whole. Hopkins' experience of the self falls within this same tradition: however inwardly turned, the self in Hopkins is never solipsistic.

11 DECISION AND PERSON-TO-PERSON INVOLVEMENT

Despite his care about procedure, in the *Spiritual Exercises* Ignatius approaches decision-making ultimately through person-to-person involvement. He feeds his thinking about human freedom with thought about divine freedom in the creation and the redemption of humankind. The 'First Principle and Foundation' (23), immediately preceding the First Week of the *Exercises*, states that God created human beings and all other things for humans' selective use or avoidance in so far as other things do or do not bring a person to God. Here the treatment of God's free choice is somewhat routine: Ignatius' text simply assumes, in accordance with common Christian doctrine, that creation is a free act of God. Ignatius attends more explicitly and insistently to God's free decision when he presents the matter for the contemplation on the Incarnation at the start of the Second Week. Here is his mise-en-scène for the First Prelude of this contemplation (102):

This will consist in calling to mind the history of the subject I have to contemplate. Here it will be how the Three Divine Persons look down upon the whole expanse or circuit of the earth, filled with human beings. ... They decree in their eternity that the Second Person would become man to save the human race. So when the fullness of time had come, they send the Angel Gabriel to our Lady.

'They decree' – a free decision, which, like all free decisions of God affecting anything outside God, is made by all three Persons, Father, Son, and Holy Spirit through the one divine will of the one God that they are.

Hopkins comments on this passage imaginatively, and again with Victorian detail, dramatizing (*S* 169):

Observe 'in sua aeternatite' [in their eternity]. The divine Persons see the whole world at once and know where to drive the nail and plant the cross. A 60-fathom coil of cord running over the cliff's edge round by round, that is, say, generation by generation, 40 fathom already gone and the rest will follow, when a man sets his foot on it and saves both what is hanging and what has not yet stirred to run. Or seven tied by the rope on the Alps; four go headlong, then the fifth, as strong as Samson, checks them and the two behind do not even feel the strain. And so on. – See this confirmed by Fr. Roothan's note.

The free divine decision or decree to redeem humankind – in Hopkins' imagery, to set a foot on the running rope – was the one on which all humankind's fate depended. Ignatius presents it anthropomorphically in a deliberative setting such as often governs human decisions: the Three Persons look over the situation, decide it would be well to do something, and decide what to do. Hopkins' presentation makes the act of decision spectacularly decisive, an abrupt intervention, a brake deliberately applied to a runaway movement – 'saving both what is hanging and what has not yet stirred to run,' for in Catholic teaching Jesus redeemed those who had died before his time as well as those not yet born. Hopkins' image here again fits the Victorian fascination with focal centres of power: the foot on the running rope and the Samson checking the plunge of his companions.

Over and over again Hopkins associates Ignatius' particularizing with his own considerations regarding the human person and freedom. In the Second Prelude of this same contemplation on the Incarnation, Ignatius had called on the exercitant to consider the different persons on the face of the earth of whom the Three Persons were thinking, 'in such diversity in dress and manner of acting.' Hopkins (S 172) highlights the diversity, and not only in their dress and behaviour but also simply as self-conscious persons: 'Each of these *persons* [italics Hopkins' own] ... wants to be the world to himself; he hates his brother whom he sees and therefore the God whom he does not see.'

Ignatius' inclusion of Mary in the scene – 'they send the Angel Gabriel to our Lady' (from Luke 1:26) – is especially significant in terms of freedom. Mary's free response to God's message delivered by Gabriel was the most crucial decision by a mere human being in all history as history appears in Christian faith. Gabriel awaits the response, which, when it comes, climaxes Luke's story. Mary simply says, 'Be it done to me according to your word.' Luke immediately concludes, 'With that the angel left her' (Luke 1:38). The event is over and the point is made. Ignatius does not advert explicitly to Mary's freedom – in his day theological reflection on human freedom had not yet moved far into this kind of psychologizing – but Hopkins zeroes in directly on the freedom of God's offer of his Son and on Mary's decision-making and freedom, working out more explicitly what Ignatius' (and Luke's) text implies for the sensitive mid-nineteenth-century consciousness (S 172–3).

It was not that she [Mary] doubted his [Gabriel's] truthfulness but that the promise 'concipies' ['you will conceive'] etc was a free offer, depending on her consent, and she was doubting whether she ought to give it, wondering what was best before God. But by telling her of her cousin Elizabeth's having already, by a less but like miracle, conceived, the angel shewed her what God's will was and that the preparations for the event had already been begun for which only her consent was wanting; so that she is no sooner thus determined and set at rest (confirmata) about God's will than she gives her submission to it: 'Ecce Ancilla' etc.

He goes into still further detail about the interaction of the human will with God's and the relation of freedom to self and persons in his essay 'On Personality, Grace, and Free Will' (S 146–59).

This free response to God's greatest offer to all the human race – the offer of his Son as redeemer – could have been made only by a woman (Ong, *Fighting* 173–6), for a man is anatomically incapable of bearing a child. The value and power of human freedom furnished a rationale for the virgin birth, for here conception takes place directly as the result of a free human decision, a 'yes.' In an excerpt from a homily that Hopkins would have read regularly in his Roman Breviary, on Christmas Day, St Leo the Great points out that Mary 'conceived Jesus in her mind' (by faith in the angel's message and her free response in faith) 'before she conceived him in her body.' In ordinary conception through sexual intercourse, having a child has no such direct connection with the free decision (or hope) to have one. Mary's response, her free assent to conceive and bear the Son, because of its pivotal place in salvation history, becomes a paradigm for all human beings, men as well as women, in every free response they make to God's grace on any occasion.

The dynamics here at work and the implications of Mary's free decision for all human beings show clearly in Hopkins' poem 'The Blessed Virgin Compared to the Air We Breathe' (P 60). Her free acceptance at Nazareth echoes in the free responses of others to God's grace: in these responses the result is not an incarnation, not the enfleshing of God's Word as man, which occurred once for all some two thousand years ago, but the complementary equivalent, a new enspiriting, as individual human persons in their own individualities, like Mary, freely open their individual lives to Christ, conceiving and, consequently, in a way, giving birth to him:

> Of her flesh he took flesh:
> He does take fresh and fresh,
> Though much the mystery how,
> Not flesh but spirit now
> And makes, O marvellous!
> New Nazareths in us,
> Where she shall yet conceive
> Him, morning, noon, and eve;
> New Bethlems, and he born
> There, evening, noon, and morn.

As human beings assimilate themselves to Christ, each enhances his or her own self:

> Bethlem or Nazareth,
> Men here may draw like breath
> More Christ and baffle death;

Who, born so, comes to be
New self and nobler me.

The human person is not diminished in Christ, is not made into
someone else or reduced to no one at all, but rather grows into a
'nobler me.' This is the self-fulfilment which comes through giving
oneself away in love. Again, as Teilhard de Chardin has it, in interpersonal relations union differentiates (63, 64, 67, 144, 152).

All the decision-making in the *Spiritual Exercises* ultimately
resolves itself not into achieving some finite end-product but in
relating one's own self personally to God through and in Jesus
Christ, in 'deciding for Christ' – though in the *Exercises* Ignatius
details what this comes to with a specificity not matched by most
evangelicals with whom this expression is commonly associated.
The meditation on the Kingdom of Christ concerns the free invita-
tion of Christ to human beings freely to choose what he chose:
'Whoever wishes to join me with me in this enterprise must be content with the same food, drink, clothing, etc., as mine' (93). In the
meditation on the 'Two Standards,' Lucifer sends out his emissaries
to cloud human beings' freedom and thereby to win them to riches,
honour, and pride, and Christ sends his apostles and disciples to try
to win people freely to choose what he chose: to live a life of poverty, to welcome insults and contempt, and to learn humility
(136–48). The meditation on the 'Three Classes of Men' considers
how free or unfree one can be in relating to wealth that pulls one
away from Christ's single-minded devotion to the Kingdom of God
(149–57); persons of the first class halfheartedly want to free themselves of possessions that are pulling them away from God, but pro-
crastinate and die unfree; persons of the second class with pseudo-
pious deception beg God to free them from undue attachment to
their possessions, provided only that God does not take away the
possessions themselves; those of the third class simply take their
problem honestly before God in prayer with no conditions, equally
willing to give up or retain the wealth that is troubling them in
accordance with what appears better before God (what is to 'the
greater glory of God'), and, so as to keep themselves truly free in
their decision-making, for the time being 'strive to conduct
themselves as though every attachment to it [the wealth] had been
broken' (155). The *Exercises* present Jesus to the exercitant as freely
inviting others to imitate even his free acceptance of an untimely

death – 'Father, into your hands I commend my spirit' (297 – from Luke 23:46) – despite attendant depression and deep repugnance (Mark 14:34–42; Matthew 26:37–46; Luke 22:41–6).

Because decision-making in the *Exercises* ultimately comes to deciding for and with Christ, its end result is the free holistic self-giving in the prayer of the 'Contemplation to Attain the Love of God' that concludes the *Exercises* (234):

Take, Lord, and receive all my liberty, my memory, my understanding, and my entire will, all that I have and possess. You have given all to me. To you, Lord, I return it. All is yours, dispose of it wholly according to your will. Give me your love and your grace, for this is sufficient for me.

The *Exercises* thus feed the particularism and self-consciousness of Hopkins' own sensibility by their own attention to detail, physical and psychic, and by their central focus on freedom in decision-making, on the free act of the will, which Hopkins styled 'the selfless self of self' (*P* 157), and ultimately by their concern with freedom as culminating in the total giving of self-conscious self to self, of the human being to God. Reference to this giving sparks many of Hopkins' brighter poems and all of his darker ones.

THREE   Academic Theology
and Hopkins'
Self-Consciousness

1   HOPKINS' THEOLOGY AND NINETEENTH-
CENTURY CONSCIOUSNESS

THE EXERCISES were not the only element in Hopkins'
training as a Jesuit that fed Victorian particularism and self-
consciousness. The Catholic theology that Hopkins studied in his
regular courses preparatory to the priesthood, together with the philosophy propaedeutic to this theology, penetrated his entire life,
from his direct ministerial work as a priest (daily celebration of
Mass, preaching, hearing confessions), through his work of teaching
and his poetry and prose writings. Some knowledge of the philosophy and theology he studied and of their setting is essential if one is
to understand the man and to hear what he is saying. More to the
present purpose, the philosophy and theology he studied provided in
abundance nourishment for Hopkins' particularism and for his acute
consciousness of his own selfhood and that of others. Scholastic philosophy provided this nourishment first of all in its protracted attention to principles of individuation (relation of the individual existent
to other individual existents and to the nonindividualized universal
concept which would represent all individuals). The same philosophy also dealt at length with freedom of the will, which Hopkins
relates specifically and intimately to the self or person. Moral
theology, a major component of the Catholic seminary education
absolutely essential to priestly ministry, also confronted the self
with itself, for it attended meticulously to the entire gamut of
human actions in so far as these actions resulted from a person's
free choices, which alone qualify as morally good or evil. Moral

theology treats in terms of principles and consequences the decision-making which the *Spiritual Exercises* attend to in terms of process. However, Hopkins' notebooks and papers make clear that the richest theological nourishment for his concern with the self came not just from philosophy and from moral theology but more especially from Trinitarian theology, the study of the Three Persons in the One God, and from Christology, the study of the Incarnate Second Person, the Son or Word of God, Jesus Christ. But philosophy and moral theology did affect his attention to the self and can be treated here first before we take up his Trinitarianism.

For most of Hopkins' Jesuit contemporaries, as for Catholic seminary students in nineteenth-century Europe generally, the potential of theology and related seminary philosophy to interact positively with the increasingly articulate self-consciousness of the age were realized very little. Nineteenth-century Catholic seminary philosophy and theology did not of themselves register very positively the deeper or more lively nineteenth-century intellectual currents, the currents that would power the evolution of consciousness in immediately succeeding generations. But they could be channelled into these currents, consciously or unconsciously, by persons familiar with the currents, where in fact Oxford had taught Hopkins to swim. Like Newman, but in his own way, Hopkins let the Catholic heritage and the mainline intellectual movements of the age come together and interact. Hopkins could do this because, as Christopher Devlin discerningly puts it (in *S* 44), Hopkins was '*inside* the doctrines of the Church.' He was also inside his own epoch in history, at home in his own age.

Hopkins' familiarity with the mainline recent philosophical thought allied to his own thought on the self and freedom was, however, mostly not at all direct. Hegel, for example, had opened new questions concerning self and freedom for generations of subsequent explorers, but Hopkins knew Hegel in the philosophy courses he followed as a Jesuit, it appears, only in the way he knew Locke, Descartes, Malebranche, even John Stuart Mill, and other 'moderns.' Seminary courses treated such persons largely as sources of 'objections' to philosophical theses which Jesuits and other believing Christians felt themselves called on to defend against these and other 'opponents' (Thomas, *Hopkins* 97; Zaniello 139). He writes Bridges on 20 February 1875, 'I have had no time to read even the English books about Hegel, much less the original, indeed I know

almost no German' (B 30–1). His unfamiliarity with German
suggests that he could hardly have read other relevant German philosophers either, such as Fichte on the transcendental ego. Yet,
Hopkins' thought was focused on intensively introspective self-and-
freedom themes as much as the thought of these philosophers was.
How did this come about?

First, as Thomas A. Zaniello has shown, in many ways Hopkins'
training in philosophy as a Jesuit actually continued some major
trends in Oxford philosophy in attacking the atomism and positivism of T.H. Huxley and John Tyndall. As an undergraduate at
Oxford in 1867 Hopkins had already stepped into the lists against
atomic materialism with his brief essay on 'The Probable Future of
Metaphysics' (J 118–21). Secondly, those who were studying and
teaching at Stonyhurst when Hopkins did his philosophy there were
to produce the Stonyhurst series of philosophical manuals, which,
though published after Hopkins' death, doubtless echoed concerns of
Hopkins' own teachers. Many of the 'Stonyhurst Philosophers' who
authored these manuals were, like Hopkins, converts to Catholicism
or the sons of converts, and had been familiar with philosophical
issues arising outside the Catholic milieu. The 'Stonyhurst
Philosophers Series' treated not only logic and epistemology but
some theological subjects as well. The best known of these
Stonyhurst philosophers was perhaps Joseph Rickaby, SJ, one year
younger (1845–1922) than Hopkins. Rickaby's most important work,
Moral Philosophy (1888), was a polemical defence of St Thomas
Aquinas against Hegelianism and positivism. Rickaby's Free Will
and Four English Philosophers (1906) treats Hobbes, Locke, Hume,
and Mill. But these engagements with the thought of the time were
dominantly defensive, concerned less with what was assimilable and
enlightening to Catholic tradition than with what was threatening
to it. Rickaby's attention to free will certainly manifests a concern
with freedom akin to Hopkins', who, however, is seldom openly
adversary-conscious in his discussion of freedom.

Hopkins' spectacularly overt preoccupation with the self and with
the freedom which certifies selfhood appears to derive in great part
from an extraordinary sensitivity to what was going on in the depths
of the psyche in his age. Hopkins' case alerts us to the fact that the
age's drift to speculation about the self and freedom was not the
result merely of linear developments in philosophical theory so
much as it was the result of deep shifts in consciousness, that is,

shifts in the ways the psyche related in its own depths to the expanding mass of knowledge about the exterior universe and about the human interior itself that was overwhelming the nineteenth century. Hopkins responded to the shift integrally. Although he studied philosophy and theology in the agonistic, defensive format retained in Catholic seminaries even as late as the 1960s (Ong, *Fighting* 137–9), Hopkins, like Newman, had very little if any of the defensiveness which betrays intellectual insecurity and freezes the mind.

2 SEMINARY PHILOSOPHY AND THEOLOGY

Hopkins studied philosophy at Stonyhurst College in Lancashire from 1870 to 1873 and theology at St Beuno's College in North Wales from 1874 to 1877. Alfred Thomas (*Hopkins*) has investigated in detail the seminary courses in these subjects that Hopkins followed.

Philosophy and theology in Catholic ecclesiastical seminaries had for some time been closely related. In Western academia from the ancient Greeks through the Renaissance 'philosophy' had a much wider meaning than it commonly has today. 'Philosophy' had included the earlier equivalents of today's physics (terrestrial and celestial), chemistry, biology, psychology, anthropology, political science, speculative mathematics (for the most part minimizing or even excluding computation, the 'rithmetic of the three r's, which was a practical skill necessary for tradesmen and women, not for university students as such), as well as the ethical and metaphysical speculation with which philosophy is commonly identified today. 'Philosophy' had been, roughly speaking, all the subjects in academia save languages, medicine, law, and theology. By the mid-nineteenth century the old alignments had shifted, largely because 'natural philosophy' had been displaced by the burgeoning modern physical and biological sciences. Seminary philosophy was narrowing itself mostly to metaphysics or ontology, epistemology, a philosophical cosmology, ethics, and some logic (quite amateur by comparison with medieval as well as with modern logic). From the seventeenth century on, Roman Catholic seminary philosophy had tended on the whole to be 'an uninspired Scholastic Aristotelianism amalgamated with ideas taken from other currents of thought, notably Cartesian and, later the philosophy of Wolff' (Copleston

2:487–8; cf McCool, 28–9; Thomas, *Hopkins* 94), and in the Jesuit milieu, in England as elsewhere, followed the scholasticism of the encyclopaedic Spanish Jesuit Francisco Suárez (1548–1617) rather than Thomas Aquinas directly (Thomas, *Hopkins* 157). It was mostly manual-based (Thomas, *Hopkins* 87, 128, 150–86). By mid-century a change was setting in that would move both philosophy and theology in the direction of neo-Thomism, but even a decade after Hopkins' study of theology, the change was hardly noticeable in England (Thomas, *Hopkins* 157; but cf 96, n 1).

Citing Edgar Hocedez, Gerald A. McCool has pointed out (17; cf Schoof) that throughout the nineteenth century Roman Catholic systematic or speculative theology in all of its 'schools' was curiously unified: the relationship between reason and faith, that is, between the order of nature and the order of salvific divine grace given to mankind through Jesus Christ – the so-called 'natural' and 'supernatural' orders – was 'the single theme which ran through the diverse systems of Catholic theology and served as the focus of theological controversy from the early years of the century to its conclusion.'

Nineteenth-century dogmatic or systematic Roman Catholic theology took shape in a largely polemic setting and tended to give a polemic tone to the philosophy associated with it. The Catholic faith was felt to be threatened by intellectual developments outside the Church and even inside. While old Protestant-Catholic disputes were still active, the greatest enemy of the Catholic faith, most felt, was rationalism, which would reduce faith to mere reason (McCool). But in the effort to counter rationalism, certain theologians, in the opinions of other theologians, sold themselves out to the faith's second greatest enemy, fideism, which would write off reason as quite irrelevant to the faith. Since it involved the relationship of the natural world and natural reason to faith, the problem besetting Catholic theology concerned not only theology itself, which dealt with Christian faith, but also philosophy, which dealt with the world of nature and natural reason.

In effect, the faith-reason question grew so acute in nineteenth-century Roman Catholic circles that many other major problems plaguing theology besides these of faith and reason were given short shrift or pretty much shelved. Roman Catholic theology responded very little to the growing awareness of the historical setting of all human thought and of Christian revelation itself. With few exceptions, it did not attend in any depth to the new discovery of biological and cosmic evolution or to the evidence of synchronic and diachronic variations in human social structures which was anthropologizing philosophy and theology elsewhere, or to the incipient existentialist and personalist currents which would psychologize the deepest accounts of existence and bring history, together with anthropology and linguistics, and the humanities generally, to focus ultimately on the history of consciousness. Being, Heidegger was to explain later, was revealing itself more and more through time, but Roman Catholic theology for the moment was too preoccupied with faith-reason problems to attend to any 'soft sift / In an hourglass' (P 28). Hopkins, however, shows himself sensitive to the new developments and indeed in many ways ahead of them, truly a protoexistentialist and a protopersonalist thinker.

The understanding of the theological and philosophical faith-reason crisis which became common among nineteenth-century Roman Catholics was worked out in complex ways and through the collaboration of many (McCool). Eventually, in the 1870 apostolic constitution of the First Vatican Council *Dei Filius* and in Leo XIII's 1878 encyclical *Aeterni Patris*, the crisis was met by referring back to the theology and philosophy of St Thomas Aquinas, who was felt to have shown for all ages how to avoid both Scylla and Charybdis, making clear the exact relationship of faith and reason. The chief designer of the theological positions and defensive strategies officially adopted was the German Jesuit Joseph Kleutgen. Kleutgen's disinclination to historical thinking, however, as it has latterly appeared, gave him a quite inaccurate understanding of the views of St Thomas Aquinas himself.

Before *Dei Filius* and *Aeterni Patris* Kleutgen had published in 1853 a work on what he called the 'traditional theology' or 'old-time theology' (*Die Theologie der Vorzeit*) of a presumably unified Middle Ages, a theology supposedly centred in the work of St Thomas Aquinas. This theology, with its concomitant 'traditional' or 'old-time' philosophy (*Die Philosphie der Vorzeit*, 1860–3), Kleutgen felt should save the Church. Kleutgen's Thomism, however, was in fact not exactly that of Thomas – whose work, moreover, by no means governed or represented all of medieval theology. Unwittingly, Kleutgen was proposing as 'Thomism' the theology of the great post-Reformation scholastics, most notably that of Francisco Suárez (McCool, 213–15), which, although it thought of itself as Thomism, was in fact not aligned with Thomas' basic insights, as mid-twentieth-century scholarship has made clear. Moreover, like the other Catholic theologians whom he opposed, such as Georg Hermes, who had tried to accommodate Kant to Catholic theology, Johann Sebastian von Drey, who had tried to accommodate Schelling, Anton Günther, who had returned to Descartes in an effort to neutralize a Hegelian pantheism, and Antonio Rosmini, who had worked out an Augustinian 'ontologism,' Kleutgen himself made the more or less tacit assumption, Hegelian rather than scholastic in its affinities, that some kind of intellectual 'system' would solve the Church's problems with the nineteenth century. The other theologians had simply opted for the wrong systems. His worked.

With few exceptions, Kleutgen's Roman Catholic opponents were as loyal to the Church as Kleutgen himself. They were, indeed, most often, devout and even saintly Catholics, trying to the best of their lights with dedicated earnestness to relate the Church to what they took to be the modern world. Although their solutions were not always entirely viable as they were presented, Kleutgen's opponents had some feel for the realities. As the theological problems of the modern world have subsequently revealed themselves more clearly, these problems have proven to be remarkably like those which Kleutgen's opponents were attempting to address and which Kleutgen wrote off as non-problems for those who followed the 'old-time theology.'

But Kleutgen's truly heroic efforts were not entirely in vain. By calling attention to the work of St Thomas Aquinas, who had been largely lost sight of in the eighteenth and early nineteenth centuries, Kleutgen unwittingly prepared the way of the present-day subject-oriented (not simply 'subjective'), historical-minded Catholic theology of Karl Rahner, Walter Kasper, and the Tübingen school, which, through the earlier work of Joseph Maréchal and others, connects at crucial points with the now better understood work of St Thomas, though it can hardly be styled simply 'Thomism,' if such an 'ism' is in fact even possible. This present-day theology would doubtless have horrified Kleutgen himself if only because of its respectful attention to the questions his opponents were trying to address and its recognition of the depths of some of his opponents' insights.

John Henry Newman, who received Hopkins into the Roman Catholic Church, produced the weightiest theology of any nineteenth-century English Roman Catholic, though not a theology that was systematically comprehensive (Strange, 157 and passim). His thinking was always clearly unassimilable to the historically and psychologically flat systematization sponsored by Kleutgen. This was evident already in *An Essay on the Development of Christian Doctrine* (1845), published on the eve of Newman's reception into the Roman Catholic Church, and it remained clear through the rest of his life, causing chronic problems for Newman in Rome with persons who identified the Catholic faith itself with theologies such as Kleutgen's. *An Essay in Aid of a Grammar of Assent* (1870), Newman's last major work, does treat the reason and faith problem, but in a psychologizing manner more akin to later phenomenology than to Kleutgen's formalism.

Hopkins' theological thinking was less opposed than Newman's to neoscholastic systematization, though Hopkins' attraction to John Duns Scotus, a medieval scholastic but in Kleutgen's view a dangerous maverick, shows a certain uneasiness with main-line manual and classroom presentation. However, Joseph J. Feeney has shown that there is no direct evidence that Hopkins' relegation to the 'short course' of theology (three years), instead of the 'long course' (four years) to which the more adept young Jesuits were assigned, was due to his Scotist views. A complex of reasons, including shortage of manpower, seemingly entered into the decision to assign him to the active ministry without a fourth year of theological studies.

Unlike Newman, who came into the Roman Catholic Church in 1845 at the age of forty-four and was ordained priest and created DD the following year, Hopkins had been received into the Church at the age of twenty-two (by Newman) and had gone through the regular seminary course of three years of philosophy and three years of theology (four for some, but not for Hopkins, as just noted). Like philosophy, the theology Hopkins was taught was mostly manual-based (Thomas, *Hopkins* 87–128, 150–86). It was 'scholastic' not in the sense that it followed Kleutgen's 'old time' thinking in any definitive way but in the sense that, like nineteenth-century seminary philosophy and theology generally, it was terminologically pre-Cartesian for the most part and thus in recognizable ways somewhat continuous with the philosophy and theology of the Middle Ages.

Despite its now evident limitations, however, the manual-based scholastic teaching that Hopkins received was far from uninformative. Philosophical analysis of being, finite and infinite, in terms of act and potency, of form and matter, or of substance, property, and accident, and in terms of the various kinds of causes, was and is still quite possible and can be made challenging, and some of the insights developed by faculty psychology (originally a part of 'physics') and a virtue-vice ethics were deep and permanently inviting. Within this setting, the great questions of Christian dogmatic or systematic theology – creation and redemption by the incarnation, passion, death, and resurrection of Jesus Christ, the Son or Word, the Second of the Three Persons in the one true God – were presented in terms with a rich patristic and later history which both invited careful analysis and left an ample residue of unsolved questions for further reflection. The other major branch of theology besides dogmatic or systematic, that is, moral theology, with impressive exactitude condensed centuries of theological (and philosophical) reflection on the right and wrong of human behaviour.

3 HOPKINS' THEOLOGICAL WRITINGS AND THE SELF

Hopkins' extant writings which are directly theological have been skilfully edited by Christopher Devlin, SJ, in *The Sermons and Devotional Writings of Gerard Manley Hopkins* (1959). These consist of three batches of material: (1) the texts of twenty-three sermons, sometimes full but in a few places quite clipped, note-like in style; (2) less than one hundred printed pages of 'Spiritual Writings,' consisting chiefly of theological reflections written out by Hopkins when he was going through the 'Long Retreat' (the unabridged thirty-day Spiritual Exercises) that was part of his year of tertianship in 1881–2, the year of spiritual renewal normally following within a few years of a Jesuit priest's ordination; (3) various isolated discourses and private notes, often of great insight and beauty. Devlin's introductions and notes provide invaluable guidelines and explanations for working through this diversified, often sketchy, but at the same time often intensely concentrated material. The material is heavily laden theologically, especially the 'Spiritual Writings.' In these, phenomenological reports on self-awareness combine with philosophical and psychological and theological theory and explication. In the sermons, mostly homilies on Sunday Gospel readings, exquisite attention to external physical detail and to interior states

of consciousness shows, among other things, the influences of the
Exercises as discussed earlier here. Everywhere, the Christological
focus of the *Exercises* (the self in personal relationship with Christ)
and the related concern with the Three Persons in the Godhead are
in evidence.

Hopkins' *Sermons and Devotional Writings* do not of course cover
all of what he studied in philosophy or theology. But they cover
enough to show that the faith-reason problem dominating
nineteenth-century Catholic theology generally, together with its
ancillary philosophy, was not at all a major centre for Hopkins'
energetic and often profound thought. At the centre of Hopkins'
theological concerns, and his related philosophical concerns, are
rather questions concerning self in relation to God and freedom,
together with the questions concerning individuation or differentiation from others which inevitably arise when the self confronts
itself. 'When I was a child I used to ask myself: What must it be
like to be someone else?' Hopkins reports (S 123), voicing a question
that most adult human beings can probably remember confronting
more or less explicitly. Recast at another philosophical level, this
question becomes: Since we are both human beings, what makes me
me and you you? Hopkins' confrontational self protrudes clearly
here.

In Hopkins' mind such questions inevitably and immediately involve themselves with Trinitarian theology, which lies at the heart
of Catholic doctrine, since Trinitarian theology treats the differences
of the three Persons, Father, Son, and Holy Spirit, within the God
who is One in nature. The three Persons are One God not just
abstractly but concretely and functionally. For all three Persons have
one and the same intellect and will – are, in a way, inside each
other existentially and operationally, though utterly distinct from
one another as Persons. Related to Trinitarian theology is Christology, which treats of the two natures, human and divine, in the Person of Jesus Christ, Word of God who became man, remaining one
Person. The liturgy brings out clearly and existentially the two-
natures-one-person in Jesus Christ, for in prayer, the same 'You'
('Thou') applies whether Christ is addressed as God or man. The
liturgy likewise brings out the Three-Persons-in-One-God doctrine:
when the Father, Son, and Holy Spirit are addressed individually in
prayer, each is a different 'You' (or 'Thou'). Hopkins' speculation in
systematic or dogmatic theology centres in this personalist theolog-

ical world of selves or, to use his own term (*S* 197), of 'selving,' human and divine.

4   MORAL THEOLOGY AND THE SELF

Before turning to the implications of dogmatic or systematic theology for Hopkins' Victorian self-consciousness, it will be well to note briefly another part of theology which Hopkins not only knew speculatively but also used practically, and which certainly intensified his concern with human freedom and thereby with the human self. This was moral theology.

Scholastic moral theology, whatever its now evident limitations, was by Hopkins' day certainly the most elaborated treatment of the morality of free human actions that the world had ever known. Simple perusal of the dozens of manuals (all in Latin, of course) from Azor (1536–1603) through de Lugo, Sanchez, Busenbaum, the Salamanca Carmelites, and Alphonsus Liguori (1696–1787) on into the nineteenth and twentieth centuries, and the innumerable sources these manuals cite, as well as a glance at the 'case books' from Francisco de Toledo (1532–96) on, proposing complex concrete moral cases for solution, shows the near-total coverage that moral theology gave (and gives) to the various kinds of human actions and their goodness or badness. Thomas (*Hopkins*, 156) notes the 'cases of conscience' gone over every Tuesday evening by Hopkins and other Jesuits studying theology at St Beuno's.

The moral theology that Hopkins knew had grown around and in great part out of the Church's penitential practices, which over the centuries had brought millions upon millions of human beings to the sacrament of penance – or the sacrament of reconciliation, as the preferred Roman Catholic terminology now has it. Over the centuries, the frequency of confession had varied, but through the Middle Ages and the Renaissance the tendency to frequent confession had grown in the West (Poschmann, 123–54), coming to a significant peak around the time of Ignatius, when consciousness, at least in the West, had interiorized itself as never before. This interiorization of consciousness, often treated simply or even grossly as growth in 'individualism,' brought the individual to decide upon and assess his or her own actions more and more by means of personally appropriated principles or reasons rather than by means of externally observed, communal behaviour. Interiorization of consciousness produces what anthropologists style a guilt culture, based more on interiorized, personal standards, as against the more archaic, more emphatically communal shame culture, in which the standards are more those which others apply to me.

One way the interiorization of consciousness showed in Protestantism was in the passion for private interpretation of the Bible (literacy fostered interiorization of consciousness – Ong, *Orality*) and for deeper personal, experiential religious conversion, which often led to behaviour running counter to many current socially accepted Christian practices (hence one reason for 'Protestant'). One way the same interiorization of consciousness showed in Catholicism was in a growing emphasis on personal, private examination of conscience and frequent confession of sins.

Quite evidently, human beings had in one way or another been examining their consciences since at least the time of the Decalogue. But by Ignatius' day, detailed examination of conscience, often taking several days, became a recommended and methodical devotional exercise, as in the *Spiritual Exercises* themselves (32–44). No doubt, the new stress on examination of conscience and the interiorization of consciousness owed much to habits of itemized personal accountability earlier fostered by writing and in Ignatius' day even more by print. Literates, whose habits of mind were more and more becoming the norm, could easily keep books on themselves. In the *Spiritual Exercises* Ignatius prescribes such bookkeeping for the particular examination of conscience, using a graph-like method, as earlier noted. Print implemented tallying one's sins in previously unthinkable detail. By the mid-1600s, the Franciscan Christoph Leutbrewer had published a tab-equipped 102-page printed manual of some one thousand different sins to expedite examination of conscience, with a title-page stating that, with its help, in less than two hours of concentrated effort, one could tally up all one's sins, large and small, for several preceding years – 'plusieurs années.' The manual was much reprinted. Without writing, no one could accumulate the quantity of statistical detail that Leutbrewer deals with, and before print, although there had been for centuries written lists of sins and penances (Poschmann 126–31, etc), these were available only in small quantities for the use of priests. Before print, it was unthinkable to mass-produce books, and only a tiny percentage of the population could read anyhow. Confession of the sort that Leutbrewer's type of manual envisions is clearly a literate, and indeed typographic, ideal.

The Council of Trent, which governed practice in Hopkins' day, had made more specific than ever before that the faithful were to seek forgiveness for their sins through confessing to a priest all their serious or 'mortal' sins (Denzinger, 889–902; Poschmann, 196–202) – by implication, after rigorous examination of conscience – with true sorrow and a determination not to sin in the future. What sins were mortal was worked out in the Church mostly as a kind of consensus, given a certain explicitness by moral theologians or by Church practice and, very infrequently, here and there, by a Church decree. Lesser or 'venial' sins could be confessed *ad libitum*, and many persons came to the sacrament of penance – still come – with nothing more than slight offences against God to ask pardon for. Serious or mortal sins, which constituted and still constitute the basic rationale for the sacrament, the Council of Trent had decreed were to be confessed not simply in general (for example, 'I have sinned seriously' or 'I have been dishonest' or 'I have been unchaste') but 'according to their specific kind and number' (*in specie et singillatim* – Denziger 899) – for example, 'I deliberately destroyed the reputation of another by lying about him on one occasion,' or 'I stole a hundred and fifty dollars,' or 'I committed adultery three times,' or 'I killed another person out of hatred and a desire for revenge,' or 'I have done grave injustice to my wife and children by wasting large sums of money on gambling and drinking,' or 'I deliberately harboured hatred against a person for months and twice sought revenge.'

The specificities were further complicated in two ways. First, in concrete cases not simply one principle but many principles were often involved, some of them seemingly conflicting. Thus Sir Thomas More knew that he had an obligation not to take the oath acknowledging Henry VIII as head of the Church in England but knew also he was obliged to take care of his family, who would be left destitute if he did not take the oath, for then all his property would be forfeit to the Crown. These two obligations More had to assess in relation to each other. Following one's conscience could mean walking a chalk line. 'Casebooks' in moral theology available in Hopkins' day worked through such realistically complex situations by the hundreds.

Second, specificities were complicated by the pastoral principle that they were to be urged always humanly or humanely. (This needs to be remembered by persons whose only knowledge of confession comes not from experience but from anecdotes with highly

fictional content or colouring.) For example, rigid enforcement of
the law 'according to their specific kind and number' could be at
times counterproductive, fostering not so much true sorrow as terrible anxiety. Overscrupulous persons (in effect, persons with
obsessive-compulsive neuroses and/or anxiety neuroses) had to be –
still have to be – counselled against 'integral' confession 'according
to ... kind and number,' and allowed or often urged, contrary to the
letter of the law, to be simply generic about their failings. The pres-
sures in adjudicating all the issues here with one penitent after
another could bear heavily on a delicately tuned sensibility such as
Hopkins'. Helping penitents practise accountability that was both
strict and humane was not always easy, and still is not easy.

The demand for specificity in confession fostered delicacy of conscience and closer and closer attention to the borders between right
and wrong, which had to be known if one was to be responsibly
free. Out of this world came, for example, the painstaking thinking
about matters such as mental reservation, associated with the
persecutions which Catholics, including many Jesuits, underwent
through the sixteenth and seventeenth centuries in the British Isles
and which Hopkins, like all educated British Roman Catholics, was
acutely aware of.

If you were questioned, often enough under torture, about actions
involving your fellow Catholics or others sympathetic to Catholics,
how could you on the one hand avoid lying – which the common
Catholic tradition held to be under all circumstances always wrong
– and on the other hand avoid revealing information that could lead
to the unjust arrest, torture, and death of your fellow religionists or
their friends? How could you frame a response to be true and yet not
betray others? Clever interrogators could so set up questions that
silence was clearly a yes or a no. Persons with less delicate consciences have never had problems of this sort: they can simply lie.
Those with delicate consciences – which Recusant Catholics must
have had, for it is conscience that makes conscientious objectors –
had somehow to hew to the truth but, so far as possible, also not
say anything to betray others. The literature on mental reservation
came into existence not to provide ploys for scoundrels but largely
to provide guidelines for persons in agonies of decision involving
their own possible deaths and the deaths of others, often their family and friends.

The moral theology Hopkins knew had matured in a stressful

world, of which the English Catholic tradition remained quite aware, and in particular the English Jesuit tradition. English Jesuits had given their lives by the score and had given counsel and comfort to hundreds of other men and women who gave their lives. English Jesuits of Hopkins' day treasured the memory of these martyrs, as Jesuits and others still do today. One of Hopkins' poems (*P* 145) deals with the heroic wife and mother Margaret Clitheroe, since declared St Margaret Clitheroe (or Clitherow). Charged with giving shelter to Roman Catholic priests and with attending Mass – capital offences – Margaret Clitherow in 1586 was pressed to death (with stones piled on planks laid on her prostrate body) because she refused to plead either guilty or not guilty, thereby making it impossible to bring her to trial. A trial, she knew, might have forced her own children to give evidence against her. English Catholic history was ridden with complex and stressful moral decisions.

Hopkins knew no way to live a vaguely moral life. Catholic moral teaching, structured to implement the self-confrontation that confession demanded, was decision-enforcing. It taught not only that some actions were right and others wrong, but also that it was wrong to act when in doubt. To act morally, one had to have assurance that one's line of action was at least morally permissible. Many theologians, including most Jesuits, urged the principle that in a doubtful case, where reasons could be seen both for and against the morality of a given action and where there was no way to decide conclusively one way or the other, if you had solid, positive reasons indicating that the action was morally permissible, so that it was genuinely doubtful that the act was forbidden, you could perform the act. The moral principle 'genuinely doubtful obligations do not bind' here enabled you to 'resolve the doubt,' to decide that the doubtfully moral action was in the practical order permissible. Such teaching was 'probabilism.' Against it stood 'probabiliorism': in a doubtful case, where reasons could be perceived both for and against the morality of a given action, you had to balance out everything totally, had to calibrate exactly which course was supported by the more probable reasons, and had to follow that course. Probabilists protested that such exact calibration of greater or lesser probabilities, involving perhaps dozens or even hundreds of pros and cons, was often psychologically impossible and in real life paralysing. (Today one might say it would call for the resources of a computer.) The differences of opinion here between probabilists and probabiliorists may seem baroque, but these people, on both sides, were, and still are, treating morality seriously and painstakingly.

Although confession was private and strictly confidential, so that the confessor could never reveal to anyone or even hint at the sins of any penitent, the Church's discipline regarding the sacrament of penance forced reflection and articulation concerning moral questions with a specificity, an exactitude, a range, and an urgency quite unknown on this scale elsewhere in human history. Nowhere, it seems, not even in rabbinic practice, have so many millions upon millions of human beings shared their problems of conscience so systematically and explicitly as in the Christian penitential tradition from the eighth century on in the West (Poschmann, 138–45) – for the Eastern Church developed a somewhat different discipline for the sacrament. The burden of conscience of course fell first on the individual penitent approaching the sacrament, but it fell in a real way even more heavily on those individual priests who over long years heard confessions by the hundreds and thousands and, in more recent times, as in the case of priests known to me, by the tens of thousands, and who felt that they were individually accountable to God for their dealings with penitents, for whatever decisions they might make or whatever counsel they might give. Was my counsel kind enough? Fully informed? Too strict? Too lax? These are not academic, but urgent practical questions. The legislation of the Society of Jesus explicitly states that Jesuits who hear confessions are to monitor themselves, reflecting afterwards in their own hearts on their performance with a view to improving themselves in the future (Loyola, *Constitutions* 202 – part IV, ch 8, no [407]).

Before ordination, the candidate for the priesthood in Hopkins' day was expected to be prepared for everything that might be brought up by penitents presenting themselves for reconciliation with God and his Church (see Thomas, *Hopkins* 176, 181–2). Moral theology undertook to educate the priest-to-be to adjudicate and advise on every conceivable kind of moral problem, always in accord with the Church's matured teaching and with Christ-like pastoral concern and love. Over-scrupulosity and laxity were equally to be avoided. Moreover, the confessor was – and still is – to be attentive to the particular state of soul of each person approaching the sacrament, the person's more or less evident intelligence, education or lack of education, good will, underlying indifference, his or her embarrassment, fear, discouragement, or whatever. The smouldering

wick was not to be extinguished. Moral rules had to be respected absolutely, yet the objective of the sacrament was forgiveness and
reconciliation and amendment of life, and the individual was to be
helped in whatever way this individual could be helped. All this
made for careful and expeditious thinking and for exquisite attention
to detail – all with reference to decision-making, since in decision-
making the person had moved or was moving to moral good or evil.
Because of the attentiveness and the responsible assessment of
human acts it calls for, hearing confessions is exhausting.

Hopkins underwent the kind of training and testing in moral
theology that the discipline of the sacrament of penance required for
priests (Thomas, *Hopkins* 155–6). The training was academically
based, but not academically oriented: candidates for the priesthood
studied moral theology to put it to use, chiefly in hearing confessions but also in counselling and other forms of pastoral work.
Hopkins put his to use in this way constantly. 'I hear confessions,
preach, and so forth,' he writes to Dixon (*D* 16). To Bridges he
writes from Liverpool 4 September 1880, that he is 'down with diar-
rhoea and vomiting, brought on by yesterday's heat and the long
hours in the confessional,' (*B* 104), later of having to miss an annual
Liverpool horse show because of work in the confessional (*B* 127),
still later of being detained at Preston 'to hear Lenten confessions
again' (*B* 143).

Back of Hopkins' sonnets about responsibility for one's acts,
about the vagaries of the human will, and about the need of each
human self ultimately to come to terms with right and wrong lies
his exposure not simply to the demands of his own conscience but
also to the problems of conscience of thousands of his fellow human
beings, whom his calling as a priest obliged him to help.

Against the background of his work as a confessor, Hopkins'
reference to 'black, white; right, wrong' in his poem 'Spelt from
Sibyl's Leaves' (*P* 61) has a more workaday background than F.R.
Leavis once assigned it (185–6). Leavis quite fancifully maintained
that the reversal ('right, wrong' instead of 'wrong, right' to corre-
spond with 'black, white') showed that Hopkins' 'absolutes waver
and change places,' leaving him in 'terrible doubt.' The terror in the
sonnet comes not from doubt about 'absolutes' but from a sense of
the irreducible seriousness of questions of conscience, reinforced by
longstanding engagement with the interiors of hundreds of human
beings, in which one self bared itself to another self, for nowhere is

the self more bare than in the sacrament of penance. The 'absolutes' are there: the problem is how this action relates to them. In the density of real existence, such a problem can be as torturing as it is real.

5 SYSTEMATIC THEOLOGY AND THE SELF: THE SCOTIST COSMOS

Moral theology nourished Hopkins' particularism and personalism largely on practical grounds, in terms of human acts and interpersonal action. Systematic theology or, as it was commonly called, 'dogmatic' theology, nourished them on theoretical and contemplative grounds, which for Hopkins, though not for the manual theology he studied, included a certain amount of careful psychologizing or protophenomenological introspection. Some of the myriad ways in which standard Catholic dogmatic theology and newer Victorian concerns with particularities and the self interacted in Hopkins' sensibility can be most handily examined in his treatment of the theology of Duns Scotus, for whom Hopkins' admiration knew almost no bounds.

Hopkins' attraction to Scotus is well known. (Thomas, *Hopkins*, 99–100, 174, 183, etc; Thomas, 'Was Hopkins' 617–29; Zaniello, 141–43; Devlin, in Hopkins *S* 338–51, also 'Essay,' 'Image,' and 'Word'). It is frequently traced to Scotus' attention to the individuality of things. Moving counter to the universalizing thrust of philosophic thought from Plato and Aristotle and through most medieval scholastics, Scotus had made a great deal of *haecceitas* – or *ecceitas*, in Hopkins' strange Italianate version (*S* 151; Devlin in *Hopkins*, *S* 293–4, 341) – the 'thisness' or individual assertiveness of each individual being. Hopkins found Scotus' attention to 'thisness' congenial to his own particularism.

As it enters into Hopkins' writings (in a rather scattered way – *S* 123–8, 146–8, 150–3), the problem of individuation has this kind of foundation: if two individuals of a species are exactly alike in their species, what is it that makes this one so utterly and totally a different being from that one? Any conceptualizable individual differentiations of one individual might also be verified in another individual. If this squirrel differs from this other of the same species by having a longer tail, there could be another individual with an exactly matching long tail which would be just as much a different

individual from the other long-tailed as the short-tailed is. And so
with any other individual characteristic or combination of characteristics. Two identical twins are just as much different individuals
– two different 'I's – as any other two individuals. What makes
them different individuals if their species and all their individual
characteristics are the same? Thomists would say each individual in
a species differs from every other by its *materia signata quantitate*
(Copleston, 2, part 2:46) or matter marked by its quantification –
which approximates saying, in today's idiom, that each individual is
from the start embarked upon a different history, a different career
in the quantified world of time and space. (One correlative of this
theory was that, since in Thomist theory angels are pure spirits
without any matter, every angel is a separate species since there are
no grounds, no matter, for distinguishing individuals within a
species.)

Other scholastic philosophers had other theories. Scotus' theory
was his own. What distinguishes one individual of a species from all
other individuals, Scotus held, cannot be explained in terms of matter or form or essence or quantity or even existence or by any combination of such elements (as the Thomists' *materia quantitate
signata*), but is simply a given with the individual itself, the being's
'thisness' or *haecceitas* (Copleston, 2, part 2:234–40). Every being is
dependent only upon the divine will and on nothing else for its being the singular or individual being it is (see Devlin in *Hopkins*,
S 283, n 122). I am I simply because God wants me to be me.
Scotus' principle of individuation, it would seem, is the most
abrupt, decisive, uncompromising, totalizing principle possible:
it has no diverse components (such as matter and quantity and
marking).

To Hopkins, as to others – for Scotus had followers aplenty,
though they were a minority – it seemed the most real principle,
truest to the way things are. Existence (which Hopkins regularly
refers to as 'being') begins not with abstract principles at all but
with full-fledged, existing things, in all their totally particularized,
existential density: in actuality, first there is God, and then there is
his real, particularized creation. Abstract principles are afterthoughts
of relatively less consequence. The only beings ever encountered are
individuals. The individuals are the data, the givens that we have to
start with. The basic problem is not how you derive individuals
from abstract species, because you never do derive individuals from

abstract species. Individuals are simply there. Rather, since individuals, particularly human individuals, are so totally different,
the more basic problem is how you can leave their individuality
behind to group them in a species at all. Our growing awareness of
the Victorians' particularist mindset has made it increasingly clear
why this individualist bent in Scotus' philosophy attracted Hopkins,
as it certainly did.

But individuation is a philosophical problem. Hopkins' deeper attraction to Scotus appears to have been theological. He was overwhelmed by Scotus' theology of the Incarnation (S 170; Devlin, in
Hopkins S 109–13, 296). This, with its implications, was what made
Hopkins 'care for him [Scotus] even more than Aristotle and *pace
tua* than a dozen Hegels,' as Hopkins put it to Bridges (20 Feb 1875
– *B* 31). Scotus, Hopkins wrote to Coventry Patmore, 'saw too far,
he knew too much ... ; a kind of feud arose between genius and
talent, and the ruck of talent in the Schools, finding itself, as his age
passed by, less and less able to understand him, voted that there was
nothing important to understand' (*FL* 349). (It should be noted in
passing that the definitive edition of Scotus is still in progress: what
Hopkins read as Scotus' text was probably Scotist enough, but
perhaps not always Duns Scotus' own personal work – Copleston, 2,
part 2:200–1).

Scotus' Christology provided a variety of food for Hopkins' thinking about the self and freedom. The Scotist view of the Incarnation
which so attracted Hopkins links creation and redemption more
closely and makes Christ more the centre of the cosmos than do
competing theories (Bonnefoy, 3–14 and passim). Most theologians
considered that the Word was made flesh because of Adam's sin in
the sense that the divine decision that the Son would become man
was God's free and generous response to humankind's plight after
the fall. Scotus thought otherwise. He did not believe that the Son
assumed human nature simply as a divinely generous response to
sin. Rather the Incarnation of the Son was God's first intent in all of
his creation. Hopkins states Scotus' position and makes it his own
(*S* 197): 'The first intention ... of God outside himself or, as they
say, *ad extra*, outwards, the first outstress of God's power, was
Christ.' The creation of the universe and of humankind followed as
a consequence of the design to have the Son take on human nature.
Adam's sin, calling for redemption as it did, gave the incarnation a
special urgency but not its real raison d'être.

Scotus' approach here was characteristically positive, not hypothetical. At least in the *Ordinatio*, his own composition, if not in the *Reportationes* drafted by his students, Scotus did not cast the issue in the hypothetical form in which it is often cast, 'If Adam had not sinned, would there have been an incarnation?' He remained within the actual economy of existence and of revelation (Carol, 27–31; Bonnefoy, 3). The actual world which we know and inhabit, in which divine revelation is given and to which divine revelation refers, was created by God because God wanted the Son to become man and share himself and his Father and the Holy Spirit with finite creatures, which are all spin-offs from the incarnation. Scotus here stays with what is real, attending to the origins of the existing world, not to possibilities.

The consequences of Scotus' view are sweeping, and especially for the mind imbued with the Victorian and present-day sense of history. If the Incarnation was the result of a divine decision to redeem a fallen human race, as it was in Thomist and other non-Scotist views, Christ is indeed established as a central figure in the cosmos but his is a figure in a history which began antecedently to himself and in this sense is thus larger than himself. New discoveries in cosmology are relatively uneventful theologically, since they relate only to nature, which does not derive from the Incarnation but is merely the situs of the Incarnation. If the Incarnation was the first divine decision or decree, so that the universe and human beings were created as a field for Christ's love to work in, Christ is antecedent to history and, instead of Christ's being in history, all history is in Christ. New discoveries in cosmology – Copernican, Newtonian, Darwinian, Einsteinian – enlarge not merely our understanding of nature but also our human insight into the mystery of the Incarnation, from which all the cosmos takes its origin. New knowledge about the cosmos (see Wildiers) is new knowledge about the consequences of the Son's becoming man. The personal yet cosmic Christ, *Christos Kosmocrator*, the anointed World-Ruler, a favourite figure in Christian iconography, especially Eastern, would seem to be in the Scotist view a far stronger figure than in competing views. It is easy to see how congenial the Scotist view was to Hopkins' Victorian enhancement of the person, the self, as well as to his vigorous Christocentrism. The Scotist view maximizes the person of Christ in a way competing views do not.

Scotus could support his view from the Bible quite as well as his opponents could theirs (see the plethora of citations in Bonnefoy 34–251). The gospel according to John and the other Johannine writings particularly favoured Scotus: 'Without him nothing was made that was made' (John 1:3). Scotus' opponents could cite the many texts stating that Christ died for our sins, but Scotus' Christology did not compromise this teaching. It even enhanced it. Coming into the real universe, which had been created so that he could enter it in human flesh, body and soul, taking on himself the human nature that was the culmination of creation and thereby im-buing finite creation with a direct share of God's life, Christ found that in fact humankind in the real universe had fallen into sin, had turned from God. He would have become incarnate if no human be-ing had ever sinned, in which case there would have been no call for his suffering and death. But, finding sin present, an aftermath of human freedom, he took it in stride, took sin on himself, too, suf-fering its racking consequences to redeem his brothers and sisters and unite them to his Father, though he himself was sinless.

Fascinated with centres of pent-up energy, Hopkins' Victorian mind could sense Christ in Scotist Christology as an energy centre more powerful than he could be in a Thomist or other Christology where the Incarnation is understood as a loving response to those suffering from sin rather than as the event in which all creation is encapsulated. In all Catholic theology, of course, Scotist, Thomist, or other, the divine act of creation had to be explained as somehow exercised through the eternal Son or Word: 'Without him nothing was made that was made' (John 1:3). Yet for the Scotist, the rela-tionship of creation to the creator lodged also, mediately, in the Word-made-flesh, in Jesus Christ, for he was the rationale, the raison-d'être of the rest of creation. All the energies of creation were centred not simply in the eternal Word but in the eternal Word-made-man, Jesus Christ.

This presentation of the God-man Jesus Christ as the major energy centre of the universe was congenial not only to the Vic-torian sensibility, with its predilection for energy centres in its representation of reality, but was also congenial to the *Spiritual Ex-ercises*, even though the Scotist presentation is not implied there. In the *Exercises* Christ's kingship is not triumphantly supervisory, as for example it appears in the iconography of the Byzantine images of *Christos Kosmocrator*, the Anointed World Ruler. Rather, in Ignatius' presentation Christ's kingship is strenuous and demanding.

Christ is an active energy centre, not only for himself but for all his followers. He is not quietly gazing out on the universe. In the meditation on the Kingdom (91–8), Ignatius imagines Christ as saying – 'Whoever wishes to join me in this enterprise [of conquering the world] must be willing to labor with me, that by following me in suffering, he may follow me in glory' (95). The entire Second and Third Weeks of the *Exercises* concentrates on the labours and the passion of Jesus. Jesus Christ's work taxes his human resources.

Over and over again, Hopkins presents Christ as energy-expending. 'Mark Christ our King. He knows war, served this soldiering through' (P 63). 'The Windhover' (P 36) where the valiant, tiny falcon 'rebuffed the big wind,' spending himself in realizing his own inscape, 'doing his thing' we would say today, Hopkins characteristically dedicates 'To Christ our Lord.' Though his suffering and death itself was a 'passion,' something undergone, Christ actively accepted it, showing his deep reserves of power in his last words, consciously and freely giving himself to the Father in his last gasp, actively accepting his own agonizing death: 'Father, into your hands I commend my spirit' (Luke 23:46). (With here 'Christ, come quickly,' the dying nun does the same, as has been seen, on the wrecked *Deutschland* – P 28). For Hopkins, God's grace comes as a 'stress' into the lives of human beings through Christ's passion and death – 'Thence the discharge of it, there its swelling to be' (P 28). Christ comes with frightening cosmic power to gather in the tall nun and the others dying on the wrecked *Deutschland*, 'Our passion-plungèd giant risen, / ... fetched in the storm of his strides' (P 28). The intensity of Christian life burst forth finally in all fullness when the Father raised Jesus up after his death to a new state of being and prepared the way for other human beings to share his joy, to be raised from a death that, as Hopkins insists, is utterly and devastatingly real – 'death blots black out' – to a new, still more real, and different order of life with him in eternity (P 72):

> Manshape, that shone
> Sheer off, disseveral, a star, | death blots black out; nor mark
>   Is any of him at all so stark
> But vastness blurs and time | beats level. Enough! the Resurrection,
> A heart's-clarion! Away grief's gasping, | joyless days, dejection.
>   Across my foundering deck shone
> A beacon, an eternal beam. | Flesh fade, and mortal trash

Fall to the residuary worm; | world's wildfire, leave but ash:
    In a flash, at a trumpet crash,
I am all at once what Christ is, | since he was what I am, and
This Jack, joke, poor potsherd, | patch, matchwood, immortal diamond,
                              is immortal diamond.

The Victorian energy centres – vortices, curled poppy buds burst open (*P* 138), clusters, Tennyson's poised eagle clutching the crag – here climax in the 'immortal diamond,' Christ and the 'I' in the poem, transformed by Christ, radiant with bursting life. Scotist Christology fosters this energy-centred presentation.

6   THE INTERIOR OF JESUS CHRIST: SELF-GIVING

For Hopkins, Christ was not merely the energy centre of the cosmos spread out around him, but also an energy centre of interior self-sacrifice or self-offering. This latter idea of Christ's self-sacrificing energy Hopkins develops at length in his treatment of what he calls the 'great sacrifice,' one of his most carefully elaborated theological discussions, to be found in his notes made during the 'Long Retreat' (*S* 196–202) and in other notes made during his tertianship year. Hopkins' theology of 'the great sacrifice' relates directly to the themes of particularization, the self, and human freedom, and it gives substance and structure to these themes in a great deal of his poetry. Downes notes how often the term 'the great sacrifice' appears throughout Hopkins' spiritual writings (*The Great Sacrifice* 42).

    The 'great sacrifice' is the *kenōsis*, the 'emptying' action of Christ, described in Philippians 2:6–11. For Hopkins the most familiar English version would be the Rheims-Douay translation of the Vulgate:

Who being in the form of God, thought it not robbery to be equal with God; but emptied himself, taking the form of a servant, being made in the likeness of men, and in habit found as a man. He humbled himself, becoming obedient unto death, even to the death of the cross. For which cause God also hath exalted him, and hath given him a name which is above all names: that in the name of Jesus every knee should bow, of those that are in heaven, on earth, and under the earth: and that every tongue should confess that the Lord Jesus Christ is in the glory of God the Father.

The 'emptying-out' of Christ, his forgoing of all honours and all else that was his due, resonates through the Church's liturgy and with special intensity through Jesuit spirituality. On the *kenōsis* of the Son and its consequences Ignatius builds his famous Third Kind (or Degree) of Humility in the *Spiritual Exercises* (167): 'I desire and choose poverty with Christ poor, rather than riches; insults with Christ loaded with them, rather than honors; I desire to be accounted as worthless and a fool for Christ, rather than to be esteemed as wise and prudent in this world. So Christ was treated before me.' It will be noted that Ignatius here follows Philippians in focusing primarily not on renunciation of honours or of anything else but on Christ – 'with Christ,' 'for Christ,' 'so Christ' – a centre of energy who here is deliberately abandoning concern about himself as a centre of wealth or resources.

The value of renunciation in Christian asceticism can be misunderstood and has been misunderstood in treatments of Hopkins. Renunciation can be practiced out of pride, for self-aggrandisement or simple power. Whatever value renunciation in itself may have for Stoics or for Christians confused by Stoicism, or simply for masochistic personalities, in itself it has no sure value at all in Christian asceticism. Christ's renunciation was out of love for the Father. His Father wished him to do things that entailed renunciation. The love was what gave renunciation its worth. Following Christ in his love of the Father and obedience to the Father does have value in the economy of Christian faith. The Son's 'emptying' of himself as God (his veiling his divinity in his real human nature, as a real man) was followed by his 'emptying' of himself as a human being, too, giving up many human things and ultimately his human life out of love and obedience to his Father for his fellow human beings. In so far as the love of Christ for his Father and obedience to him called for these renunciations, the Christian is also called to renunciation – out of love of Jesus Christ and a desire to be like him in every way possible, and thus to assimilate himself or herself to the Son in relationship to the Father in the Holy Spirit, not out of devotion to the idea of renunciation, even to the idea of renunciation as ego-strengthening or character-building.

Full understanding of why the Son 'emptied' himself and suffered and died for human beings remains forever elusive in Christian theology, but the faithful know that these actions flow from the Son's love for the Father and the love of Father and Son and Holy

Spirit for human beings. Jesus acts somewhat as the *go'el* in ancient Hebrew culture, the reliable and resourceful kinsman whose obligation it was to take responsibility on himself for suffering and helpless relatives, to redeem them from slavery, rescue them from starvation, or otherwise extricate them from disaster. Sin, estrangement from God, brought the greatest disaster of all, and Jesus took sin and its consequences on himself in his life, and especially through his passion and death. He became a human being, kinsman of us all, to serve as *go'el*, the responsible one, the one who shoulders the burden of estrangement that his kinsfolk cannot carry.

Around the *kenōsis* or 'emptying' of the Son, Hopkins builds an elaborate theory about a cosmic Eucharistic presence of Christ which made him existent as man to the angelic world in non-human, angelic, or, in Hopkins' own term 'aeonian' time, before he became existent as man in cosmic and human time (Devlin in *S*:110-15). Hopkins spins further related theory around the meaning of the battle waged by Michael and other angels against the dragon, the battle depicted in chapter 12 of Revelation. But the power of Hopkins' insight into the human, ascetic, and devotional implications of Christ's *kenōsis* is quite independent of such theories, however curiously insightful they may be – much as the power of Hopkins' verse is independent of his metrical theories. 'Supposing,' Christopher Devlin writes (in Hopkins, *S* 114), in a passage cited in part earlier,

... that one rejected the distinction just mentioned [between the two kinds of time framing the Incarnation], supposing also that one rejected all the paraphernalia of the battle in heaven, Hopkins' devotional insight would still be a valid and most fruitful one. True devotion, to be born, requires close union with a personal savior; but to be nourished it must be able to move at ease on the great heights of revelation. Any experience which puts one *inside* the doctrines of the Church is of the utmost value. Such an experience, for Hopkins, was the perception of Christ adoring the Father. It took him as nearly as possible to the heart of theology and, one might say, to the heart of God.

It might be noted that in the cosmology of Pierre Teilhard de Chardin adoration is likewise central.

Because he is indeed 'inside' the doctrines of the Church, Hopkins effectively brings his Victorian sensitivities to his sense of

the *kenōsis*. He feels the *kenōsis* not as something conveyed to him
through manualized explanation but something he has appropriated
totally into his own being, where he finds it existentially related to
the world around him. Meditating on Philippians 2:6–11, Hopkins
psychologizes more than earlier interpreters had done, or could do,
seeing the *kenōsis* as an action deep in the interior of Christ, profoundly secret, intimately personal, buried in the mystery of
Christ's own particular self. In a letter to Bridges (*B* 175 – 3 Feb
1883), he writes:

Christ's life and character are such as appeal to all the world's admiration,
but there is one insight St. Paul gives us of it which is very secret and seems
to me more touching and constraining than everything else is: This mind he
says, was in Christ Jesus – he means as man: being in the form of God –
that is, finding, as in the first instant of his incarnation he did, his human
nature informed by the godhead – he thought it nevertheless no snatching-
matter for him to be equal with God, but annihilated himself, taking the
form of servant; that is, he could not but see what he was, God, but he
would see it as if he did not see it, and be it as if he were not and instead of
snatching at once at what all the time was his, or was himself, he emptied
himself or exhausted himself so far as that was possible, of godhead and
behaved only as God's slave, as his creature, as man, which also he was,
and then being in the guise of man humbled himself to death, the death of
the cross. It is this holding of himself back, and not snatching at the truest
and highest good, the good that was his right, nay, his possession from a
past eternity in his other nature, his own being and self, which seem to me
the root of all his holiness and the imitation of this the root of all moral
good in other men.

Philippians 2:6–11 is all but certainly an early liturgical hymn,
drawing some inspiration from Isaiah 52:13–12 (Fitzmyer, in Brown
et al, 2:250), which Paul is simply quoting. Here, at the heart of the
early liturgy, Hopkins' attention is caught by the interior action of
Christ, which Hopkins immediately interprets in relation to Christ's
'own being and self.' In Colossians 2:3 and Ephesians 3:8 and elsewhere Paul treats of the great mystery (*mysterion*), the summation
in Christ of all God's wisdom and knowledge. This *mysterion* is
suggested in the present passage: God the Father perceives something in Christ which is not evident from the externals of his death
on the cross, and in consequence of this deeply embedded something

the Father exalts Christ. Paul's theology is deeply interiorized in the sense that, here as elsewhere, it attends to an intimate, personal relationship with Christ, and perhaps nowhere does Paul communicate a sense of interiority more forcefully than when treating of the *mysterion*. Hopkins, however, intensifies interiority and privacy even more in his own reflections on this passage. Paul's insight itself Hopkins qualifies as 'secret' and 'touching' in its intimacy. The insight is also 'constraining' (the Victorian love of condensed force again, of pent-up energy, ready to burst out). Hopkins zeroes in explicitly on Christ's 'own being and self,' Christ's inscape, his own distinctive interiority and self-possession that makes him utterly unique. Hopkins psychologizes with a specificity beyond Paul's reach.

Hopkins' hermeneutic here is undoubtedly valid and exact. For hermeneutic or interpretation of a text means integrating the text into the living thought of the milieu where the interpreter interprets. Showing what a text means consists in relating it in its own original context to our own thought (which is not to say reducing it to our own thought). Hopkins here is bringing the meaning of the earlier text into articulation with Victorian awarenesses. Consciousness had developed a more exquisitely articulate self-awareness since Paul's day, and there was now no way to approach Paul's text effectively without exercising this more articulate self-awareness. The result is that the Victorian sensibility here, far from causing God to 'disappear,' is making the work of salvation more humanly and personally evident than ever before. Hopkins is truly 'explicating' Paul's text, unfurling what had earlier been unavoidably less discernible, getting in a certain way to the interior of Paul's message even more effectively than Paul himself had, revealing even more than Paul had been able to do what it had hidden, though of course simultaneously allowing for a certain darkness in matters which to Paul had seemed more clear.

7   INCARNATION AND TRIUNE GOD: PERSONAL INTERACTION AND DECISION

Two theological subjects closely related to each other and to the *kenōsis* of the Son elicit from Hopkins further comment having to do with the person or self, with individuation and freedom. These two subjects are the Incarnation and the Trinity of Persons in God.

The divine decision that the Son, the Second Person, would become man figures centrally in the *Spiritual Exercises*. As already noted, it is on this decision that Ignatius focuses the meditation on the Incarnation at the beginning of the Second Week of the *Exercises*. Hopkins attends to this meditation in his notes for the Second Week made during his Long Retreat in November and December of 1881 (*S* 171). Ignatius had recommended that for the Composition of Place in this meditation the exercitant imagine 'the great bulk and extent of the earth' (*magnam capacitatem et ambitum mundi*). In following Ignatius' directive here to call the imagination into play, Hopkins' post-Ignatian, Victorian imagination far outdoes Ignatius' particularizations with an enterprising image, the pomegranate. Inside its skin, a pomegranate is a mass of hundreds of small granular seeds – *pomum granatum*, the 'grainy fruit.' The whole world is a pomegranate, and so is 'each species in it, each race, each individual.' The mass of particulars represented by the mass of seeds can be further particularized, for the fruit can be sliced through in any direction to produce an infinite number of different surfaces, plane or curved, each cross-section or 'cleave' of the fruit and its enclosed seeds representing the actualization of a given set of possibilities. Hopkins is undertaking to represent particularization without limit.

Even 'the sphere of the divine being, a steady "seat or throne" of majesty,' has, from our human point of view, its own cleaves, that is, God's individual decrees or decisions. The decision that the Son will take to himself a human nature, will enter the material world is one 'cleave' or decision of God's, out of an infinite possible number of divine decisions. Hopkins' attention to cleaving shows the high voluntarist charge in Hopkins' (as in Ignatius') thinking: deciding something is like cleaving something for it is 'definitive' (border-making), partitive (this rather than that), we decide 'between' issues, separating them in our act of deciding. The term *decide* derives from the Latin *de-*, meaning 'off,' and *caedere*, meaning 'cut.'

Hopkins' full passage follows (*S* 171–2):

'Magnam capacitatem et ambitum mundi' – This suggests that 'pomegranate,' that *pomum possibilium* [fruit, berry, apple of possibilities]. The Trinity saw it whole and in every 'cleave' the actual and the possible. We may consider that we are looking at it in all the actual cleaves, one after another. This sphere is set off against the sphere of the divine being, a steady 'seat or throne' of majesty. Yet that too has its cleave to us, the entrance of Christ on the world. There is not only the pomegranate of the whole world but of each species in it, each race, each individual, and so on. Of human nature the whole pomegranate fell in Adam (Aug. 26 '85)

'Videre Personas' – See for this pp. 121, 122 MS.[5] [In printed text S 186.] The Trinity made man after the image of Their one nature but They redeem him ('*faciamus* redemptionem') by bringing into play with infinite charity Their personality. Being personal They see as if with sympathy the play of personality in man below Them, for in his personality his freedom lies and this same personality playing in its freedom not only exerts and displays the riches and capacities of his one nature (see Fr. Roothaan's note ... 'unam eandemque' sqq) but unhappily disunites it, rends it, and almost tears it to pieces. One of Them therefore makes Himself one of that throng of persons, a man among men, by charity to bring them back to that union with themselves which they have lost by freedom and even to bring them to a union with God which nothing in their nature gave them

The freedom distinctive of human beings, Hopkins makes clear, entails risk. Risk means that human beings can tear themselves apart through freedom as well as pull themselves together ('disunites ... rends ... almost tears to pieces ... back to that union ... ').

Ignatius' age could not bring off an imaginative recreation with this intense and exquisite particularism: the infinite number of 'cleaves' of all actual and possible reality, then 'all the actual cleaves, one after another,' the 'cleave' of the entrance of Christ. The sixteenth-century and seventeenth-century metaphysical poets could exploit unlikely imagery with uncanny skill and precision, as John Donne exploits the image of the draftsman's compass in 'A Valediction Forbidding Mourning,' but they did not produce clinically explanatory texts of this analytic detail. Hopkins' particularism admits no limits, running from the Godhead to each individual human person. In this field of particularities the Persons in the Trinity – totally distinct as Persons from one another yet mysteriously One God, united in one nature, one intellect, one will – because they are themselves distinct Persons, 'see as if with sympathy the play of personality in man below Them, for in his personality his freedom lies.'

Elsewhere he conceives of the procession of the Son from the Father and of the Holy Spirit from the Father and the Son explicitly as a 'selving' in God, connecting this 'selving' with the previously mentioned 'cleave' which is the free decision by all Three Persons that the Son become man, (S 197):

Why did the Son of God ... go forth from the Father not only in the eternal and intrinsic procession of the Trinity but also by an extrinsic and less eternal, let us say aeonian one? – to give God glory and that by sacrifice, sacrifice offered in the barren wilderness outside of God, as the children of Israel were led into the wilderness to offer sacrifice. This sacrifice and this outward procession is a consequence and shadow of the procession of the Trinity, from which mystery sacrifice takes its rise; ... It is as if the blissful agony or stress of selving in God had forced out drops of sweat or blood, which drops were the world, or as if the lights lit at the festival of the 'peaceful Trinity' through some little cranny striking out lit up into being one 'cleave' out of the world of possible creatures.

The interior dynamism of the Three Persons in One God was not for Hopkins some sort of formula for theological juggling acts but was rather the centre of his personal devotional life and thus of his own 'selving.' His prayer and his daily activities were embedded in his felt relationships in faith to Father, Son and Holy Spirit. He writes to Bridges 24 October 1883, from Stonyhurst (B 187–8):

For if the Trinity, as Francis Newman [younger brother of the cardinal, completely at odds with the cardinal on matters of Christian faith] somewhere says, is to be explained by grammar and by tropes, why then could he furnish explanations for himself; but then where wd. be the mystery? the true mystery, the incomprehensible one. At that pass one should point blank believe or disbelieve: he disbelieved; his brother, at the same pass, believed. There are three persons, each God and each the same, the one, the only God; to some people this is a 'dogma,' a word they almost chew, that is an equation in theology, the dull algebra of schoolmen; to others it is news of their dearest friend or friends, leaving them all their lives balancing whether they have three heavenly friends or one – not that they have any doubt on the subject, but that their knowledge leaves their minds swinging; poised, but on the quiver. And this might be the ecstasy of interest, one would think.

Hopkins' acute sense of the three diverse relationships of the Christian to Father, Son, and Holy Spirit had earlier marked

Ignatius' own thought and prayer. In his *Autobiography* (37-8) Ignatius mentions as the first of five cardinal spiritual experiences of his life an overwhelming illumination regarding the Trinity, which, Karl Rahner has it (*Spirituality* 50) marked the end of Ignatius' 'night of the soul.' Ignatius adds that 'great devotion while praying to the Most Holy Trinity has remained with him throughout his life.' 'Visions,' sensory experiences, often in the visual field, representing sometimes God the Father, sometimes Father, Son, and Holy Spirit individually, often were granted him to confirm, he was convinced, various decisions he had come to in drawing up the *Constitutions* of the Society of Jesus (Loyola, *Autobiography* 93). Ignatius' important *Spiritual Diary* consists largely of personal notes on his varying day-to-day relationship to each of the Three Persons of the Trinity in his prayer. Assessing the significance of these varying relations to one or another of the Persons, he tried to calculate the validity of his decisions regarding the prescriptions he was writing into the *Constitutions*. Coldness or disturbance in his prayer might possibly be due to a decision faulted by too much selfishness or other failings. The *Spiritual Exercises* treat such delicate and demanding assessments of interior states of consciousness under 'Discernment of Spirits' (6-10, 313-36).

In the *Autobiography* (89), reporting the incident after his ordination now known as the vision or experience at La Storta (the River Bend), near Rome, in a Church there dedicated to Mary, he records how the awareness overwhelmed him that God the Father had 'placed him with his Son.' A deep sense of being not merely united with God in some generic way, but rather of being placed by the Father 'with' Jesus, adopted by the Father into Jesus' own place among the Persons of the Trinity, underlies Ignatius' insistence that the order he founded be called the *Societas Jesu*, the *socii* or companions of Jesus. Since all Christians are companions of Jesus, who is their Brother by their adoption into the Trinity, the name that Ignatius clung to for his new order marked not a differentiation from other Christians but rather an intense focus on this central Incarnational and Trinitarian Christian teaching.

The objection might be made, and sometimes is, that despite the Trinitarian complexion of his thought, Ignatius was not fully sensitive to all Three Persons in the *Spiritual Exercises* because he says relatively little there explicitly about the Holy Spirit, the Third Person, although he over and over again adverts explicitly to the Father

and the Son. This very nonmention, however, shows how accurately
Ignatius senses the quite differentiated relationship of the believer
to each of the Persons, including the Holy Spirit. The Church does
not normally address public prayers to the Holy Spirit, though in
Catholic belief he is God with the Father and the Son, and the equal
of the Father and the Son. For in Christian belief prayer itself is the
work *of* the Holy Spirit, the *Paracletos* or Advocate, who shapes
prayer in the hearts of the faithful, pleading with and for them.
Typically, outbursts – hymns, antiphons – express the Church's
relation to the Spirit, who 'fills' the hearts of individuals and of the
Church as a whole. 'The Spirit himself makes intercession for us'
(Romans 8:26). He is an abiding presence throughout the cosmos,
the one who, in Hopkins' words, 'over the bent / World broods with
warm breast and with ah! bright wings' (*P* 31, echoing Genesis 1:2,
'and the spirit of God moved over the waters'). Ignatius takes all
this for granted in the *Spiritual Exercises*, which bear the name of
the Spirit in their title and thereby in their entirety acknowledge the
presence of the Spirit. In his *Spiritual Journal* (tr Young, 137–8, 145)
Ignatius records his own overwhelming experiences of intimate
prayer with the Holy Spirit, and throughout notes over and over
again the deep awareness of the utter distinctness of the Three Persons as Persons that frequently overpowered him in prayer and
reduced him to tears. Ignatius' kind of intense and passionately
articulate, deeply interiorized devotion to the Three Persons individually would seem to be a relatively new development, theologically a continuum with what went before but activated by a new
state of self-consciousness that marks the sixteenth century.

As the era he lived in contoured Ignatius' Trinitarian devotion, so
Hopkins' era contours his. But here again, in the Trinitarian centre
of his thought, Hopkins is ahead of his age. Hopkins' articulation of
the self that marks his Christology and Trinitarian theology does
more than register the Victorian stage of consciousness. It presages
what was to come in the evolution of thought and of consciousness.
It presages, first, the existentialist personalism and phenomenology
and depth psychology that would flower in the mid-twentieth century. It also presages major developments in present-day Roman
Catholic and other Christology and Trinitarian theology, notably
that of the Tübingen School. Since Hopkins, Christology, as earlier
noted here, has been more and more deeply psychologized, for example, in the work masterfully synthesized and advanced by Walter

Kasper (*Jesus the Christ*) and by Edward Schillebeeckx (*Jesus* and *Christ*). Jesus' human nature and existence, most particularly his self-consciousness as well as his consciousness of his Father, have been gone into with a psychological specificity and depth never before reached or even attempted.

Trinitarian theology has become so active that mid-twentieth-century theologians, Protestant, such as Karl Barth, and Catholic, such as Karl Rahner and Wilhelm Thüsing, have even tried to fine-tool the concept long expressed by the established term 'person' in Trinitarian theology (Porter, and references there). Today Three Persons suggest three centres of consciousness, whereas in God there is only one centre of consciousness in the sense that there is one nature, one intellect, and one will, and whereas in Jesus Christ, though he is one Person, one 'I' or 'You,' there are two centres of consciousness, it would seem, because there are two natures, two intellects, and two wills. The new terms modestly proposed by Barth ('mode or way of being') and Rahner ('distinct manner of subsisting') are suggested as supplementary or auxiliary terms – for neither theologian wishes at all to do away with 'person.' The new terms, however, may in fact create more problems than they solve, for the Church's liturgy as well as its New Testament background makes it clear that each of the three Persons is a different 'you' ('thou'). One can readily think of addressing a person as 'you,' but hardly of addressing a 'mode of being' or a 'distinct manner of subsisting' as 'you' or as anything else, for the terms do not seem to stand for any*one* and thus seem to foreclose dialogue. Yet the flurry that has generated these terms is perhaps the liveliest in Trinitarian theology for centuries, and it shows how modern concern with self or person interlock with and activate absolutely central teachings of Christianity. In his attention to the 'selving' in the Godhead, Hopkins was moving in a current that was not dying but that was destined to grow in force.

8 LATIN ACADEMIC THEOLOGY AND HOPKINS' VERNACULARISM

Hopkins' development of his sense of self relates intimately to the seemingly workaday Latin-vernacular issues that have surfaced in recent Roman Catholicism. Seminary theology and most related academic theology was still in Latin in Hopkins' day for the Latin

Rite in the Roman Catholic Church, that is, for around ninety-eight per cent of the Roman Catholic Church across the world. (The seventeen Roman Catholic rites other than the Latin, taken together, include only some two per cent of the Roman Catholics in the world.) Latin textbooks transmitted theological understanding to clergy generation after generation. The vernacular catechisms which provided the laity with their basic and often their only systematic theological instructions were in effect vernacular adaptations of the Latin manual materials.

Hopkins studied all his formal theology in Latin – that is dogmatic or systematic theology and moral theology – for ancillary courses such as canon law, Church history, or scripture might be in English (Thomas, *Hopkins* 97, 158). He had previously studied all his philosophy as a Jesuit in Latin as well. I also studied philosophy and theology in Latin in essentially the same way as Hopkins (Ong, *Fighting* 137–9), and in both was always orally examined in Latin throughout the entire philosophy and theology courses. I also have taught Latin, briefly, and have written some Latin poems, as other Jesuits in studies with me did, exhibition pieces, tours de force. My notes to my philosophy and theology courses I took in Latin – a fact that I have verified for my purposes here by consulting these still extant notes in my files. I do not know whether Hopkins' notes for his courses were in Latin or in English. I do know that the kind of traffic with one's own unconscious and consciousness that Hopkins commonly carries on in his poetry and in much of his prose could not then as it cannot now be carried on in Latin.

It might have been carried on in Cicero's day, when Latin was still a vernacular, if, *per impossibile*, the psyche had at that stage of history been interiorized enough to be on the verge of producing a Freud. But consciousness was too young in classical antiquity to render possible such articulate scrutiny of the psyche. Cicero's traffic with the unconscious and with his consciousness was real enough, but even in his letters, it is channelled over relatively communal, oratorical routes – which does not keep it from being in its own way expertly tooled and exquisitely sensitive. Cicero exploits the rhetorical *topoi* or *loci communes* as conspicuously in his personal letters as in his orations, perhaps even more conspicuously. All Cicero's writings betray in varying degrees the public, oratorical tone that marks elaborated discourse in oral or residually oral cultures generally.

Since Cicero's day, in addition to its inherited oratorical, relatively external communality, Latin had acquired a new kind of externality. It had severed the immediate ties with home and mother which it had enjoyed as a vernacular when, between the sixth and ninth century, it had finally become exclusively a public, tribal language, learned in extrafamilial school settings, a distancing medium by contrast with vernaculars or mother tongues. Over the centuries it had had millions of skilled speakers, but not a single one of them knew it as a first language and not a single one knew it as only a spoken language. Every one of its millions of users could write it. By comparison with oral speech, writing creates distances (Ong, *Orality* 101–8). Latin could be forceful and moving in Hopkins' milieu. It could hardly be fully intimate.

The overall effects of Latin-bound theology on Roman Catholic thought are absolutely massive and have yet to be assessed, though some of the effects are evident enough. Encasement in Latin kept the theology 'safe' largely by insulating it from other thought and notably from the deeper unconscious and subconscious currents that power all fresh thinking. Efforts to relate Catholic theology seriously in depth to the more lively currents of the ages, such as the efforts of Hermes, Drey, Günther, Rosmini, or Newman, were regularly in the vernacular and as regularly considered heterodox or, for example, in Newman's case, at least suspect – though they did have the result of luring writers of refutations, such as Kleutgen, into the vernacular, too.

The psychologizing and anthropologizing turns in Hopkins' Christological and Trinitarian theology were connected with the fact that, despite the Latin academic theological tradition, all his thinking was rooted deep in the vernacular. This is not to say that it was not influenced by Latin, on which vernacular English had been drawing for some two thousand years to gain much of its sophistication and depth. Hopkins himself knew Latin thoroughly and Greek as well, and he drew heavily on the central Latin theological tradition (for example on Scotus, whom he read in Latin of course) and to a lesser extent on the Greek patristic theologians. He taught both Latin and Greek and he wrote a few minor poems in Latin as well as a few in Greek (and a few in Welsh). But virtually everything else from his pen is in English, including his theological works. As his poems spectacularly show, English powered Hopkins' thought and his sense of being-in-the-world, not simply his expression, with an intensity realized in few other English-language writers. In his theology he did not – could not – merely transfer into English words what he learned from Latin manuals: he reprocessed the material into the vernacular fibre of the nineteenth-century psyche. The way in which the new self-consciousness of the century enters into Hopkins' theological reflections shows the process at peak.

In *An Essay on the Development of Christian Doctrine* and even more in *An Essay in Aid of a Grammar of Assent*, Newman also undertook to develop Catholic doctrine in vernacular ways which could relate it in depth to the psychological, anthropological, and historical concerns of the time. In *A Grammar of Assent* he worked out a circumstantial analysis of acts and states of the mind in an effort to show that the Lockean and scholastic stress on formal logical proofs as the actual grounds for valid assent was untrue to the realities of the human lifeworld. Newman's attentive introspection here would, to say the least, have been difficult to work out in Latin. It is too involved in the continuum of conscious, subconscious, and unconscious existence. But, despite his attention to the dense depths of human thought, neither in his prose nor in his verse does Newman ever achieve the intimacy that marks Hopkins, even in the latter's designedly theological prose: 'pitch' for personality, 'bare self,' 'freedom of play,' 'freedom of field' and so on. Newman's English is far less responsive than Hopkins' to the unconscious, for Newman, as his penchant for disputation and his somewhat lapidary grace shows, was still very much in the old rhetorical – that is, fundamentally public, oratorical – tradition.

In the 1852 edition of *The Idea of a University* (1927, rpt 1852) Newman had included a chapter about how to develop a Latin prose style, in the course of which he refers to a series of lectures delivered in Latin by a Latin scholar to 'a large, cultivated, and critical audience' in a nineteenth-century classical Latin style remarkable for its lucidity as well as its ornateness. Even though the actual incident may be fictional, for it is adduced by Newman in a fictional conversation about the acquiring of a good Latin style, it shows how, with some verisimilitude, perhaps mingled with wishful thinking, one could still in 1852 imagine original Latin expression as relating speaker and audience with an urgency comparable to that which the vernacular could create. The chapter evaporated from later editions, for Latin was on its way out as a medium of discourse.

One effect of Latin on Newman shows in his beautifully tailored English platform style. His *Apologia pro Vita Sua* is thoroughly honest, thoroughly real, and deeply moving account of its author's profound religious convictions and their effects on his life, but it is far more conspicuously public in stance than Hopkins' intimate prose, or even than Hopkins' prose generally, including his sermons (*S* 13–104). As the occasion for this beautifully earnest platform performance, providence had given Newman in Charles Kingsley what every orator secretly covets, a publicly identifiable, unwittingly vulnerable, and demonstrably unjust assailant. Newman responded with fitting rhetorical flair.

Though Hopkins knew Latin as well as Newman did, by comparison with Newman's English style Hopkins' English style had rather less to do with the Latin rhetorical tradition. Perhaps this was one reason why Hopkins failed as a preacher: congregations still generally expected something of the old-line, formally distanced orotundity. Hopkins' idiosyncratic musings disoriented his hearers somewhat, and his superiors even more (Devlin in *Hopkins*, S 4–12). But if his preaching suffered, Hopkins' deep resonance to the distinctively vernacular idiom, creatively attuned to the unconscious, gives his theological writings a human immediacy quite new among Roman Catholics, even when Newman is included in the comparison. Hopkins' theology lives where his poetry lives, in intimate contact with today's human lifeworld and the articulately self-conscious self. It does this because although it drew on vast Latinate sources, its roots were sunk directly and deeply into living vernacular English.

FOUR

Modernity: Faith beyond Scandal

1 NAMING, THE NAMELESS SELF, AND MODERNISM

HOPKINS' RESOLUTE CONFRONTATION OF THE SELF situates him in a consciousness-raising movement that had been in progress for thousands of years. Self-consciousness, in all its human existential intimacy, had registered all through history wherever a human being could say 'I,' but articulate attention to what is involved in saying 'I' developed only with glacial slowness. Discourse about a subject requires distance or 'objectivity' as well as proximity: the known has to be set off somehow from the knower. The unique intimacy of the 'I' makes any such distance difficult to achieve. For here the known is the knower: the two coincide.

Simple naming, with common nouns or with proper nouns or individuals' names, is the most archaic, and still the most basic operation for setting off the known intellectually from the knower, and thereby setting off known objects from one another. A two-year-old just learning to talk, working through a picture book with his mother, points, and shouts, with great satisfaction, 'Tree!' or 'Mary!' He puts the tree or the person 'out there' by naming it or her, advertising that what is named is not himself, nor mother, but something or someone quite different, distanced from him and from her as well, yet within his and her grasp. As two knowers speaking and hearing the same name, he and she can share both the distance and the grasp. It's great fun. A name is often referred to in slang as a 'handle,' a hold on something or someone. A handle both sets an object apart from me and assures its proximity and manoeuvrability.

Of course, as has been seen (ch 1, sect 9) names, and especially proper names of persons, can also become reservoirs of emotions that feed intimacy, although subordinately to the non-name, the pronoun 'you,' by comparison with which even proper names of persons are thing-like.

Even high-technology cultures still use names, of things and of processes, as the most basic operation for setting off the known from the knower: you cannot learn biochemistry or electronic engineering, for example, without mastery of a vast nomenclature. But high-technology cultures also have innumerable, supplementary distancing techniques in the abstract noetic structures set up by writing, print, and now the computer: these distancing technologies make possible and keep enlarging our gigantically elaborated and abstractly organized fields of learning. Before writing, noetic distance was hard to come by (Havelock, *Preface*) and simple naming was often the only resort for achieving it. Hence in oral cultures, or in writing cultures with high residual orality, human consciousness is hyperattentive to names and naming. This can be seen in the importance imputed in Adam's naming of the animals in Genesis 2:19–20, in the name-calling taunt songs and other fliting common in oral and residually oral cultures, in the strings of names such cultures like to put together in praise poems and litanies, and in such productions as the Neo-Platonic treatise on the divine names by the sixth-century Pseudo-Dionysius and the similar treatises that continue through the residually oral Middle Ages and Renaissance. In their attentiveness to names earlier peoples strike those from today's high-technology cultures as expecting names to deliver more than they possibly can. But high-technology peoples' common explanation that 'primitive' peoples, unlike more advanced peoples (such as ourselves), think that names give power over things is often simple-minded and patronizing. Names do give power over things by distancing things from the knower and from each other and thereby implementing knowledge.

The same earlier peoples who were fascinated with names experienced difficulty in developing elaborate discourse about the 'I,' even under the guise of 'the self,' precisely because 'I' is not a name, as has earlier been explained here at length. A book – and a title – such as Martin Buber's *I and Thou* (first German edition 1922) could be only a late development in the evolution of the consciousness. Buber's line of thought here was not entirely without antecedents yet was the first of its kind in the 'revolutionary simplicity' of its directly confrontational as well as poetic approach to the 'I' and to the corresponding 'you' or 'thou' which its title encapsulates (Smith, in Buber, *I and Thou* v–vii). This kind of confrontational attention to the 'I' emerges at a later, and transmuted, stage of the 'utilitarian individualism' whose early spokesman had been Thomas Hobbes. The rise of this individualism marked a shift of authority 'from the external world – God, nature, or society – to the interior of individuals,' displacing religion 'from its role as guardian of the public world-view' (Bellah, 17–19). By Buber's day – and earlier in Hopkins – privatization of the psyche had developed more human and more deeply personalized emphases than in Hobbes. In Hopkins and Buber, far from deemphasizing religious faith, this privatization of consciousness intensifies such faith and the personal relation of man to God. The new, deeply interiorized, personal individualism shows in the various forms of theistic existentialism and phenomenology with which Buber's thinking connects.

The privatization of the psyche, whether theistic or atheistic, is a distinctive element, though by no means the only element, in the late stage of consciousness or, better, of self-consciousness that we call modernism. Hopkins' constant and compelling confrontation of the self certifies him as belonging to this late stage, the modern world. Long before Buber, but riding the same general currents of consciousness that Buber was to ride, Hopkins, like Buber, explicitly and passionately situated everything – not only the deeper concerns of philosophy but also the life of faith – in the ambit of the 'I,' the utterly distinctive, unique self, now becoming manageable with an articulate directness and fullness never possible before. Not Aristotle's 'universals' or Samuel Johnson's 'generalities,' but 'all things counter, original, spare, strange' (*P* 37) called forth the best of Hopkins' psychic energies. And nothing was more 'counter, original, spare, strange' than each 'I,' each of the unique, induplicable, unclassifiable selves that made up humankind. 'Selving' centred human existence, and centred each human being's relationship to God.

Modernism as a movement in literature and art is not easy to define. Accounts of it, however, uniformly attend to its preoccupation with the self (Howe, 1967). Wendell Stacy Johnson (*Gerard Manley Hopkins* 171) notes that 'the great preoccupations of modern writers remain those defined by Romanticism. These are not so much questions of theology, ethics, or social reform as they are questions about the self.' This inward turning of consciousness, as earlier explained (chap 1), develops in counterbalance with the extreme outward turning implemented by the distancing or 'objectivizing' technologies of writing, print, and computers, so that it is clear that self-consciousness is not the only feature marking the modern sensibility. But it is a major feature. It has as concomitant and related phenomena the subjectivity or solipsism with which modern art and literature are often charged, the modern sense of alienation (the self feels itself in the extreme isolation of the nameless, pronominal 'I') the sense of loss (the world of names has spent its force, become secondary to the anonymous self), a certain rejection of history (the 'I,' as earlier noted, is historically free-floating, though it can and eventually does bring vast reaches of history into itself), the rejection of organized society (which relates named people in namable structures) in favour of community (which relates people personally, on an I-you basis). Attention to community, to communes, to all sorts of person-to-person sharing marked the late modernist 1960s and 1970s. Selves were to link with other selves, ideally in pure I-thou relationships. When names were used, intimate first names were preferred to more distancing family names. Even the modernist preference for the unconscious over consciousness relates directly to the confrontation of the self, for consciousness has a preference for the distancing effected by names. Close attention to the nameless self involves something deeper than consciousness alone.

Seen in these perspectives, certain other features of modernism become more understandable. Modernism set out to abolish the old classically grounded rhetoric partly because rhetoric was the seedbed of name-consciousness and of externalized societal relationships. Such rhetoric has been constantly, if often unjustly, charged with being only 'words, words, words.' In *Burnt Norton*, T.S. Eliot bemoans the way words persistently decay in their referential or naming function. Deconstructionists, such as Jacques Derrida, downgrade naming, by denying its implied referential values, even while practising it vigorously. Important modern writers have preoccupied themselves directly with namelessness in human life, as James Baldwin in *Nobody Knows My Name*, Samuel Beckett in *The Unnamable*, and Ralph Ellison in *Invisible Man*. Martin Buber had anticipated them all: he had called his seminal work simply, and more positively, but namelessly, *I and Thou* (*Ich und Du*, 1923). For Paul Ricoeur, as for Martin Heidegger, 'words, the only way toward self, prove unending detours' (Regan, 18) – except for the *pronomen*, the surrogate name, the almost non-word 'I' (and its correlative 'you' or 'thou') and their plurals ('we,' 'you').

The anonymity that modernism attends to here is not at all the same as the ineffability which implies the numinous, the *mysterium tremendum*, the holy (Hebrew *kadosh*, separated), the tabu, the distanced. The anonymity of the modern 'I' and the 'thou' (or 'you') is an anonymity of intimacy, even when, as in much of Buber's book, the 'Thou' whom the 'I' relates to is God. The modernist world quickly became a close-in, intimate world, with personal, intimate meanings conveyed by such creations as abstract expressionist paintings, which do not represent namable objects but imply that the nonrepresentational conveys some meaning that sensitive viewers can intimately share. The isolation enforced by the nonrepresentational is, moreover, somehow communally experienced. Sharing a nonrepresentational, abstract expressionist painting, savouring its ineffable significance, we all are enabled to be intimately alone together. The typically modern Imagist movement, in principle if not in fact an antirhetorical phenomenon, called for punctilious verbal precision but at the same time downgraded names in its dogma that clear, visual impressions evoked by a poem were to produce the effect to which the names and their referential functions were somehow peripheral (though essential). 'A poem should not mean / But be,' Archibald MacLeish proclaimed in his modern 'Ars Poetica.'

Hopkins was unmistakably a modern in his uncompromising confrontation of the nameless self. Relatively few of Hopkins' coevals, of whatever faith or of none, were yet as at home as he was in the new world of modern consciousness so intent on the self as self, the mysterious 'I' that underlies and eludes all naming. Few Catholic intellectuals were involved in this world at all creatively. The kind of domestic integralism and categorization fostered by nineteenth-century Catholic seminary theology in Kleutgen's and others' systematics had no way of dealing with, or indeed of imagining, the deep psychic changes that were taking place. The Copernician, Galilean, and Newtonian discrediting of Aristotelian cosmology and the consequent dissolution of medieval syntheses of theology with the natural world had left Roman Catholics and other Christians with an acosmic and thereby seriously weakened theology and philosophy (Wildiers, 211 and passim). Discomfort with the state of affairs led many orthodox Catholics and other Christians in Hopkins' Europe to retreat from the modern world to a purportedly more unified world typified by the European Middle Ages, wistfully understood as 'the Age of Faith' and still represented by the Roman Catholic Church, which had retained into Victorian times so many of the medieval trappings that Protestantism had discarded.

Fascination with the Middle Ages marked Hopkins' milieu. This fascination had continued strong in England since Romanticism, as Dante Gabriel Rossetti, Holman Hunt, John Everett Millais, and others of the Pre-Raphaelite Brotherhood devoted themselves programmatically to medieval religious themes and William Morris culminated his achievements in the graphic arts with his pseudo-medieval Kelmscott Press edition of Chaucer. Romantic medievalism at its worst could be crippling but at its best it resulted in tremendous literary and artistic creativity, for it put the psyche in touch with neglected archaic symbols and the fertility of the unconscious. It also had large-scale intellectual consequences: the scholarly attention drawn to the Middle Ages resulted eventually, in the twentieth century, in a newly sophisticated understanding of this complex and rich period in Western history – an understanding which often destroyed many oversimplifying myths that had made the period so attractive to the unconscious in the first place. Kleutgen's and others' vaunting of Thomism in Roman Catholic circles, it has already been noted, attracted to the works of St Thomas Aquinas scholars who soon became aware that Thomas was indeed vitally important, but not on the grounds that Kleutgen and others had projected.

Hopkins was not totally untouched by the medieval revival. He shared with many if not most Roman Catholics, especially converts, a yearning for a completely Catholic England suggesting that of medieval times. Yet, this completely Catholic England would be a modern England (P 28, st 35). Hopkins, like Newman, shows no tendency deliberately to retreat from the real, modern world he lived in by medievalizing his faith or anything else. He used medieval scholastic frames of reference in discussing philosophical questions such as the principle of individuation, but not programmatically or nostalgically: he was familiar with them from his philosophy and theology courses and found them useful analytic tools. His attraction to Scotus was not to the age or milieu but to the thought of the man, as his attraction to Plato was. His poem 'Duns Scotus' Oxford' (P 44) exploits the obvious continuity between medieval Oxford and the Oxford Hopkins knew, with many of its medieval buildings still standing, but it signals no adulatory medievalism, such as one might find later in the writings of Gilbert Keith Chesterton or Hilaire Belloc or in Ralph Adams Crams' architecture or in James J. Walsh's curious book, *The Thirteenth, Greatest of Centuries* (1907). Hopkins had no serious problems with the new scientific understanding of the cosmos. He did not undertake to provide theology with a comprehensive cosmology, as Pierre Teilhard de Chardin was later to undertake to do, but Leggio has called attention to Hopkins' not infrequent efforts to align current scientific thought and Catholic theology and has contrasted these efforts with Newman's 'elegant evasions.'

Hopkins felt no need to retreat to the past. He really showed no signs that intellectual or other developments of his time, including some forms of Darwinian evolution (Collins, 'Philosophical Themes'; Zaniello, 151–6), created any particular crises for his Roman Catholic faith. Zaniello (136) notes that in the 'Stonyhurst Group' only Hopkins could be called an amateur scientist. Hopkins had patriotic, even chauvinistic, problems with Gladstone, 'the Grand Old Mischiefmaker' (B 257) who 'negotiates his surrenders of the empire' (B 210), problems with English-Irish politics, problems with the dirt and squalor of cities, with ecological nonplanning that destroyed the countryside and nature ('even where we mean to mend her, we end her' – P 43), with the depressed industrial surroundings and the sufferings of his poor parishioners at Bedford Leigh, with the style of some contemporary (and earlier) writers, but seemingly no great trouble at all in keeping his faith afloat in the intellectual and cultural world of the nineteenth century. He did not find a neatly identifiable epicentre of evil in the Victorian world as Newman did somewhat in inveighing against 'liberalism.' Whatever anguish Hopkins experienced was not typically of the sort, either, that David Strauss' *Das Leben Jesu* (1835) had been causing for many. Hopkins was 'modern' in the deepest and most positive sense of the term: at home in the real world, and certainly in its attentiveness to the self as self.

2   SELF-CONFRONTATION: EUPHORIA AND ANGUISH

In his confrontation of the self as self Hopkins faced up in a major way to the tensions from which a sentimental medievalism retreated. A highly articulate self-consciousness was even more distinctively a part of nineteenth-century reality than scientific understanding was. Thinking of the self could give rise to Hopkins' greatest enthusiasm: 'new self and nobler me' (*P* 60), 'God, beauty's self and beauty's giver' (*P* 59), or 'The sweet alms' self is her' (*P* 60). At other times, it was associated with interior anguish: 'selfwrung, selfstrung, sheathe- and shelterless, | thóughts agaínst thoughts ín groans grínd' (*P* 61).

This interior anguish, tied up with an intense self-awareness, was greatest, though not unremitting, in his later, Dublin years (Robinson, 129–33). It appears in his letters, but the most moving evidence comes from his later poems (Mariani, *Commentary* 196), particularly the so-called 'dark' or 'terrible' sonnets of desolation which, with some other later poems, have to do most directly with the self, not simply as the object of close philosophical attention but rather as the real, reflexively obtrusive, insistent, inescapable person present in all Hopkins' conscious hours. 'I wake and feel the fell of dark, not day' (*P* 67). 'I am gall, I am heartburn' (*P* 67). 'I'll not, carrion comfort, Despair, not feast on thee' (*P* 64). 'I am all at once what Christ is ... / This Jack, joke, poor potsherd ... immortal diamond' (*P* 72).

The later poems which treat so much of the self are highly autobiographical, as are many others of Hopkins' poems, perhaps most of his mature poems. It has become a tiresome commonplace that poetry can never be pure autobiography, and indeed that in a certain sense no literature, and especially no poetry, can ever be purely autobiographical at all. In poetry, even of the most intimate sort, the poetic voice, the person speaking in the poem, is never quite the same as the extrapoetic voice of the real, living author who creates the persona of the poem. But neither are these two voices ever

unrelated. A fictional voice does not float into the world from
nowhere.

Relationships between the two voices are infinitely varied. The
fictional voice can be close to or distant in countless ways from the
real-life voice of the author, the voice he uses to purchase shoes or
to give someone directions how to get from one place to another. In
Hopkins they are relatively distinct, but very similar. The tones of
voice in the poems dealing with the self and the tones of voice in
many of Hopkins' conversational, personal letters often ring very
much the same (though even personal letters, of course, are texts,
not conversation). Poetic expression distances, especially if the
poetry is composed in writing, for, in Wordsworth's formulation,
such poetry 'takes its origin from emotion recollected in tranquility.' But what is distanced has often an identifiable place in
extrapoetic life. Hopkins is insistent about this in the case of 'The
Wreck of the Deutschland' and elsewhere. As Robinson has suggested (138–58), Hopkins' most anguished poems may well have
been written in part precisely to distance the experience out of
which each grew – we might even say to tranquillize it, in Words-
worthian fashion – and thereby to help Hopkins manage the experience better in its original extrapoetic context. The self in Hopkins'
poems and his self outside his poems interface.

3   THE ANGUISHED SELF IN POETRY, EARLY AND LATE

Poems about the anguished self are common in Western culture and
probably in all cultures in one form or another (see Johnson, *Gerard
Manley Hopkins* 23–4). Hopkins was working in a longstanding, but
evolving, tradition. In Hopkins' case, the chief ancient connections
of his anguished-self poems are biblical. At times Hopkins advertises
such connections. The untitled sonnet (*P* 74) that ends

> ... birds build – but not I build; no, but strain,
> Time's eunuch, and not breed one work that wakes.
> Mine, O thou lord of life, send my roots rain

has as its opening lines Hopkins' translation of the Vulgate Latin
text of Jeremiah 12:1, which Hopkins makes the epigraph to his
poem:

> Thou art indeed just, Lord, if I contend
> With thee; but, sir, so what I plead is just.
> Why do sinners' ways prosper?

Hopkins' idiom here is a bit out of line with most translations. In Hopkins' day English-speaking peoples were not – as today some still are not – used to having the Bible presented to them in language close to their own lifeworld: the convention was that everyone from Adam and Eve through Jesus' Apostles spoke only sixteenth-century and early seventeenth-century English, as in the King James version or in the Douay-Rheims version used by nineteenth-century English Roman Catholics:

> Thou indeed, O Lord, art just, if I plead with thee, but yet I will speak what is just to thee: Why doth the way of the wicked prosper?

Hopkins honours the convention minimally, retaining 'thou art' and 'thee,' but the 'sir' is new and, like Hopkins' 'contend' as compared with the Douay 'plead,' is more confrontational: the idiom has been desolemnized and the I-thou relationship foregrounded. Hopkins intensifies the I-thou relationship further with his own added query

> ... and why must
> Disappointment all I endeavour end?

Instead of an Elizabethan Jeremiad, we have here a renegotiated, more interiorized or personalized Victorian Jeremiad.

Biblical quotations and echoes in Hopkins' poetry are beyond counting, but a great many relating to the self can be identified by cruising through Mariani's *Commentary* (eg, 65, 69, 97, 156–7, 201, etc). Hopkins supplements biblical citations and echoes with para-biblical material, often from ascetical writings or the liturgy. Mariani (199–209) has called attention to the fact that 'Spelt from Sibyl's Leaves' (*P* 61) is an Ignatian meditation on the condition of souls in hell, duly fitted with a composition of place. In addition, one might note that the poem's dissolution of all colours into fateful black and white at nightfall echoes several of the hymns for Vespers in the *Breviarium Romanum*, from which, after ordination to the priesthood, Hopkins prayed daily. In these liturgical hymns we find 'black chaos falls' (*Illabitur tetrum chaos*, Sunday Vespers), the

Creator who keeps mingled things distinct from each other (*qui mixta ne confunderet*, Monday Vespers), 'The fiery sun disappears / ... Pour light into our hearts (*Jam sol recedat igneus* / ... *Infunde lumen cordibus*, Saturday Vespers). The resolution of all colours at nightfall is the resolution of all life into right and wrong that leaves all thoughts 'selfwrung, selfstrung, sheath- and shelterless' (*P* 61). Job 9:16–18 (being overwhelmed in a tempest) and 1 Kings 19:11 ('the Lord was not in the wind') echo in another Hopkins 'dark' sonnet – 'creep, / Wretch, under a comfort serves in a whirlwind' (*P* 65). Still another sonnet of anguish, 'Carrion Comfort' (*P* 64), calls to mind Jacob's wrestling with God in Genesis 32:22–3 as well as Ezechiel 20:33, 35 'I will reign over you with a strong hand ... and with fury' (Mariani, *Commentary* 228–30). And so on and on.

Between biblical times and Hopkins' own day lie countless other antecedents for Hopkins' anguished-self poems. Augustine's 'Our hearts are restless till they rest in you' had set the tone of many postbiblical religious treatments of the anguished self in the West, but there are innumerable other treatments independent of Augustine. Old English literature especially exploited the theme, from the solemn speech of Byrhtwold in *Maldon* (lines 312–19), 'My life has been long. Leave it I will not, / but beside my lord I will sink to earth, / I am minded to die by the man so dear,' through laments such as those in the 'Seafarer' and the 'Wanderer.' The courtly love tradition of the Middle Ages produced poems about the spurned and anguished selves of lovers in quantities earlier unheard of, and the Petrarchan tradition kept such lovers alive – though always barely so – well through the Renaissance (Regan). The devotional poetry of St John of the Cross treats of the anguished self, but more positively, for the poems commonly end with the union, not always painless, of the human lover and God.

Sixteenth-century and seventeenth-century English religious poetry develops more distinctively confrontational ways of treating the self that begin to suggest Hopkins' later stark self-confrontation. In 'Astrophil and Stella,' Sir Philip Sidney sensitively voices the Petrarchan sense of self with new plangency. But his conspicuous display of the self – as in 'I may, I must, I can, I will, I do' (Sonnet 47) or 'I, I, I may say that she is mine' (Sonnet 69) – remains a clearly public rhetorical exercise, openly conventional, though presented with great sensitivity in settings of often matchless wit. From Donne and Herbert on, English devotional lyric can avail itself of the new directness worked out in the dialogue of the Elizabethan stage, which was composed in intimate contact with vernacular colloquialism as well as with classical rhetoric. Herbert could declaim with histrionic urgency, as in 'The Collar':

> I will abroad.
> What? Shall I ever sigh and pine?
> My lines and life are free, free as the road.
> ...
> But as I raved and grew more fierce and wild
>   At every word,
> Me thought I heard one calling, Child!
>   And I replied, My Lord.

And Donne could call out to God even more abruptly:

> Batter my heart, three-personed God, for you
> As yet but knock, breathe, shine, and seek to mend;
> That I may rise and stand, o'erthrow me; and bend
> Your force to break, blow, burn, and make me new.

This face-to-face directness was not so articulable in earlier ages. It is more immediate than the most urgently voiced Psalms or than medieval introspective writing. But the self is not so exposed even in the seventeenth century as it would be in Hopkins' age. In the Elizabethan and Jacobean era, the pervasively oratorical, public cast of thought and expression, the heritage of the ubiquitous rhetorical tradition, still insulated the self somewhat from its own direct gaze, and even lyric poetry could not shed all the insulation. Donne's poem is personal and certainly deals with the self, but there is in Donne nothing quite like Hopkins' confrontational 'self ín self steepèd and páshed.' Nor is there in Herbert, who in his poetry typically holds his self at arm's length – 'so did I weave myself into the sense.' Barbara Leah Harman observes that Herbert's poems about the self and God are ultimately typological, so that 'representation of *individual* persons never takes shape' (196). Hopkins' self, including his body, is more urgent and obtrusive than this. Compared to Hopkins, Herbert sounds Platonic – which is not to say Hopkins is Aristotelian. Aristotle is far too genteel for Hopkins' sense of self. Nor is all this to say that earlier authors were not dealing with the self. They were, but not so confrontationally as Hopkins was to do.

The self fares much the same way in prose as in poetry. In her book *The Eloquent 'I': Style and Self in Seventeenth-Century Prose* the late Joan Webber has shown how the self made its characteristic appearance in prose in this crucial preromantic period. She states (4) that by 'seventeenth-century literary self-consciousness' she means 'the writer's crucial and unremitting awareness that he is the subject of his own prose, whether or not he is literally writing autobiography.' Donne, Bunyan, John Lilburne, Robert Burton, Richard Baxter, Sir Thomas Browne, John Milton, and Thomas Traherne, all of whom she reports on, 'contributed to the development of a self-conscious language, and of man's capacity for self-analysis and self-expression in life and in art' (255). She finds their works 'interesting to study for the sake of the personae, the world, and the expected audiences.' But in the development of self-consciousness at this time, she adds, 'no writer has either the desire or the terminology to represent himself as uniquely individual, but wishes only to find a significant meaning for his sense of self in terms of his own traditions' (255).

Writers at this stage of consciousness could articulate their self-awareness in new ways, but they still commonly worked in the old rhetorical framework of public address in which the speaker organizes his expression in the communally possessed topoi that publicly and conspicuously bind together society and thought. Montaigne designedly binds the self and his text (Marc Eli Blanchard, 157–78). The pastoral self is distanced (Blanchard, 167–80), or, in present terms, 'cool,' where Hopkins' self is 'hot,' insistent, assertive. The Christian sense of God's immanence, or of Christ's, the God-man's, immanence in the universe registers some sense of self, to which the immanence is manifest, but sixteenth-century and seventeenth-century poets who treat of this immanence – Southwell, Donne, Herbert, Vaughan, Traherne, and Edward Taylor – discussed by Ira Clark in *Christ Revealed*, also work more in the rhetorical tradition and with less self-confrontational urgency than Hopkins in the 'Deutschland' (P 28) or 'The Windhover' (P 36) or elsewhere.

By the eighteenth century, although the old public rhetorical framework still supported much in the writer's psyche – as can be seen in Gibbon's historiography, for example, or in Samuel

Johnson's declamatory pronouncements as reported by Boswell and even in Johnson's written compositions, such as his famous *Dictionary* letter to Chesterfield – nevertheless poetry such as Cowper's or Blake's, as well as the developing novel, shows that the age was disengaging or isolating the self from society more than ever before, thereby making the self in Western culture a kind of 'stranger within,' in the words of Edward Young, (Cox, 3, 159; cf Jean A. Perkins). On many fronts the 'search' for the 'true self' was on (Lyons) and with it the cultivation of 'sensibility.' Jean-Jacques Rousseau's view of the 'inner self' as constitutive of human nature marked the beginning of the modern sense of self-possession (Hartle 155–7).

In one way, Hopkins connects with the eighteenth-century self-isolation enterprise. Despite Hopkins' classical learning, and his often conscious use of classical rhetorical forms, the self in his poetry (and prose) emerges free of the older, classically grounded, rhetorical, communal encasements, disengaged, decidedly bare. But in another way Hopkins diverges from the eighteenth-century tradition in that he is not searching for a 'true self' nor indeed searching for any self at all. As has been seen, the self Hopkins deals with does not have to be found: it is simply there, whether he likes it or not – the 'I' that he knows, that is with him the moment he awakes, that he cannot avoid or escape, transcending and trivializing any definition, corresponding to, though totally different from, the utterly distinctive 'I' that each other human person knows. Hopkins allows the 'I' to speak in its starkness as earlier poets never quite had. 'The lost are like this, and their scourge to be / As I am mine, their sweating selves' (*P* 67). 'I cast for comfort I can no more get / ... than blind / Eyes in their darkness' (*P* 69). 'I am all at once what Christ is / ... immortal diamond' (*P* 72). The self addresses itself point-blank:

> My own heart let me more have pity on; let
> Me live to my sad self hereafter kind,
> Charitable ...
>
> (*P* 69)

This is not the declamation more or less evident in earlier self-talk, but confrontational self-address. The idiom is not oratorical in the sense in which Hamlet's highly introspective soliloquy is patently oratorical at the very same time that it is highly personal:

To be or not to be; that is the question.
Whether 'tis nobler in the mind to suffer
The slings and arrows of outrageous fortune,
Or to take arms against a sea of troubles,
And by opposing end them. To die; to sleep;
No more ... (III.i.56–61)

The Shakespeare passage haunts us, it conveys an interior anguish of
the self, but it is nonetheless an academic exercise on a set theme –
the respective advantages of bodily existence and its cessation – exactly the kind of exercise, rooted in declamatory rhetoric, that
Shakespeare often had to do in school. This does not mean that the
passage is not genuine. But, the pros and cons of Shakespeare's
showpiece do not have the deeply self-confrontational tone of
Hopkins'

O the mind, mind has mountains; cliffs of fall
Frightful, sheer, no-man-fathomed ... (P 65)

or his

Soul, self; come, poor Jackself, I do advise
You, jaded, let be; call off thoughts awhile
Elsewhere; leave comfort root-room ... (P 69)

This is direct, point-blank self-address.

It is address dramatically heightened, of course, wrought to a
pitch of expression hardly credible in any extraliterary address to
oneself or to any conceivable nonliterary audience. For Hopkins'
work is truly literary, addressed to readers, taking the forms and
shapes generated by habits of composing in writing for circulation in
print. Though Hopkins liked to insist that his poems be read 'in
loud, leisurely, poetical (not rhetorical) recitation' (B 246, cf 51–2),
they are not oral compositions but texts to be retrojected into the
oral world.

In fact, literariness, textuality, is one of the factors making for
Hopkins' extreme self-consciousness: writing and reading are both
lonely activities, especially as they became maximally interiorized
from the Romantic Age on (Ong, *Rhetoric*). They encrust the self in
privacy. Look at a writer at work – if you can find his or her hide-

out. Glance around a library reading room and sense the private
worlds into which the readers (who may also be writing as they
read) have individually withdrawn themselves. Yet this privacy sets
up a special intimacy of discourse not only with oneself but also
with others. The reader of a book can often feel more intimate with
the absent – or, often enough, dead – author than with a speaker
who is alive and personally present. This is especially so after print,
when silent reading gradually established itself as normative and
small-sized books became common. Typically, handwritten books,
whether scrolls or codices, were relatively large, hard to curl up
with in cozy intimacy. They often invited declamation and were
commonly read aloud, even when the reader was alone. Printed
books are more private, often easy to carry in one's pocket, and
print eventually made the silent reader the norm. Hopkins' plea for
audible vocalization would have been superfluous in earlier ages.

The deeper and deeper penetration of textuality into the psyche,
especially printed textuality, has been a major factor in producing
the modern solitary self who is also the avid interpersonal commu-
nicator. This increasing penetration figures in the evolution of self-
representation from Wordsworth (Romantic) to Roland Barthes
(modern) which Paul Jay so well traces in *Being in the Text*,
although Jay seems not to allude to textual penetration of the
psyche as such. Reading became less and less a social activity
through the period he treats. Well through the eighteenth century
even reading alone was often done aloud, though less often than in
earlier ages (Ong, *Presence* 58–65, *Orality* 119–20), and well through
the nineteenth century individuals regularly read to others and even
to large public groups. Dickens wore himself out reading from his
novels and other stories to paying audiences. In modern times, reading is typically a totally isolated activity (if we do not count radio
and teleprompters, where the fact that reading is going on is assidu-
ously concealed – textuality is in effect denied). The text has been
driven more deeply inward. Isolation in quiet with another consciousness creates such intimacy as to bring Mariann Sanders Regan to
venture flatly, 'I would suggest that the literary text can be an
equivalent self' (19). The absence of the author's person fuses him
or her with the reader's own consciousness. But since the other
consciousness (that of the author) is accessible to a limitless number
of readers, each in his or her own personal isolation, the ultimate result is a system of intersecting privacies, an intense communality of

idiosyncratic awarenesses. Such communalized isolation characterizes the lonely-cum-socially-sensitive modern and postmodern
world, with its publicly secret meanings found in Dada, expression-
ism, existentialism, and virtually all subsequent modernisms. No
wonder that the modern poets coopted Hopkins as soon as Bridges
got his *Poems* into print in 1918.

4   THE SELF-CONFRONTING SELF AND GOD

In *The Disappearance of God* (343) Hillis Miller finds that for
Hopkins a person's selfhood 'is not naturally Christ-like. It is diabolically idiosyncratic. The self has no likeness to any natural being.
All things rebuff it with blank unlikeness.' Idiosyncratic, yes, but, it
would seem, in Hopkins' Christian view hardly diabolically idiosyncratic. For utter difference from every other 'I,' with full reflective
awareness of this difference, necessarily marks every human self, as
has earlier been seen, and in the creation of the world, God's chief
focus is on the creation of such unique, 'idiosyncratic' selves, as
Hopkins is clearly convinced. Thinking of creation in terms of this
inside world of isolated, idiosyncratic selves rather than simply of
the outside world of things makes the concept of creation itself
more spiritually edifying, so that, as Hopkins has it, the idea of
creation thereby 'takes on the mind more hold' (S 122). Moreover,
only such 'idiosyncratic' interiors as each of us are can form true
communities, that open our isolation to sharing love.
    The world within the self, or, better, the 'I' or 'me' – in Hopkins'
words 'my selfbeing, my consciousness and feeling of myself, that
taste of myself, of *I* and *me* above and in all things' (S 122–3) – is
holy in its very idiosyncratic isolation. The human self implies a
creator God who is, in Hopkins' explicit words, precisely a 'selfmaking power' (S 125). Hopkins (S 128; cf 285, n 4) quotes Augustine's
observation that God is 'interior to my innermost being' (*interior in-
timo meo*), the innermost being that knows it has no duplicate. A
human being in all his or her personal, idiosyncratic differentiation,
indeed especially in this idiosyncratic differentiation, somehow
resembles God in his 'selfexistence' (S 128) who is One and unique
in nature and yet is known to the Christian through faith as also differentiated or (idiosyncratically) 'selved' into Three Persons (S 197)
('The Utterer, Uttered, Uttering' – P 145). No one of these 'selvings'
is either of the others, as the so-called Athanasian creed makes re-

soundingly clear, though all three are the One True God with the same one nature, one intellect, and one will.

Miller is certainly deeply sensitive to the human interior. 'No words can describe directly what goes on in the ineffable regions of the soul's solitude,' he goes on perceptively to observe, pointing out how Hopkins resorts to one metaphor after another in speaking of the secret solitude of the self because none works adequately. But it is precisely in 'the ineffable regions of the soul's solitude' that God is chiefly present to Hopkins, as Hopkins knows God in faith. God's presence to the human self is more interior and secret than the human self's own interiority and secretness to itself. And more idiosyncratic – for God made this very idiosyncratic interiority and secretness, that is, the 'I.' According to Hopkins, this is the greatest and principal thing that God made, the centre of each human being and the ultimate focus of exterior creation, of the physical cosmos. An Indian Jesuit ascetical theologian, Anthony De Mello, writing out of an intimate acquaintanceship both with Ignatius' *Spiritual Exercises* and with Eastern religious sensibility, puts it this way (49): 'For you there is no reality that is closer to God than yourself. You will experience nothing closer to God than yourself. St. Augustine would therefore rightly insist that we must restore man to himself so that he can make of himself a stepping stone to God.'

Ignatius clearly makes the axis of human existence and of God's entire physical creation the relationship between the interior selves of individual human beings and God – which, of course, entails relationship to other interior human selves, for the second great commandment, 'love your neighbour as yourself,' is 'like' the first commandment to love God above all else (Matt 22:36–8). Everything in Ignatius' universe God made subservient to the union of human beings with God (*Spiritual Exercises* 23). The end even of exterior creation is in the last analysis the personal, interior, union of unique, idiosyncratic selves and God. All exteriority, though utterly real in itself, ultimately faces inward through the human psyche.

Hopkins expressly thought of his poetry in this framework of self-in-relation-to-God, as he thought of everything else in this framework. As it values other created things, he writes Dixon (D 93), 'our Society values ... literature ... as a means to an end,' the end being interior union of the human person with God. Poetry was not salvific in itself at all but, like other human creations, it was truly worthwhile and could serve salvific ends because and in so far as, under the given circumstances, it related one's own self and other selves to God, in any number of possible ways (*D* 93–6), many of them elusive to description. This is not to say that Hopkins always judged correctly, or could always feel sure that he judged correctly (*D* 93) the ways his poetry did or did not fit into this framework. Like all of us, he anguished over such decisions. From our point of vantage it appears that Hopkins at times judged his poetry too negatively on this point. The poetry has contributed not only to poetic enjoyment but also to the faith of thousands of readers far more than Hopkins at times seemed to have allowed for even as a possibility.

Hopkins' most exuberant poems, such as 'Pied Beauty' or 'Hurrahing in Harvest' or 'Henry Purcell' or 'As kingfishers catch fire,' often have to do with the delights of inscape and instress and the joys of selfhood. But the self has a sombre side, too, as in 'The Wreck of the Deutschland' (in part, for the self has also a joyous side here) or in 'Spelt from Sibyl's Leaves' or in the 'dark' or 'terrible' sonnets (*P* 65–9). Sombreness attends the self most when the self is in isolation. Hopkins' poem that most isolates the self would appear to be the untitled sonnet beginning 'I wake and feel the fell of dark, not day' (*P* 67):

I wake and feel the fell of dark, not day.
What hours, O what black hoürs we have spent
This night! what sights you, heart, saw; ways you went!
And more must, in yet longer light's delay.

With witness I speak this. But where I say
Hours I mean years, mean life. And my lament
Is cries countless, like dead letters sent
To dearest him that lives alas! away.

I am gall, I am heartburn. God's most deep decree
Bitter would have me taste; my taste was me;
Bones built in me, flesh filled, blood brimmed the curse.

Selfyeast of spirit a dull dough sours. I see
The lost are like this, and their scourge to be
As I am mine, their sweating selves; but worse.

Why does Hopkins here feel the isolated self so loathsome? Elsewhere (*S* 125) he explicitly associates shame, guilt, and his fate with self-isolation. One answer particularly applicable to Hopkins' case seems to be that, when unable to fix on other things besides itself, other sensory objects, imaginations, thoughts, the self is regularly somehow quite intolerable to itself. Eric Neumann (115) has discussed how ego consciousness, growing in each individual (and phylogenetically, over the centuries, in the entire human species), 'brings a sense of loneliness ... [and] introduces suffering, toil, trouble, evil, sickness, and death ... as soon as these are perceived by an ego.' At this point the person, the 'I,' finds the 'other,' the 'you' to be a crucial need. Mijuskovic (6) has suggested that human thought and action is all found in 'a desire to avoid the feeling of existential human isolation.'

The drive to overcome isolation appears to be one reason why solitary confinement turns out to be maximal severe punishment, and why survival tactics in solitary confinement include setting up and solving problems, reciting lists – anything to spin attention off the isolated self. The speaker in Hopkins' poem here has been unable to manage any such diversionary tactics: in uttering the poem, the self has not been able to imagine even a separate interlocutor. The 'you, heart' that the self addresses is here only another version of 'I' or 'me,' and the earlier 'we' has the same reference. It is strictly a factitious plural, not really two persons at all.

Night is normally a time of reduced sensory input, of sensory deprivation, leaving the self more or less to itself, isolated, or to sleep. The sonnet opens after a horrible night of psychologically as well as physically 'black hoürs' (Hopkins' diacritical mark indicates that the diphthong in this word is to be more than normally split in reading and the word thus dragged out: *ow—ers*). Night is yielding to day, but the poet feels even day as only prolonging night's sensory deprivation and isolation. Day itself is still covered with the 'fell' or pelt of night. The speaker is still deprived of everything but the feel of self. Well, not quite everything, as his metaphors show – if sensory deprivation were complete in sleep, no one could be shaken awake – but he is in effect deprived of virtually everything. The metaphors all lead back to the self.

However, while it is true that the 'I' in this poem has no interlocutor other than itself, it is not true that there is no other person referred to in the poem. The poet brings in one other, numerically a second person though introduced grammatically in the third person: God, as known by Hopkins' Christian faith, a providential God, car-

ing personally for each isolated self in the most agonizing suffering
as much as in time of greatest joy. Almost a decade and a half before
this and other sonnets of desolation, in 'The Wreck of the
Deutschland' (*P* 28) Hopkins had already declared God 'lighting and
love ... a winter and warm; / Father and fondler of heart thou hast
wrung,' the God who 'Hast thy dark descending and most art merci-
ful then.' God's providence within sickness as in health had been
proclaimed to Hopkins over and over and over since he entered the
Jesuit novitiate in 1868. Suffering is not good in itself, but accepted
in union with another, Jesus Christ, it has positive, redemptive
value. Every month in the various Jesuit communities where
Hopkins lived from the novitiate on, he heard or read, as prescribed
(27 – no 53), the *Summary of the Constitutions of the Society of
Jesus*, which includes the statement (27 – no 50) that illness is 'a
gift from the hand of our Creator and Lord' and indeed 'a gift no less
than is health.' This means all sickness, without any exception, including the deepest psychological suffering.

The statement is an ascetical commonplace. Indeed, intense suffering, primarily internal rather than external, normally or, more
likely, always, accompanies growth in the life of faith. Any suffering, accepted with love, has positive value; this conviction marks
Christian belief from its beginnings, through Hopkins and Teilhard
de Chardin (Ward). The various 'dark nights' which the soul can go
through are much worse not only in reality but also in ascetical
literature than they appear in T.S. Eliot's genteel assessment of St
John of the Cross in *Burnt Norton*. Absolutely everything but God
must go – friends, family, intellectual and other interests, political
loyalties, enjoyment of food, games, everything – to be known again
in God. Hopkins knew this from the Bible and the Church's common teaching, reinforced strongly by the *Spiritual Exercises* with
their stress on 'indifference,' detachment from everything but God
and his love for us. 'Nothing is God but God' is in fact the bearing
of the first of the Beatitudes, central to Jesus' message: 'Blessed are
the poor in spirit, for theirs is the Kingdom of Heaven' (Matthew
5:3). The 'poor in spirit' here are not, as is sometimes comfortably
thought, those who carry their wealth gracefully, with winsome in-
souciance, without gross attachment to it or esteem of it. 'Poor in
spirit' refers to no such self-consciously gracious, privileged persons.
Echoing Isaiah 61:1, it renders quite certainly Jesus' Aramaic term
anawim, which means the deprived, those destitute economically

materially, spiritually, psychologically, emotionally, those drained so that they have nothing and no one in all creation to rely on, only God (McKenzie, 'The Gospel according to Matthew,' in Brown et al, *Jerome Biblical Commentary*, vol 2, p 70). Luke's version of the first of the Beatitudes (6:20) is more direct: 'Blessed are you poor; the reign of God is yours.' Blessed are those with absolutely no resources of their own, unable to assert themselves, totally poor, with only God as support. Theirs is the kingdom of heaven. The utterly naked self knows God's love as the highly accoutred self hardly can. In so far as we are aware of ourselves standing destitute before God, we are close to him, and he is close to us. This is hard, it is frightening, it is tough, and it is at the heart of Christian faith. It is also a declaration of total love. It is the cross on which Jesus died, stripped naked.

From early New Testament times Christians have been made aware that no loss of whatever sort can be any indication of loss of God or of a lack of love on God's part for me. This utterly extremist position has been an explicit part of Christian faith from the start. 'Who will separate us from the love of Christ?' Paul asks in Romans 8:35, meaning, as the preceding verses make clear, not his love for Christ but the love which Christ has for him, Paul. 'Trial, or distress, or persecution, or hunger, or nakedness, or danger, or the sword?'' None of these or anything else that had already happened or could happen to him will convince Paul that Christ does not love him. 'I am certain,' Paul goes on, 'that neither death nor life, neither angels nor principalities, neither the present nor the future, nor powers, neither height nor depth nor any other creature, will be able to separate us from the love of God that comes to us in Christ Jesus, our Lord' (Romans 8:38–9).

Hopkins was fully aware of this text. God comes in 'lightning and lashed rod' as well as in 'lovely asunder / Starlight' (*P* 28). Like Paul ('nor any other creature'), Hopkins sets no limits to the sufferings that may come one's way. One of his sonnets of desolation (*P* 65) begins, 'No worst, there is none.' His term is not 'worse,' but 'worst.' Suffering has no limit. There is no 'worst.' You can never cheer yourself by thinking you have survived the maximum. It can always get still worse: 'No worst, there is none. Pitched past pitch of grief / More pangs will, schooled at forepangs, wilder wring.' Any present suffering can make the next onset of greater suffering even greater still, and not just additively but geometrically – the later suffering will be 'schooled' by the earlier. Each wound intensifies sensitivity to the next wound. But, even so, one can live it through. Christian faith, clung to with hope and love, is always threatened, yet always beyond scandal. The sonnet ends, 'Here! creep / Wretch, under a comfort serves in a whirlwind: all / Life death does end and each day dies with sleep.' As earlier noted, the lines echo, 'The Lord answered Job out of a whirlwind' (Job 38:1). In utter extremity, at times all one can do is wait with the sufferings. And waiting of course means, ultimately, waiting for death. 'Patience, hard thing!' (P 68) is still a fully positive and strong psychic and Christian response. Patience is one of the fruits of the Holy Spirit (Galatians 5:22), the more positive and strong here in Hopkins' poem because the psychic resources here available to it are so minimal. The sonnet of Hopkins' on patience occurs in the same manuscript as his desolate 'I wake and feel the fell of dark, not day' (P 67), to which it serves as a kind of antiphonal response.

Suffering attendant upon total isolation of the self was known to much earlier ascetical writers, as has been seen. *The Cloud of Unknowing*, previously cited in chapter 1, treats of the 'naked knowledge and feeling of your own being' (ed Johnston, 103-4), indicating that suicidal urges brought on by psychic isolation should never be yielded to. 'Never / does he [the devout Christian] desire not-to-be, for this is the devil's madness and blasphemy against God.' Nevertheless, Hopkins' experience differed from antecedent experiences of others in the sense that he could articulate agonies of the self more circumstantially and urgently than had been possible in earlier ages. Articulation of a situation, even metaphorically, makes the situation in a way more real – though at the same time, as earlier suggested, it can also in another way distance the speaker from the situation and make it more bearable, and, paradoxically, more sharable. Articulation socializes the situation by uttering it, that is, etymologically, by 'outering' it, putting it into words that others can understand. Hopkins' newly intense isolation was not so unique that his contemporaries and subsequent generations could not realize it empathetically, as we are undertaking to do here.

Hopkins never expresses the belief that compensatory or balancing mechanisms or manoeuvres would make his, or anyone else's, suffering less real or less painful. They may make it endurable. Nothing in the Gospels suggests that thoughts of the Resurrection reduced the agonies of Jesus' crucifixion. Hopkins' understanding of the cross was not docetic, as though Jesus had been just playing a game, had been not really a man but, rather, simply God playing a charade. Hopkins' view of death had no such pietistic overcoating. It was forthright, all the way through his mature poetry, as in 'That Nature Is a Heraclitean Fire' (*P* 72), where Hopkins faces unflinchingly the removal effected by death:

> Manshape, that shone
> Sheer off, disseveral, a star, | death blots black out; nor mark
> Is any of him at all so stark
> But vastness blurs and time | beats level.

His view of the crucifixion was equally forthright. The truth was that what Jesus was working for, what he had planned, turned out a total and spectacular failure. It still appears a failure and always will to those without belief and hope in the Resurrection. This state of affairs is no scandal to Christian faith, but an expected situation. Hopkins comments directly on the failure of Jesus' plans in a letter to Dixon (*D* 137–8):

His career was cut short and, whereas he would have wished to succeed by success – for it is insane to lay yourself out for failure, prudence is the first of the cardinal virtues, and he was the most prudent of men – nevertheless he was doomed to succeed by failure; his plans were baffled, his hopes dashed, and his work was done by being broken off undone. However much he understood all this he found it an intolerable grief to submit to it. He left the example: it is very strengthening, but except in that sense it is not consoling.

In Christian teaching, God the Father had let Jesus' 'career' work out as a failure not to cancel out the failure later but because he had plans about the consequences of the failure. The failure was never cancelled out and never will be. Jesus redeemed us not by his own human plans, which fell crashing around him, but 'by ... obedience' (Romans 5:19), freely aligning his reluctant human will with the divine. 'He learned obedience by the things which he suffered' (Hebrews 5:8). He became 'obedient unto death, even to the death of the cross' (Philippians 2:8). Jesus' self was devastated: 'My soul is sorrowful even unto death' (Matthew 26:38). 'My Father, if it be possible, let this chalice pass from me' (Matthew 26:39). 'My God, my God, why hast thou forsaken me?' (Matthew 27:46 – a quotation of the opening lines of the messianic Psalm 22). In the teachings of the faith that Hopkins lived, though Jesus was not only a human being but also God, he went through the same torment that any other human person would have gone through: he was 'one who was tempted in every way that we are, yet never sinned' (Hebrews 4:15).

A modern Protestant theologian, Jürgen Moltmann, points out (19–20) that for the believer, as for the nonbeliever, 'death is real death and decay is putrefying decay. Guilt remains and suffering remains. ... Faith does not overstep these realities into a heavenly utopia. ... It can overstep the bounds of life ... only at the point where they have in actual fact been broken through. It is only in following Christ who was raised from suffering, from a god-forsaken death and from the grave, that it gains an open prospect in which there is nothing more to oppress us. ... There faith can and must expand into hope.' The Catholic theologian Walter Kasper (121) makes a similar point.

This is Hopkins' position and the rockbottom position of his Church. Hopkins' Catholic faith made a lot of the cross, iconographically as well as metaphorically, and indeed would appear to many or most Protestants to be unhealthily addicted to crucifixes. When at the end of his two-year novitiate a Jesuit pronounces his vows of perpetual poverty, celibate chastity, and obedience in the Society of Jesus, he commonly receives as a memento the 'vow crucifix' which each Jesuit retains all his life as a reminder of his offering of himself to God. Because of fears of the Penal Clause in the Emancipation Act (1829) forbidding the presence of Jesuits in England, novices in Hopkins' time took their vows without any such presentation or special ceremony (Thomas, *Hopkins* 86), and Hopkins received his crucifix from his master of novices, Father Peter Gallwey, two days later. One focus of Hopkins' asceticism was the interior suffering self of the crucified Jesus Christ. There is no reason to believe that this suffering of Jesus was any less intense than the suffering portrayed in Hopkins' sonnets or that Hopkins thought it was any less intense.

Some earlier Hopkins critics, unfamiliar with Catholic asceticism, had thought that Hopkins' attention to the depth of suffering revealed in his 'dark' sonnets, or even any mention of such suffering, much have indicated a wavering faith. Quite the contrary: it signalled unwavering faith. As Miller perceptively points out, the problem in considering these sonnets is not whether Hopkins wavered or not. 'Let there be no misunderstanding, Hopkins wavers neither in his faith nor in his vocation. His experience is not incompatible with Catholicism' (*Disappearance* 352). The problem is whether Hopkins' experience of the isolated self as registered in this poem and other poems means that in some special new sense God has 'disappeared' for him, as Miller explains God had for many Victorians, whether Hopkins ends in a place similar to that of other Victorians, believing in God but 'unable to reach him' (*Disappearance* 359) so that God for Hopkins is only 'transcendent, not immanent' (358). Behind these problems and responses lies the question as to whether Hopkins in plunging so point-blank into the self had somehow found God out of reach.

Everything Hopkins says and everything in his ascetical background suggests that Hopkins' point-blank thrust into the suffering self, far from being a threat to Christian faith that somehow made God 'disappear,' in fact provided an opportunity to know more deeply what the faith entailed and to embrace the faith's full consequences with a degree of explicit awareness unattainable before. 'God's most deep decree / Bitter would have me tase; my taste was me' (*P* 67). Self-confrontation is part of God's plan. The mystery of the cross, of the suffering interior self of Christ, as appropriated in faith, does not admit of total articulation, but it can admit of fuller and fuller conscious appropriation as consciousness evolves to become more and more articulately self-conscious. The fuller articulation of the self entails suffering as inevitably as it entails joy.

Commenting on another of the sonnets of desolation, the one known by its editorially supplied title 'Carrion Comfort' (*P* 64), Mariani (*Commentary* 230) notes that Hopkins' position in the face of desolation and death is less passive than that of Newman's Gerontius in *The Dream of Gerontius*, 'in which the soul dissolves with a whimper before the oncoming flood of darkness.' Hopkins' poem protests, 'I'll not ... / Cry *I can no more*. I can; / Can something, hope, wish day come, not choose not to be.' 'The responsibility to "not choose not to be," ' Mariani explicates, 'cannot be surrendered; death is the surrender of the body only, not of the self.' The toughness of Hopkins' ego structures, commented on by Mariani ('Hopkins'); as noted in chapter 1, as well as the firmness of Hopkins' faith, shows here. Hopkins' stance suggests, though it is not by any means the same as, Dylan Thomas' 'Do Not

Go Gentle into That Good Night' 'Rage, rage against the dying of the light.'

Hopkins' sonnets of desolation all bear more than a little resemblance to his earlier 'God's Grandeur' (P 31), an exultant poem which nevertheless includes the forthright facing of utter discouragement:

> And though the last lights off the black West went
>   Oh, morning, at the brown brink eastward, springs –
> Because the Holy Ghost over the bent
>   World broods with warm breast and with ah! bright wings.

The sonnets of desolation in fact all end, every one of them, with an upbeat such as this, the more remarkable when faint, for it is even then absolutely irrepressible. 'Birds build – but not I build; no, but strain, / Time's eunuch, and not breed one work that wakes' (P 74). And then, with pained but confident hope, 'Mine, O thou lord of life, send my roots rain.' Even 'I wake and feel the fell of dark, not day' (P 67) ends on an upbeat: the suffering of the damned is like that reported in the poem – 'but worse.' The poet is not really at the bottom of the pits, after all. When Hopkins felt most isolated, most abandoned, most arid, he kept himself always open to any 'released shower, let flash to the shire' (P 28). This is not to say that the abandonment and aridity were enjoyable, but that they were under-laid with hope and love.

Although he lived as everyone does, with some unresolved ten-sions, and lived also with what he regarded as imperfections in his life of Catholic faith, Hopkins' person and his activities constituted an unusually integrated whole. By activities here I mean all that he did, pastoral, academic, literary (in poetry and in prose), ascetic (his own life of Christian faith lived out finally as a member of the Society of Jesus and a priest), recreational, or whatever else. Writing of Hopkins' poetry principally, Robinson (p x) has to include a view of the man's whole life: 'So completely was Hopkins involved in his purposes that he gives the appearance of leaving himself no still center from which he might protect himself against the vicissitudes of experience.' Hopkins' joy and his anguish were part of a con-tinuum, the continuum of his own person, his own self. This self was unique, as every self is. Though the ingredients for Hopkins' kind of achievement were central to the evolution of consciousness in the West and were present in the environment of many, only Hopkins put them together the way he did.

5 HOPKINS' OWN INSCAPE

Hopkins' relationships to the past and to his own Victorian age are rich and manifold. They are nowhere deeper than in the two developments surveyed in the present work: his exquisite sensitivity to differentiation or particularity in the external world – to 'all things counter, original, spare, strange' (P 37) – and his equally exquisite sensitivity to the differentiation or particularity that constitutes the internal world, to the deeply interiorized, individual, isolated, yet communally oriented self. Both these interests certify him as Victorian, and, as he cultivates them, they also certify him as belonging to the post-Victorian twentieth-century, which coopted him as its own as soon as his poems became known after their publication in 1918.

Hopkins' articulate self-consciousness, outstanding in an unprecedentedly self-conscious age, followed the direct line of development in the West leading to the more and more interiorized consciousness and more and more articulate self that are part of the modern world and of 'modernism' in all its forms. This development has been commonly interpreted hitherto largely as a secular development, as it certainly in great part was. However, as Hopkins' case makes clear, much in Catholic ascetical tradition as well as in academic philosophy and theology, moral and systematic or dogmatic, fostered interiorization of consciousness and ultimately greater and greater articulation of the self. The history of the key term 'person' shows that from the fourth-century and fifth-century Hellenic world on, Christian theology was the principal locus in which questions concerning person were raised and faced. The secular concern with 'person,' a concept unavailable in ancient Hebrew or ancient Greek, grew in great part out of and alongside the heated Trinitarian and Christological disputes of the early Christian centuries and has marked the consciousness of the West ever since.

Even among the decidedly self-conscious Victorians, Hopkins stands out in his preoccupation with the self as a subject of discourse – not only his own self, but the selves of others – and his correlative preoccupation with free decision, the free act of the will, which he identifies as 'the selfless self of self' (P 157). In his case the widespread Victorian preoccupation with these correlative themes of self and freedom was reinforced by Hopkins' Catholic faith and by his theological and ascetical training. This is not to say that all his confrontations of the self were joyful or could be expected to be. In the Catholic faith tradition, the person or self or 'I,' who comes to be more and more directly attended to over the centuries leading into the nineteenth, is a self dwelling both in joy and in suffering. To such a tradition, the idea of 'self-fulfilment,' as this is often cheerily understood in popular psychology today, sounds feeble and unreal. Dealing with the self inevitably involves suffering. The sufferings which inevitably engage the self 'in extremity' (as John Robinson's book title effectively has it) are in Catholic asceticism not estranging but part and parcel of the individual's closeness to God, situating the Christian with Jesus on the cross. Hopkins knew this and there is no evidence that he thought accepting it as part of Christian teaching would alleviate suffering, though it would give suffering transcendental redeeming value.

Besides the particularism of the interior self (the most particular of particulars), the other kind of Victorian particularism which so strongly marks Hopkins' poetry and prose is the particularism of existents in the exterior world – of 'rose-moles all in stipple upon trout' (P 37), of the falcon 'riding / ... the rolling level underneath him steady air' (P 36), of oak trees whose 'determining planes are concentric, a system of brief contiguous and continuous tangents' (J 144), of 'all things counter, original, spare, strange' (P 37). This kind of detailed verbal description, especially from the eighteenth century on, develops pari passu with the more and more intensively articulated attention to the self as self. For the advances in accumulating and articulating ultraspecific, particularized knowledge implemented by print spills into both the exterior and interior worlds.

Of the two worlds, interior and exterior, which consciousness had become more and more capable of dealing with in verbalized detail, the interior was in the last analysis the more important for Hopkins, as it had clearly been for Ignatius Loyola in the Spiritual Exercises and for the Christian faith tradition generally, and as it has also been in certain ways for modernism generally, with its close attention to the human self. In Christian teaching, it is in their interiors, their most intimate selves, that human beings relate to God and are redeemed. In creation God's central intent was to create human selves, each in its own idiosyncratic uniqueness. The external world is there to support interior consciousness and, as Ignatius Loyola reiterates, is to be used by human beings in ways which relate their interior consciousness to God, and which relate the external world to God through their consciousness. 'Glory be to God for dappled things' (P 37) – the human recognition, giving 'glory' and thanks, realizes the full potential of external nature.

But the external world and the interior world of the self are not entirely separate. Our bodies are both part of ourselves and part of the external world. In his sense of 'inscape' and 'instress' Hopkins finds the interior world of consciousness appropriating the exterior in its most particularized, individualized form. Inscape refers to the utter individuality and distinctiveness that marks each individual existence, its 'thisness,' *haecceitas.* Instress refers to the fusion of the inscape of a given being with a given human consciousness in contact at a given moment with that being in all its uniqueness. Because the exterior universe can thus relate in its particular reality to human consciousness, to the self, the 'I' – and not only to believing human selves, but to anyone with ordinary human sensitivity – the exterior universe can be related in Christian faith through the human self to God, who is 'selfmaking' and who welcomes the exterior universe to himself through the human selves he has made.

But with regard to the vast external world in its entirety as it was revealing itself to human beings in Hopkins' age, inscape and instress had their limitations. The focus on particulars worked consummately well by bits and pieces: a bluebell here, a soaring falcon there, a farrier at his anvil or a labouring ploughman, the 'rollrock highroad' of the brook at Inversnaid. And at times inscape and instress could be much more encompassing. 'The world is charged with the grandeur of God. / It will flame out like shining from shook foil,' Hopkins cries in one of his best known sonnets, 'God's Grandeur' (P 31). 'Nature is never spent; / There lives the dearest freshness deep down things.' Nature's 'black West' bears promise of 'morning, at the brown brink eastward' – and all this 'Because the Holy Ghost over the bent / World broods with warm breast and with ah! bright wings.' Here Hopkins focuses on the terrestrial globe. At other times, as in 'The Wreck of the Deutschland' (P 28), he turns from the globe out to interstellar space, finding God's presence in 'Starlight, wafting him out of it.'

In one of his greatest sonnets, 'That Nature is a Heraclitean Fire' (P 72), Hopkins expresses a deeper cosmic vision of 'nature.' Nature is a power 'million-fuelèd,' whose 'bonfire burns on,' life-giving but ultimately absolutely fatal to each utterly unique 'Manshape that shone off, disseveral, a star.' For ultimately, every trace of every human person 'death blots black out.' Every mark that any and all human beings have left on earth at long last 'vastness blurs and time beats level.' Hopkins is unrelenting in his acknowledgment of death and entropy. Death is death, all-encompassing. Nothing in nature, but only participation in Christ's resurrection – not mere resuscitation, but transformation into a new bodily state – makes it possible to override all this when

> In a flash, at a trumpet crash
> I am all at once what Christ is, ⏐ since he was what I am, and
> This Jack, joke, poor potsherd, ⏐ patch, matchwood, immortal diamond,
> Is immortal diamond.

The prospect is breathtaking, but in the last analysis the cosmology is more Heraclitean than nineteenth-century. Hopkins' relationship to the exterior world is simply not so total in his poems or his other writings nor by any means so precocious as his relationship to the world of the self, of the 'I.' The paths into the self and out again were well trodden theologically, those into the new cosmology, with its new scenario for humankind, were theologically untrodden, or virtually so. In his comprehensive access to the exterior cosmos, even Hopkins, the only one of the 'Stonyhurst group' who could qualify as an amateur scientist (Zaniello, 136), still represents the Catholic tradition generally of his day, and to a great extent, even of the present. He works with no urgent, modern, comprehensive cosmological vision. For, as has been seen, since the collapse of the old Aristotelian cosmology, Catholic theology and indeed the entire Catholic ethos had never got the newly emerging cosmos fully into theological focus. The sense of the universe and of human beings in the universe was undergoing profound alteration in and before Hopkins' time – since, for example, Sir William Herschel (1738–1822) and his son Sir John Herschel (1792–1871) had opened insights into the true size of the universe, where, as would come to be known in our century, our entire galaxy is only one of billions of similar systems in creation. Sensing the inscape and instress of such a creation as a whole would challenge the imaginative and emotional resources of anyone, including Hopkins, and I suspect that he sensed that it would. Sir Charles Lyell's new uniformitarian explanation of change in his *Principles of Geology* (1830), J. Clerk Maxwell's electromagnetic theory of light, Ludwig Boltmann's kinaesthetic theory of gases, John Dalton's experimental foundation for the concept of atomic weight, and much else, most of all Charles Darwin's report *On the Origin of Species by Means of Natural Selection*, were establishing a context for *Homo sapiens* far beyond any imagined by Heraclitus.

Darwin's and Alfred Russel Wallace's joint paper on natural selection was read to the Linnean Society in 1858 and Darwin's book appeared the next year, when Hopkins was fifteen years old. Hopkins refers to Darwin in passing (*B* 172, 281, 290) and appears everywhere singularly free of hostility or even uneasiness regarding Darwin's or other new discoveries that were reshaping the cosmic scenario (Collins, 96). But Hopkins' poetry of inscape and instress pretty well passes up the new discoveries, dwelling in a sense of the enveloping and poetically inspiring 'nature' familiar since the early Romantics.

It could hardly have been otherwise. St George Jackson Mivart and a few others were working for a more mature Catholic cosmology, but, in effect, Hopkins would have had to build his own pretty much from scratch. The new physics had engendered no new Catholic metaphysics. The Catholic theology of the past four or five centuries to the present has been what Wildiers (211) has styled an 'acosmic theology,' with no integral relationship to the fifteen-billion-year-old evolving universe that we now know, to the thirty-thousand-year or longer history of *Homo sapiens*, or to the countless hundreds of thousands of years of human existence that, for all we can tell, lie ahead. Individual Catholics by the hundreds of thousands or millions are acutely aware of what modern science has shown the real universe to be and are aware that their faith teaches that God created the actual universe that is, not the construct imagined by Aristotle or even the one imaginatively pictured in Genesis. But with rare exceptions, such as Pierre Teilhard de Chardin, who was to enter the Society of Jesus in 1899, just ten years after Hopkins' death, few have undertaken to theologize about the cosmos as we now know it to be, to discourse about human redemption through Christ in the framework of the total known physical reality in which human beings have come into existence and live.

Modern cosmology in Hopkins' day of course had not advanced so far as it has now, but it was well out on its present trajectory. Hopkins, as has been seen, had no hankering for a cosmology of the past, he was no nostalgic medievalist or antiquarian, and, as has also been seen, he was to a considerable degree interested in interpreting the Church's teaching in the light of what we know of the real physical universe. But he had other things to do and he did not work at such interpretations very hard. The clinically detailed physical description at which Hopkins excelled was the coefficient of the science that had produced and was improving the modern understanding of the external universe. But this modern understanding of the universe Hopkins and almost all of his fellow Catholics left lying theologically fallow. Not so the interior self. Articulate understanding of the self had developed vastly since antiquity and was to develop still further, but it had never had to be revised as cosmology had had to be. God may have been distanced in some sense from the external cosmos, the macrocosm, in the minds of many believers in Hopkins' age and since. But not from the microcosm of the self. This is and always had been terrain open from the inside to each human person who can or could say 'I.' Here is where the most intimate action of the Catholic faith has always occurred, though the action has evolved different forms in different ages. Here Hopkins was at home. Here he felt, for himself and for all others, is the meeting point of each human person with God.

References

Arekelian, Paul G. 'A Winter and Warm: The Shape of "The Wreck of the Deutschland."' ' *Studies in English Literature*, 22 (1982), 659–70

Augustine of Hippo, St. *The Confessions of St. Augustine*. Trans John K. Ryan. Garden City, NY: Image Books (Doubleday) 1960. Citations are by book and chapter.

Barthes, Roland. *Sade, Fourier, Loyola*. Paris: Editions du Seuil 1971

Bataillon, Marcel. *Erasme et Espagne: recherches sur l'histoire spirituel du XVIe siècle*. Paris: E. Droz 1937

Bellah, Robert H. 'Religions and the University: The Crisis of Unbelief.' *Religion and Intellectual Life*, 1 (1938), 13–26, 40–56

Bergonzi, Bernard. *Gerard Manley Hopkins*. New York: Macmillan 1977

Bettelheim, Bruno. *Freud and Man's Soul*. New York: Knopf 1983

Blanchard, Marc Eli. *Description: Sign, Self, Desire – Critical Theory in the Wake of Semiotics*. Approaches to Semiotics, 43. The Hague: Mouton 1980

Bochenski, I.M. *A History of Formal Logic*. Trans and ed Ivo Thomas. Notre Dame, Ind: University of Notre Dame Press 1961

Bonnefoy, Jean-Francois, OFM *Christ and Cosmos*. Trans and ed Michael D. Meilach, OFM. Paterson, NJ: St Anthony Guild Press 1965

Boyle, Marjorie O'Rourke. 'Angels Black and White: Loyola's Spiritual Discernment in Historical Perspective.' *Theological Studies*, 44 (1983), 241–57

Boyle, Robert, SJ. 'Time and Grace in Hopkins' Imagination.' *Renascence*, 29 (1976), 7–24

Brandt, Anthony. 'Self-Confrontations.' *Psychology Today*, 14 (1980), 78–101

Brown, Raymond E., Joseph A. Fitzmyer, and Roland E. Murphy, eds. *The*

Jerome Biblical Commentary. Vol 1, *The Old Testament.* Vol 2, *The New Testament.* Englewood Cliffs, NJ: Prentice-Hall 1968

Bruns, Gerald L. 'Energy and Interpretation in Hopkins.' In his *Inventions: Writing, Textuality, and Understanding in Literary History.* New Haven and London: Yale University Press 1982, pp 125–42

– 'The Idea of Energy in the Writings of Gerard Manley Hopkins.' *Renascence,* 29 (1976), 25–42

Buber, Martin. *I and Thou.* With a Postscript by the author. Translated by Ronald Gregor Smith. 2nd ed of English translation. New York: Charles Scribner's Sons 1958. First appeared in German as *Ich und Du* in 1922.

Buckley, Jerome Hamilton. *The Victorian Temper: A Study in Literary Culture.* Cambridge, Mass: Harvard University Press 1951

Bynum, Caroline Walker. *Jesus as Mother: Studies in the Spirituality of the High Middle Ages.* Berkeley, Calif: University of California Press 1982

Carol, Juniper B., OFM. *The Absolute Primacy and Predestination of Jesus and His Virgin Mother.* Chicago: Franciscan Herald 1981

Christ, Carol T. *The Finer Optic: The Aesthetic of Particularity in Victorian Poetry.* New Haven and London: Yale University Press 1975

Clancy, Thomas H., SJ. *An Introduction to Jesuit Life: The Constitutions and History Through 435 Years.* St Louis, Mo: Institute of Jesuit Sources 1976

Clark, Ira. *Christ Revealed: The History of the Neotypological Lyric in the English Renaissance.* University of Florida Monographs, Humanities, no 51. Gainesville, Fla: University Presses of Florida 1982

[*The Cloud of Unknowing,* modernized version.] *The Divine Cloud.* Ed Henry Collins. With Notes and a Preface by Augustine Baker, OSB. London: T. Richardson and Son 1871

The Cloud of Unknowing and the Book of Privy Counselling. Ed Phyllis Hodgson. Early English Text Society, Original Series, no 218. London: Humphrey Milford, Oxford University Press, for the Early English Text Society 1944

The Cloud of Unknowing and the Book of Privy Counselling. Ed in a modern English version by William Johnston, SJ Garden City, NY: Doubleday and Co 1973

Cohen, Patricia Cline. *A Calculating People: The Spread of Numeracy in Early America.* Chicago and London: University of Chicago Press 1982

Collins, James D. 'Kierkegaard's Imagery of the Self.' In *Kierkegaard's Truth: The Disclosure of the Self.* Ed Joseph H. Smith. Psychiatry and the Humanities, vol 5. New Haven and London: Yale University Press 1981, pp 51–84.

- 'Philosophical Themes in G.M. Hopkins.' *Thought*, 22 (1947),
  67–106

Copleston, Frederick. *A History of Philosophy.* 9 vols. London: Burns,
  Oates, and Washbourne 1946–75

Cotter, James Finn. *Inscape: The Christology and Poetry of Gerard Manley
  Hopkins.* Pittsburgh, Pa: University of Pittsburgh Press 1972

Cox, Stephen D. *'The Stranger Within Thee': Concepts of the Self in Late-
  Eighteenth-Century Literature.* Pittsburgh, Pa: University of Pittsburgh
  Press 1980

Daly, Peter Maurice. *Literature in the Light of the Emblem: Structural
  Parallels Between the Emblem and Literature in the Sixteenth and Seventeenth Centuries.* Toronto and Buffalo: University of Toronto Press 1979

De Mello, Anthony, SJ. *Sadhana: A Way to God – Christian Exercises in
  Eastern Form.* 5th ed. St Louis, Mo: Institute of Jesuit Sources (in cooperation with Gujarat Sahitya Prakash, Anand Press, Anand, India), 1978

Denziger, Henricus, ed. *Enchiridion Symbolorum Definitionum et Declara-
  tionum de Rebus Fidei et Morum.* Quod post Clementem Bannwart et
  Ioannem B. Umberg S.I. denuo edidit Carolus Rahner, S.I. Barcelona,
  Freiburg-im-Breisgau, and Rome: Herder 1957.

Derrida, Jacques. *Of Grammatology.* Trans Gayatri Chakravorty Spivak.
  Baltimore and London: Johns Hopkins University Press 1976

Devlin, Christopher, SJ. 'An Essay on Scotus.' *The Month*, 182 (Nov–Dec
  1946), 456–66

- 'The Image and the Word – I and II.' *The Month.* ns 3 (Feb–Mar 1950),
  114–27, 191–202

- 'Time's Eunuch.' *The Month*, ns 1 (May 1949), 303–12

Dilligan, Robert J., and Todd K. Bender. *A Concordance to the English
  Poetry of Gerard Manley Hopkins.* Madison and London: University of
  Wisconsin Press 1970

Divine Cloud, The. See *Cloud of Unknowing.*

Downes, David Anthony. *Gerard Manley Hopkins: A Study of His Ignatian
  Spirit.* New York: Bookman Associates 1959

- *The Great Sacrifice: Studies in Hopkins.* Lanham, Md: University Press of
  America 1983

- *Victorian Portraits: Hopkins and Pater.* New York: Bookman Associates
  1965

Dumoulin, Heinrich, SJ. *Christianity Meets Buddhism.* Trans John C.
  Maraldo. LaSalle, Ill: Open Court Publishing Co 1974

Duns Scotus, Joannes. *Opera Omnia.* 26 vols. Parisiis: Vives 1891

- *Opera Omnia.* Ed Pacificus M. Peratonus. Studio et cura Commissionis

Scotisticae ad fidem codicum edita, praeside Carolo Balic. Civitas Vaticana: Typis Polyglottis Vaticanis 1950 –

Egan, Harvey D., SJ. *The Spiritual Exercises and the Ignatian Mystical Horizon*. Foreword by Karl Rahner, SJ. St Louis, Mo: Institute of Jesuit Sources 1976

Evenett, H. Outram. *The Spirit of the Counter-Reformation*. Ed John Bossy. Cambridge, England: The University Press 1968

Feeney, Joseph J., SJ. 'Grades, Academic Reform, and Manpower: Why Hopkins Never Completed His Course in Theology.' *Hopkins Quarterly*, 9 (1982), 21–31

Fessard, Gaston, SJ. *La Dialectique des Exercises spirituels de S. Ignace de Loyola*. [Vol 1,] *Temps, liberté, grace*. [Vol 2,] *Fondement, péché, orthodoxie*. Paris: Aubier 1956, 1966

– See also Pousset, Edouard, SJ, below.

Freeman, Rosemary. *English Emblem Books*. London: Chatto and Windus 1948

Garber, Frederick. *The Autonomy of the Self from Richardson to Huysmans*. Princeton, NJ: Princeton University Press 1982

Garcia Villoslada. See Villoslada.

Gardner, W.H. *Gerard Manley Hopkins: A Study of Poetic Idiosyncrasy in Relation to Poetic Tradition*. 2 vols. 2d ed. Foreword by Gerard Hopkins. London: Oxford University Press 1969

Georgiana, Linda. *The Solitary Self: Individuality in the 'Ancrene Wisse.'* Cambridge, Mass, and London, England: Harvard University Press 1981

Glavin, John J. ' "The Wreck of the Deutschland" and "Lycidas" ': Ubique Naufragium Est,' *Texas Studies in Literature and Language*, 22 (1980), 522–46

Goldsmith, Robert H. 'The Selfless Self: Hopkins' Late Sonnets.' *Hopkins Quarterly*, 3 (1976), 67–75

Greenblatt, Stephen. *Renaissance Self-Fashioning: From More to Shakespeare*. Chicago and London: University of Chicago Press 1980

Guibert, Joseph de, SJ. *The Jesuits: Their Spiritual Doctrine and Practice: A Historical Study*. Trans William H. Young, SJ. Chicago, Ill: Institute of Jesuit Sources in Cooperation with Loyola University Press 1964

Guntrip, Harry J.S. *Psychoanalytic Theory, Therapy, and the Self*. New York: Basic Books 1971

Harding, M. Esther. *The 'I' and the 'Not-I': A Study in the Development of Consciousness*. Bollingen Series, 79. New York: Pantheon Books 1965

Harman, Barbara Leah. *Costly Monuments: Representations of the Self in George Herbert's Poetry*. Cambridge, Mass: Harvard University Press 1982

Hartle, Ann. *The Modern Self in Rousseau's 'Confessions': A Reply to St.*

Augustine. Notre Dame, Ind: Notre Dame University Press 1983

Havelock, Eric A. *Preface to Plato*. Cambridge, Mass: Belknap Press of Harvard University Press 1963

Holland, Norman N. *The I*. New Haven and London: Yale University Press 1985

Hopkins, Gerard Manley. Works are here listed in the alphabetic order of the abbreviations used in the present work for each title. Note that in the case of *P* the numbers used in the present work refer to the numbers of the poems, not to pages.

- *B The Letters of Gerard Manley Hopkins to Robert Bridges*. Ed Claude Colleer Abbott. 2nd (revised) impression. London: Oxford University Press 1955. (The index to this volume and to *D* are found combined at the end of *D*, where without notice *B* is treated as vol 1 and *D* as vol 2.)

- *D The Correspondence of Gerard Manley Hopkins and Richard Watson Dixon*. Ed Claude Colleer Abbott. 2nd (revised) impression. London: Oxford University Press 1955 (see note with *B* here above)

- *FL Further Letters of Gerard Manley Hopkins, including His Correspondence with Coventry Patmore*. Ed Claude Colleer Abbott. 2nd ed, revised and enlarged. London: Oxford University Press 1956

- *J The Journals and Papers of Gerard Manley Hopkins*. Ed Humphrey House and Graham Storey. London: Oxford University Press 1959

- *N The Note-Books and Papers of Gerard Manley Hopkins*. Ed Humphrey House. London: Oxford University Press 1937. Superseded by *J* (1959) and *S* (1949), which include what is in this volume together with much other material.

- *P The Poems of Gerard Manley Hopkins*. Ed W.H. Gardner and N.H. MacKenzie. 4th ed, revised and enlarged. London: Oxford University Press 1970. For this volume, numbers in the text of the present work refer to poem numbers, not to pages.

- *S The Sermons and Devotional Writings of Gerard Manley Hopkins*. Ed Christopher Devlin, SJ. London: Oxford University Press 1959

Horner, Winifred Bryan, ed. *Historical Rhetoric: An Annotated Bibliography of Selected Sources in English*. Boston, Mass: G.K. Hall 1980

Howe, Irving, ed. *The Idea of the Modern in Literature and the Arts*. New York: Horizon Press 1967

Howell, Wilbur Samuel. *Logic and Rhetoric in England 1500–1700*. Princeton, NJ: Princeton University Press 1956

Hume, David. *A Treatise of Human Nature*. Ed L.A. Selby-Bigge. 2nd ed (of 1888 edition), revised by P.H. Nidditch. Oxford: Clarendon Press 1978. (This work was first published 1739–40.)

Iparraguirre, Ignacio, SJ. *Historia de los Ejercicios de San Ignacio*. Vol 2,

Desde la muerte de San Ignacio hasta la promulgación del Directorio oficial (1556–99). Vol 3, *Evolución en Europa durante el siglo XVII.* Roma: Institutum Historicum Societatis Iesu 1955, 1973

James, William. *The Principles of Psychology.* New York: Dover 1950. Rpt of original 1890 edition

Jay, Paul. *Being in the Text: Self-Representation from Wordsworth to Roland Barthes.* Ithaca and London: Cornell University Press 1984

Jerome Biblical Commentary, The. See Brown, Raymond E., Joseph A. Fitzmyer, and Roland E. Murphy.

Johnson, Wendell Stacy. *Gerard Manley Hopkins: The Poet as Victorian.* Ithaca, NY: Cornell University Press 1968

– 'Sexuality and Inscape.' *Hopkins Quarterly,* 3 (1976), 59–65

Johnstone, Henry W., Jr. *The Problem of the Self.* University Park, Penn: Pennsylvania State University Press 1970

Joseph, Gerhard. 'Tennyson's Optics: The Eagle's Gaze.' *PMLA,* 92 (1977), 420–8

Jung, C.G. *The Undiscovered Self.* Trans R.F.C. Hall. Boston: Little, Brown, and Co 1957

Kahler, Erich. *The Inward Turn of Narrative.* Trans Richard and Clara Winston. Princeton, NJ: Princeton University Press 1973

Kasper, Walter. *Jesus the Christ.* Trans V. Green. New York: Paulist Press 1977

Kerrigan, William. 'The Articulation of the Ego in the English Renaissance.' *Psychiatry and the Humanities,* vol 4, *The Literary Freud: Mechanisms of Defense and the Poetic Will.* Ed Joseph H. Smith. New Haven and London: Yale University Press 1980, pp 261–307

Kretz, Thomas, SJ. 'Advents Three for Three: A Study of "The Wreck of the Deutschland." ' *Victorian Poetry,* 11 (1973), 252–4

Lanham, Richard A. *The Motives of Eloquence: Literary Rhetoric in the Renaissance.* New Haven and London: Yale University Press 1976

Lavelle, Louis. *The Dilemma of Narcissus.* Trans W.T. Gairdner. London: George Allen and Unwin; New York: Humanities Press 1973

Leavis, F.R. *New Bearings in English Poetry.* London: Chatto and Windus 1932, rpt Ann Arbor, Mich: University of Michigan Press 1960

Leggio, James. 'The Science of a Sacrament.' *Hopkins Quarterly,* 4 (1977), 55–67

Leutbrewer, Christoph, OFM. *Nouvelle methode pour se disposer aisement a une bonne et entiere confession de plusieurs annees en moins de deux heures.* 5th edition. Paris: Nicolas et Jean de la Coste 1657. This is the edition in the St Louis University Library. Since the approbation is dated

28 April 1649 and the Privilège du Roys 26 January 1650, the book was probably first published in 1650. An 8th edition had appeared by 1663 and there were many subsequent editions (see Bibliothèque Nationale and British Museum catalogues of printed books).

Lévi-Strauss, Claude. *Myth and Meaning*. The 1977 Massey Lectures (CBC Radio Series, *Ideas*). New York: Schocken Books 1979

Loyola, Ignatius. *The Autobiography of St. Ignatius Loyola with Related Documents*. Trans Joseph F. O'Callaghan. Ed John C. Olin. New York: Harper and Row 1974

- *The Constitutions of the Society of Jesus*. Trans George E. Ganss, SJ. St Louis, Mo: Institute of Jesuit Sources 1970

- *Diario espiritual 2 febr. 1544-27 febr. 1545*. In his *Obras completas*. Ed Ignacio Iparraguirre, SJ, and Candido de Dalmases, SJ. 3rd ed rev Madrid: Biblioteca de Autores Cristianos 1977, pp 321-410

- *The Spiritual Exercises of St. Ignatius: Based on Studies in the Language of the Autograph*. Trans and ed Louis J. Puhl, SJ. Chicago: Loyola University Press 1951. References to the text of the *Spiritual Exercises* are to the section numbers, not to the pages, of this edition.

- *Spiritual Journal* [also called in English *Spiritual Diary*] *of Ignatius Loyola, February 2, 1554, to February 27, 1545*. Trans William H. Young, SJ. In Simon Decloux, *Commentaries on the Letters and Spiritual Diary of St. Ignatius Loyola, with the Autograph of the Spiritual Diary*. Rome: Centrum Ignatianum Spiritualitatis 1980, pp. 124-96.

Lyons, John O. *The Invention of the Self: The Hinge of Consciousness in the Eighteenth Century*. Carbondale, Ill: Southern Illinois University Press 1978

Magliola, Robert R. *Phenomenology and Literature: An Introduction*. West Lafayette, Ind: Purdue University Press 1977

Mahler, Margaret S. 'A Study of the Separation-Individuation Process and Its Possible Application to Borderline Phenomena in the Psychoanalytic Situation.' In *The Psychoanalytic Study of the Child*, vol 26. Ed Ruth Eissler. New York: Quadrangle Books 1971, pp 403-24

Mariani, Paul L. *A Commentary on the Complete Poems of Gerard Manley Hopkins*. Ithaca and London: Cornell University Press 1970

- 'Hopkins: Toward a Poetics of Unselfconsciousness.' *Renascence*, 9 (1976), 43-9

McCool, Gerald A. *Catholic Theology in the Nineteenth Century: The Quest for a Unitary Method*. New York: Seabury Press 1977

Mijuskovic, Ben Lazare. *Loneliness in Philosophy, Psychology, and Literature*. Assen, Netherlands: Van Gorcum 1979; Atlantic Highlands, NJ:

Humanities Press 1983

Miller, J. Hillis. 'The Creation of the Self in Gerard Manley Hopkins.' *ELH*, 22 (1955), 293–319

– *The Disappearance of God: Five Nineteenth-Century Writers*. Cambridge, Mass: Belknap Press of Harvard University Press 1963

– 'The Disarticulation of the Self in Nietzsche.' *The Monist*, 64 (1981), 247–61

Milroy, James. *The Language of Gerard Manley Hopkins*. London: André Deutsch 1977

Milward, Peter, SJ. *A Commentary on G.M. Hopkins' 'The Wreck of the Deutschland.'* Tokyo: Hokuseido Press 1968

– *Landscape and Inscape: Vision and Inspiration in Hopkins' Poetry*. Photography by Raymond V. Schoder, SJ. Grand Rapids, Mich: Eerdsmans; London: Paul Elek 1975

Milward, Peter, SJ, and Raymond V. Schoder, SJ, eds. *Readings of 'The Wreck': Essays in Commemoration of G.M. Hopkins' 'The Wreck of the Deutschland.'* Chicago: Loyola University Press 1976

Moltmann, Jürgen. *Theology of Hope: On the Ground and the Implications of a Christian Eschatology*. London: SCM Press 1965

Motto, Marylou. *Mined with a Motion: The Poetry of Gerard Manley Hopkins*. New Brunswick, NJ: Rutgers University Press 1984

Neumann, Erich. *The Origins and History of Consciousness*. With a Foreword by C.J. Jung. Trans R.F.C. Hull. Bollingen Series, 62. Princeton, NJ: Princeton University Press 1954

Newman, John Henry. *Apologia pro Vita Sua: Being a History of His Religious Opinions*. Ed Martin J. Svaglic. Oxford: Clarendon Press 1967

– *An Essay in Aid of a Grammar of Assent*. Ed Charles Frederick Harrold. New York: Longmans, Green 1947

– *An Essay on the Development of Christian Doctrine*. Ed Charles Frederick Harrold. With an Appendix on Newman's textual changes by Ottis Ivan Schreiber. New York: Longmans, Green 1949

– *The Idea of a University Defined and Illustrated:* I, In Nine Discourses Delivered to the Catholics of Dublin; II, In Occasional Lectures and Essays Addressed to the Members of the Catholic University. Author's dedication and Preface dated 21 Nov 1852. London: Longmans, Green 1927

O'Daly, Gerald J.P. *Plotinus' Philosophy of the Self*. New York: Barnes and Noble (Harper and Row) 1973

O'Malley, John W., SJ. 'The Fourth Vow in Its Ignatian Context: A Historical Study.' *Studies in the Spirituality of Jesuits*, 15:1 (Jan 1983), 1–60. St Louis, Mo: American Assistancy Seminar on Jesuit Spirituality 1983

Onesta, P.A. 'The Self in Hopkins.' *English Studies in Africa*, 4 (1961), 174–81

Ong, Walter J., SJ. ' "A.M.D.G.": Dedication or Directive?' *Review for Religious*, 11 (1952), 257–64

– *Fighting for Life: Contest, Sexuality, and Consciousness*. Ithaca and London: Cornell University Press 1981

– *Interfaces of the Word*. Ithaca and London: Cornell University Press 1977

– *Orality and Literacy: The Technologizing of the Word*. London and New York: Methuen 1982

– *The Presence of the Word*. New Haven and London: Yale University Press 1967

– *Ramus, Method, and the Decay of Dialogue: From the Art of Discourse to the Art of Reasoning*. Cambridge, Mass: Harvard University Press 1958

– *Rhetoric, Romance, and Technology*. Ithaca and London: Cornell University Press 1971

– 'St. Ignatius' Prison-Cage and the Existentialist Situation.' *Theological Studies*, 15 (1954), 34–51

– 'System, Space, and Intellect in Renaissance Symbolism.' *Bibliothèque d'Humanisme et Renaissance*, 18 (1956), 222–39

Organ, Troy Wilson. *The Self in Indian Philosophy*. The Hague: Mouton and Co 1964

Peckham, Morse. *Beyond the Tragic Vision: The Quest for Identity in the Nineteenth Century*. New York: George Braziller 1962

Percy, Walker. *The Message in the Bottle*. New York: Farrar, Straus, and Giroux 1981

Perkins, Jean A. *The Concept of the Self in the French Enlightenment*. Geneva: Librairie Droz 1969

Porter, Lawrence B., OP. 'On Keeping "Persons" in the Trinity: A Linguistic Approach to Trinitarian Thought.' *Theological Studies*, 41 (1980), 530–48

Poschmann, Bernhard. *Penance and the Anointing of the Sick*. Trans and rev Francis Courtney. New York: Herder and Herder 1964

Pousset, Edouard, SJ. *Life in Faith and Freedom: An Essay Presenting Gaston Fessard's Analysis of the Dialectic of the Spiritual Exercises of St. Ignatius*. Trans Eugene L. Donahue. SJ. St Louis, Mo: Institute of Jesuit Sources (in cooperation with Gujarat Sahitya Prakash, Anand Press, Anand, India) 1980

Rahner, Hugo. ' "Be Prudent Money-Changers": Toward the History of Ignatius' Teaching on the Discernment of Spirits.' Epitomized and trans by Harold E. Weidman. In *Ignatius of Loyola: His Personality and Spiritual Heritage 1556–1956*. Ed Friedrich Wulf. St Louis, Mo: Institute of Jesuit

Sources 1977, pp 272–9
- *Ignatius the Theologian*. Trans Michael Barry. New York: Herder and Herder 1968
Rahner, Karl. 'The Ignatian Process for Discovering the Will of God in an Existential Situation.' Epitomized and trans Harold E. Weidman. In *Ignatius of Loyola: His Personality and Spiritual Heritage 1556–1956*. Ed Friedrich Wulf. St Louis, Mo: Institute of Jesuit Sources 1977, pp 280–93
- *Mary, Mother of the Lord: Theological Meditations*. Trans W.J. O'Hara. New York: Herder and Herder 1963
- *The Spirituality of St. Ignatius Loyola*. Trans F.J. Smith, sj. Westminster, Md: Newman Press 1953
Rahner, Karl, and Wilhelm Thüsing. *A New Christology*. Trans David Smith and Verdant Green. New York: Seabury Press 1980
Regan, Mariann Sanders. *Love Words: The Self and the Text in Medieval and Renaissance Poetry*. Ithaca and London: Cornell University Press 1982
Ricoeur, Paul. *Freedom and Nature: The Voluntary and the Involuntary*. Trans Erazim V. Kohak. Evanston, Ill: Northwestern University 1966
Robinson, John. *In Extremity: A Study of Gerard Manley Hopkins*. Cambridge, England: Cambridge University Press 1978
Rosenberg, Morris. *Conceiving the Self*. New York: Basic Books 1979
Schillebeeckx, Edward. *Christ: The Experience of Jesus as Lord*. Trans John Bowden. New York: Seabury Press 1980
- *Jesus: An Experiment in Christology*. Trans Hubert Hoskins. New York: Seabury Press 1979
Schneider, Elizabeth. *The Dragon in the Gate: Studies in the Poetry of Gerard Manley Hopkins*. Berkeley and Los Angeles: University of California Press 1968
Schoof, Mark, op. *A Survey of Catholic Theology, 1800–1970*. Trans N.E. Smith. Paramus, nj and New York: Paulist Newman Press 1970
Shoemaker, Sydney. *Self-Knowledge and Self-Identity*. Ithaca ny: Cornell University Press 1963
Sidney, Sir Philip. *The Poems of Sir Philip Sidney*. Ed William A. Ringler, Jr. Oxford: Clarendon Press 1962
Smith, Joseph M., ed. *Kierkegaard's Truth: The Disclosure of the Self*. New Haven and London: Yale University Press 1982
Sprinker, Michael. *'A Counterpoint of Dissonance': The Aesthetics and Poetry of Gerard Manley Hopkins*. Baltimore and London: Johns Hopkins University Press 1980
Storey, Graham. *A Preface to Hopkins*. London and New York: Longman 1981

Strange, Roderick. *Newman and the Gospel of Christ*. New York: Oxford University Press 1981

Sulloway, Alison G. *Gerard Manley Hopkins and the Victorian Temper.* New York: Columbia University Press 1972

Summary of the Constitutions [of the Society of Jesus]. In *Rules of the Society of Jesus*. Woodstock, Md: Woodstock College Press 1956, pp 5–27

Sutton, Max Keith. 'Selving as Individuation in Hopkins: A Jungian Reading.' *Hopkins Quarterly*, 2 (1975), 119–29

Sypher, Wylie. *Loss of the Self in Modern Literature and Art*. New York: Random House 1962

Tanner, Tony. *The Reign of Wonder: Naivety and Reality in American Literature*. Cambridge, England: Cambridge University Press 1965

Teilhard de Chardin, Pierre. *Human Energy*. Trans J.M. Cohen. New York: Harcourt Brace Jovanovich 1969

Thomas, Alfred, SJ. *Hopkins the Jesuit: The Years of Training*. London: Oxford University Press 1969

– 'Was Hopkins a Scotist Before He Read Scotus?' *Studia Scholastica-Scotistica*, 4 *De Doctrina Ioannis Duns Scoti*, vol 4, *Scotismus decursu Saeculorum*. Rome 1968, pp 617–29

Tyrrell, George. *Lex Orandi, or Prayer and Creed*. London: Longmans, Green, and Co 1903

Tzougros, Penelope. ' "The Selfless Self of Self" in Hopkins' Two Beautiful Young People.' *Hopkins Quarterly*, 7 (1980), 5–8

Villoslada, Ricardo García, SJ. 'Rasgos caracteristicos de la Devotio Moderna.' *Manresa*, 28 (1956), 315–50

– 'San Ignacio ... y Erasmo ...' *Estudios eclesiasticos*, 16 (1942), 235–64, 399–426; 17 (1943), 65–103

Walhout, Donald. *Send My Roots Rain: A Study of Religious Experience in the Poetry of Gerard Manley Hopkins*. Athens, Ohio, and London, England: Ohio University Press 1981

Walliser, Stephan. '*That Nature Is a Heraclitean Fire and of the Comfort of the Resurrection*': A Case Study in G.M. Hopkins' Poetry. Bern, Switzerland: Franke Verlag 1977

Ward, M. Eucharista. 'Suffering and Passivity: Pierre Teilhard de Chardin as a Gloss on Gerard Manley Hopkins.' *Victorian Poetry*, 10 (1972), 321–32

Watt, Ian. *The Rise of the Novel: Studies in Defoe, Richardson, and Fielding*. Berkeley: University of California Press 1967

Webber, Joan. *The Eloquent 'I': Style and Self in Seventeenth-Century Prose*. Madison, Wis, and London: University of Wisconsin Press 1968

Weyand, Norman, SJ, ed. *Immortal Diamond: Studies in Gerard Manley*

Hopkins. New York: Sheed and Ward 1949

Whelan, Edward J. 'The Rhetoric of Early Renaissance Meditation.' Diss, St Louis University 1972

Wildiers, N. Max. *The Theologian and His Universe: Theology and Cosmology from the Middle Ages to the Present*. New York: Seabury Press 1982

Wolter, Hans. 'Elements of Crusade Spirituality in St. Ignatius.' Trans Louis W. Roberts. In *Ignatius of Loyola: His Personality and Spiritual Heritage 1556-1956*. Ed Friedrich Wulf. St Louis, Mo: Institute of Jesuit Sources 1977, pp 97–134

Wulf, Friedrich, sj, ed. *Ignatius of Loyola: His Personality and Spiritual Heritage 1556-1956*. St Louis, Mo: Institute of Jesuit Sources 1977

Wylie, Ruth C. *The Self Concept: A Critical Survey of Pertinent Research Literature*. Lincoln, Neb: University of Nebraska Press 1961

Zaniello, Thomas A. 'The Stonyhurst Philosophers.' *Hopkins Quarterly*, 9 (1983), 133–56

Index

The Alexander
Lectures

The Alexander lectureship was founded in honour of Professor W.J.
Alexander, who held the Chair of English at University College, University
of Toronto, from 1889 to 1926. The Lectureship brings to the university a
distinguished scholar or critic to give a course of lectures on a subject
related to English literature.

1928–9
L.F. Cazamian (Sorbonne): 'Parallelism in the Recent Development of
English and French Literature.' Included in *Criticism in the Making* (Mac-
millan 1929).

1929–30
H.W. Garrod (Oxford): 'The Study of Poetry.' Published as *The Study of
Poetry* (Clarendon 1936).

1930–1
Irving Babbit (Harvard): 'Wordsworth and Modern Poetry.' Included in 'The
Primitivism of Wordsworth' in *On Being Creative* (Houghton 1932).

1931–2
W.A. Craigie (Chicago): 'The Northern Element in English Literature.'
Published as *The Northern Element in English Literature* (University of
Toronto Press 1933).

1932–3
H.J.C. Grierson (Edinburgh): 'Sir Walter Scott.' Included in *Sir Walter Scott,
Bart* (Constable, 1938).

1933–4
G.G. Sedgewick (British Columbia): 'Of Irony, Especially in Drama.'
Published as *Of Irony, Especially in Drama* (University of Toronto Press
1934).

1934–5
E.F. Stoll (Minnesota): 'Shakespeare's Yonge Lovers.' Published as *Shakespeare's Young Lovers* (Oxford 1937).
1935–6
Franklin B. Snyder (Northwestern): 'Robert Burns.' Included in *Robert Burns, His Reputation, and His Art* (University of Toronto Press 1936).
1936–7
D. Nichol Smith (Oxford): 'Some Observations on Eighteenth-Century Poetry.' Published as *Some Observations on Eighteenth Century Poetry* (University of Toronto Press 1937).
1937–8
Carleton W. Stanley (Dalhousie): 'Matthew Arnold.' Published as *Matthew Arnold* (University of Toronto Press 1938).
1938–9
Douglas Bush (Harvard): 'The Renaissance and English Humanism.' Published as *The Renaissance and English Humanism* (University of Toronto Press 1939).
1939–41
C. Cestre (Paris): 'The Visage of France.' Lectures postponed because of the war and then cancelled.
1941–2
H.J. Davis (Smith): 'Swift and Stella.' Published as *Stella, A Gentlewoman of the Eighteenth Century* (Macmillan 1942).
1942–3
H. Granville-Barker (New York City): 'Coriolanus.' Included in *Prefaces to Shakespeare* volume II (Princeton 1947).
1943–4
F.P. Wilson (Smith): 'Elizabethan and Jacobean.' Published as *Elizabethan and Jacobean* (Clarendon 1945).
1944–5
F.O. Matthiessen (Harvard): 'Henry James: the Final Phase.' Published as *Henry James, the Major Phase* (Oxford 1944).
1945–6
Samuel C. Chew (Bryn Mawr): 'The Virtues Reconciled: A Comparison of Visual and Verbal Imagery.' Published as *The Virtues Reconciled, an Iconographical Study* (University of Toronto Press 1947).
1946–7
Marjorie Hope Nicolson (Columbia): 'Voyages to the Moon.' Published as *Voyages to the Moon* (Macmillan 1948).

1947–8
G.B. Harrison (Queen's): 'Shakespearean Tragedy.' Included in *Shakespeare's Tragedies* (Routledge and Kegan Paul 1951).
1948–9
E.M.W. Tillyard (Cambridge): 'Shakespeare's Problem Plays.' Published as *Shakespeare's Problem Plays* (University of Toronto Press 1949).
1949–50
E.K. Brown (Chicago): 'Rhythm in the Novel.' Published as *Rhythm in the Novel* (University of Toronto Press 1950).
1950–1
Malcolm W. Wallace (Toronto): 'English Character and the English Literary Tradition.' Published as *English Character and the English Literary Tradition* (University of Toronto Press 1952).
1951–2
R.S. Crane (Chicago): 'The Languages of Criticism and the Structure of Poetry.' Published as *The Languages of Criticism and the Structure of Poetry* (University of Toronto Press 1953).
1952–3
V.S. Pritchett. Lectures not given.
1953–4
F.M. Salter (Alberta): 'Mediaeval Drama in Chester.' Published as *Mediaeval Drama in Chester* (University of Toronto Press 1955).
1954–5
Alfred Harbage (Harvard): 'Theatre for Shakespeare.' Published as *Theatre for Shakespeare* (University of Toronto Press 1955).
1955–6
Leon Edel (New York): 'Literary Biography.' Published as *Literary Biography* (University of Toronto Press 1957).
1956–7
James Sutherland (London): 'On English Prose.' Published as *On English Prose* (University of Toronto Press 1957).
1957–8
Harry Levin (Harvard): 'The Question of Hamlet.' Published as *The Question of Hamlet* (Oxford 1959).
1958–9
Bertrand H. Bronson (California): 'In Search of Chaucer.' Published as *In Search of Chaucer* (University of Toronto Press 1960).
1959–60
Geoffrey Bullough (London): 'Mirror of Minds: Changing Psychological

Assumptions as Reflected in English Poetry.' Published as *Mirror of Minds: Changing Psychological Beliefs in English Poetry* (University of Toronto Press 1962).

1960–1

Cecil Bald (Chicago): 'The Poetry of John Donne.' Included in *John Donne: A Life* (Oxford 1970).

1961–2

Helen Gardner (Oxford): 'Paradise Lost.' Published as *A Reading of Paradise Lost* (Oxford 1965).

1962–3

Maynard Mack (Yale): 'The Garden and The City: The Theme of Retirement in Pope.' Published as *The Garden and the City* (University of Toronto Press 1969).

1963–4

M.H. Abrams (Cornell): 'Natural Supernaturalism: Idea and Design in Romantic Poetry.' Published as *Natural Supernaturalism* (W.H. Norton 1971)

1964–5

Herschel Baker (Harvard): 'The Race of Time: Three Lectures on Renaissance Historiography.' Published as *The Race of Time* (University of Toronto Press 1967).

1965–6

Northrop Frye (Toronto): 'Fools of Time: Studies in Shakespearian Tragedy.' Published as *Fools of Time* (University of Toronto Press 1967).

1967–8

Frank Kermode (Bristol): 'Criticism and English Studies.'

1967–8

Francis E. Mineka (Cornell): 'The Uses of Literature, 1750–1850.'

1968–9

H.D.F. Kitto (Bristol): 'What is Distinctively Hellenic in Greek Literature?'

1968–9

W.J. Bate (Harvard): 'The Burden of the Past and the English Poet (1660–1840).'

1970–1

J.A.W. Bennett (Cambridge): 'Chaucer at Oxford and at Cambridge.' Published as *Chaucer at Oxford and at Cambridge* (University of Toronto Press 1974).

1971–2

Roy Daniells (British Columbia): 'Mannerism: An Inclusive Art Form.'

1972–3
Hugh Kenner (California): 'The Meaning of Rhyme.' Publication planned.
1973–4
Ian Watt (Stanford): 'Four Western Myths.' Publication planned.
1974–5
Richard Ellmann (Oxford): 'The Consciousness of Joyce.' Published as *The Consciousness of Joyce* (Oxford 1977).
1975–6
Henry Nash Smith (Berkeley): 'Other Dimensions: Hawthorne, Melville, and Twain.' Included in *Democracy and the Novel: Popular Resistance to Classic American Writers* (Oxford 1978).
1976–7
Kathleen Coburn (Toronto): 'Some Perspectives on Coleridge.' Published as *Experience into Thought: Perspectives in the Coleridge Notebooks* (University of Toronto Press 1979).
1977–8
E.P. Thompson (Worcester): 'William Blake: Tradition and Revolution 1789–1793.' Publication planned.
1978–9
Ronald Paulson (Yale): 'The Representation of Revolution 1789–1820.' Published as *The Representation of Revolution (1789–1820)* (Yale 1983).
1979–80
David Daiches (Edinburgh): 'Literature and Gentility in Scotland.' Published as *Literature and Gentility in Scotland* (Edinburgh 1982).
1980–1
Walter J. Ong, sj (St. Louis): 'Hopkins, the Self, and God.' Published as *Hopkins, the Self, and God* (University of Toronto Press 1986).
1982
Robertson Davies (Toronto): 'The Mirror of Nature.' Published as *The Mirror of Nature* (University of Toronto Press 1983).
1983
Anne Barton (Cambridge): 'Comedy and the Naming of Parts.' Published as *The Names of Comedy* (University of Toronto Press 1990).
1984
Guy Davenport (Kentucky): 'Objects on a Table: Still Life in Literature and Painting.'
1985
Richard Altick (Ohio): 'The Victorian Sense of the Present.'
1985

Jerome J. McGann (California) Various Subjects
1986

Inga-Stina Ewbank (London) 'The World and the Theatre: Strindberg, Ibsen and Shakespeare.'
1987

Christopher Ricks (Boston) 'Allusion and Inheritance 1784–1824.'
1988

John Burrow (Bristol) 'Langland's *Piers Plowman*: The Uses of Fiction.'
1989

John Fraser (Dalhousie) 'Nihilism, Modernism, and Value.'
1990

Mary Jacobus (Cornell) 'First Things: Reproductive Origins.'
1991

Peter Conrad (Oxford) 'To Be Continued ...'
1992